HIP-HOP RIVALRIES

Ran into Gator, from Jungle Fever,

He's my people and my neighbor, I said I need a favor,

He said for ten dollars, and for ten Whoppers

From Burger King, I'll tell you the nigga who gotcha,

Gave him what he wanted plus the extra large fry,

He said, "Blue eyes, blonde hair, a White guy,"

I said... "What the fuck going on?

A White guy interrupting my fuck flowing on?"

So I copped some new ammo, reloaded my flare gun,

Stalking like Rambo, mixed with Commando,

Gator pushed the 10-speed bike, I'm on the handle,

Crashed into something 'cause he high off my man blow...

"Soopaman Luva 5 (Pt. 2)" - Redman

HIP-HOP RIVALRIES:
EAST COAST VERSUS WEST COAST

NJASANG NJI

WHITE OWL
AN IMPRINT OF PEN & SWORD BOOKS LTD
YORKSHIRE – PHILADELPHIA

First published in Great Britain in 2025 by
PEN AND SWORD WHITE OWL
An imprint of
Pen & Sword Books Ltd
Yorkshire – Philadelphia

Copyright © Njasang Nji, 2025

ISBN 978 1 03611 418 3

The right of Njasang Nji to be identified as Author of this work has been asserted by him in accordance with the Copyright, Designs and Patents Act 1988.

A CIP catalogue record for this book is available from the British Library.

All rights reserved. No part of this book may be reproduced, transmitted, downloaded, decompiled or reverse engineered in any form or by any means, electronic or mechanical including photocopying, recording or by any information storage and retrieval system, without permission from the Publisher in writing.
NO AI TRAINING: Without in any way limiting the Author's and Publisher's exclusive rights under copyright, any use of this publication to "train" generative artificial intelligence (AI) technologies to generate text is expressly prohibited.
The Author and Publisher reserve all rights to license uses of this work for generative AI training and development of machine learning language models.

Typeset in Times New Roman 11/15 by
SJmagic DESIGN SERVICES, India.
Printed and bound in the UK by CPI Group (UK) Ltd, Croydon, CR0 4YY.

The Publisher's authorised representative in the EU for product safety is Authorised Rep Compliance Ltd., Ground Floor, 71 Lower Baggot Street, Dublin D02 P593, Ireland.
www.arccompliance.com

For a complete list of Pen & Sword titles please contact

PEN & SWORD BOOKS LIMITED
George House, Units 12 & 13, Beevor Street, Off Pontefract Road,
Barnsley, South Yorkshire, S71 1HN, England
E-mail: enquiries@pen-and-sword.co.uk
Website: www.pen-and-sword.co.uk

or

PEN AND SWORD BOOKS
1950 Lawrence Rd, Havertown, PA 19083, USA
E-mail: uspen-and-sword@casematepublishers.com
Website: www.penandswordbooks.com

MIX
Paper | Supporting
responsible forestry
FSC® C013604

Contents

Acknowledgements 7

Introduction 9
    A. What's Beef? 9
    B. Honorable Mentions 16
    C. The Buildup 20

1 The Backdrop and AAVE 28

2 What's Beef? 40
    A. Tupac Shakur vs. The Notorious B.I.G. (aka "Biggie") 40
    B. Nas vs. Jay-Z 67
    C. Ice Cube vs. N.W.A. 85
    D. Pusha T vs. Drake 94
    E. Nicki Minaj vs. Everybody (Yes, including Lil Kim, Cardi B, Meg the Stallion, Coi Leray, and even the ex-wife of the big homie Papoose, et al.) 116
    F. Cassidy vs. Freeway 117
    G. Jadakiss and The LOX vs. 50 Cent and G-Unit 127

3 Eminem vs. Everybody 145

4 The Culture Today 174

5 The URL and The Future of Battle Rap... 182
   A. Smack and Beasley 182
   B. Honorable Mentions (and A Message For Lil Durk) 185

6 Poetic Justice 189

7 Conclusion 190
   A. What Is To Come? 190
   B. Diddy Do It? 196
   C. Diddy Kong 199

Afterword 207

Battle Rap Playlist Suggestion 209

Appendix 212

Acknowledgements

- Yahuah God, The Biggest Homie
- Favour
- Mom and Dad - Rest in Perfect Peace
- Edward Bozek - My HBI brother forever
- Auntie Cecilia, Uncle Johnson, Mama Colette, Auntie Irene, Ma Ndangoh, Ma Ngwe Anastasia Awasum - Thank you all for the wisdom, strength, foresight, forbearance, and perspicacity with which you raised me. Rest in Perfect Peace
- All those who have died or been imprisoned and/or tortured during the Ambazonian War of Independence - Rest in Perfect Peace, Honor, and Courage - ASAWANA
- My son and his new wife: Mr. and Mrs. Tasheem and Kirsten Feliciano - with great joy and hope for a better future for you both, I will always love you
- Sula Sula (and her twin, Juliana Allen) - Forever and a Day...
- Jonathan Wright, History, Transport and White Owl Publisher, Pen and Sword Books Limited - a hearty thank you for giving me this opportunity to shine
- Cameron Neill - the check cutter (lol) - thanks for explaining how the finances work. Ngl, I'm still a bit clueless
- Charlotte Mitchell, former Junior Commissioning Editor & Marketing Executive, Pen & Sword Books Limited - an equally hearty thank you for your patience and many insights
- Mélanie Dangereuse de Clegane, Author and Editor - thanks for not being so brutal on the chopping block. You really had me sweating through the rereads

- Marc Burrows, Writer, Thespian, Musician, Comedian, and literary scout (of sorts, lol) - you found me and led me to my new home, for which you will always have my profound gratitude
- Everyone else who helped and encouraged me during the writing process, especially my Ambazonian brothers and sisters (Samuel Wazizi will live forever)
- Rest in peace to the big homie, Irv Gotti
- Solange Tabit Egbe - you are greatly appreciated for everything you have done for us in this shithole. Thank you for all your sacrifices.

Introduction

A. What's Beef?

Google describes "beef," in part, as "a complaint or grievance." To "The Culture" (that is, Black people as a whole, with emphasis on Blacks in America), those of us living in high poverty and high crime areas throughout the United States of America, describing beef as merely "a complaint or grievance" is insulting. I grew up in all the boroughs in New York City, sometimes in good neighborhoods, sometimes in not-so-good neighborhoods, but speaking from the perspective of an African male who moved to New York City in the late 1980s as a preteen, I can speak with authority that, if you said you had beef with somebody, or somebody said they had beef with you, it was "on sight." This meant, as soon as you saw each other, there would likely be some sort of physical altercation. That was what "beef" meant when I was growing up.

In the 1970s and the early 1980s, when hip-hop was at its nascence, beefs were settled between rivals by danceoffs, occasions where crews or street gangs would meet up and at which their members would dance "against" each other. Whoever was deemed to have danced better, won, and this was how "breaking," or breakdancing, was born (think of the movie "Breaking" and "Breaking 2: Electric Boogaloo"). "Breakdancing is a style of street dancing that incorporates coordination, acrobatic and intricate body movements, style, and aesthetics. It evolved from the hip hop movement during the early 1970s and is the most widely known of all hip hop dance styles. Old-style breakdancing was popular until the late 1970s when the Freak took over."

Hip-Hop Rivalries: East Coast Versus West Coast

It's (also) said that this style "was based on the debut album 'Freak Out!' by the band the Mothers of Invention." The Rock Steady Crew, formed in 1979 and 1980, introduced acrobatic moves that had never been seen before, nor practiced, like headspins, hand glides, and backspins. With the advent of the crack epidemic ushered in by the CIA and ostensibly enforced, regulated, and promoted by the FBI (specifically J. Edgar Hoover), breakdancing began fading out as those of us in the impoverished underbelly of America started settling beefs with knives, clubs, and other really nasty weapons, while federal and local authorities sought out Black Americans like Frank Lucas, Alpo, and Rich Porter, who thought nothing of supplying crack and heroin to the people in their own communities, just so they could get out of those same communities and move on up to the East Side like the Jeffersons. This is the ubiquitous "they" that Jay-Z refers to in his song *"Watch Me"* - the *ubiquitous* White people, *primarily* those in high positions of authority in America and throughout the world who are dedicated to destroying Black culture by giving us drugs and then investigating us for using them.

The Culture knew what was going on, saw what hard drugs were doing to our communities, and we were almost helpless to fight what "they" seemed to be trying to do: exterminate Black people. After all, was that not the entire premise underpinning the Counterintelligence Program ("COINTELPRO")? "Under then-FBI Director J. Edgar Hoover, COINTELPRO included legal harassment, intimidation, wiretapping, infiltration, smear campaigns, and blackmail, and resulted in countless prison sentences and, in the case of Black Panther Fred Hampton and others, murder. This scope of operations can hardly be described as 'limited.'" In addition, "these tactics were employed against every national civil rights organization, the antiwar movement (particularly on college campuses), Students for a Democratic Society, the American Indian Movement, the Puerto Rican Young Lords, and others."

COINTELPRO was a secret operation designed to infiltrate, bankrupt, and ultimately shut down organizations regarded as "radical" and which could later on become a problem for the U.S. government. Several associations that had been sighted and were being investigted by COINTELPRO were the Communist Party, Black Panther Party, and the American Indian Movement. But mainly the "Black Panther Party (BPP) bore the brunt of the FBI's surveillance. In the wake of COINTELPRO, 295 documented actions taken by the FBI against Black nationalist groups were discovered.

Introduction

233 of these confirmed actions specifically targeted the Black Panther Party." In addition to the Black Panther Party, the activities of other Black nationalists were discredited and wrongfully exposed as malign. At least, that was part of what an old FBI document detailed that COINTELPRO was to be doing. COINTELPRO was also apparently keeping a close eye on Reverend Dr. Martin Luther King Jr., Malcolm X, and Eldridge Cleaver.

On 8 March, 1971, a group of activists from the Citizens Commission snuck into an FBI office in Pennsylvania and stole at least 1,000 confidential documents. They immediately sent copies of these documents to a variety of news agencies all over the country, as well as to the country's political leaders. The Washington Post was the only news association that ran the story. Thus exposed, this indicated the beginning of the end of COINTELPRO. As soon as the information went public, there was no retracting previously shady statements on the said subject of the reason behind COINTELPRO's creation.

J. Edgar Hoover's unjust and draconian (Rockefeller) drug laws further punished primarily Black people to whom these same authorities were providing drugs. However, The Culture survived and became stronger. "The Rockefeller drug laws, when they were enacted in 1973, were intended to combat drug abuse by providing such harsh sentences for drug offenses that users and dealers would be deterred from continued involvement in drugs. It did not work. John Dunne, one of the original sponsors of the laws, has admitted 'beyond any shadow of a doubt that these laws are not working.'"

One Chief Judge Judith Kaye of the New York Court of Appeals called for reform. "The New York State Catholic Conference has issued a statement calling for more effective policies focusing on treatment. The newspapers, including The New York Times, Newsday and the Times Union have printed numerous articles, editorials and letters calling for the legislature to recognize the obvious: that these laws don't work, they result in serious injustices and they need to be changed."

Furthermore, what they ended up realizing "is that drug use is a criminal problem only because we have made it one. When drug use becomes drug abuse it is first and foremost a medical problem. Yet by seeking to impose criminal sanctions to limit both use and abuse of drugs, we have taken what is at worst a medical problem and turned it into a crime problem."

♪ ♪ ♪ ♪

In the meantime, The Culture also noticed how consumed with one specific hard drug White people had become. Heroin was fast becoming the drug of choice for the (primarily poor) White American population. We already knew how ensorcelled with cocaine Whites were - it was rare for Black people to indulge in that drug, a phenomenon that remains true to this day. But from cocaine, many Caucasians leapt into the arms of a singularly unkind gorilla. Perhaps because of the presence of alcohol, cocaine, and marijuana at social gathering events, music and the music industry became intertwined with smoking joints and doing lines (snorting cocaine). Joints became blunts as marijuana use became part of The Culture. After all, marijuana had been used in ancient African rituals, used to reduce pain, and used to invoke visions throughout millennia and in various civilizations worldwide.

Weed is not smoked by every Black person in America, but I would go so far as to say that over half of the African-American population smokes marijuana recreationally. With the revamping of the Rockefeller Drug Laws and the eventual decriminalization of marijuana, the so-called "War on Drugs" recently continued with two objectives in mind:

1. Catch and/or kill as many Black hard drug pushers and users as possible; and
2. Bust and/or confiscate a remarkable (and genuine) amount of heroin, cocaine, and the newest rage: methamphetamines.

I have never seen anyone openly smoke crack or shoot heroin (openly) at a rap/hip-hop event, but there are sure to be clouds of marijuana smoke at said events. There are now hookahs available for use at almost every social gathering, and at every club or similar environment. (For those who are not aware, a hookah is just a fancy name and fancier apparatus for what we knew as "bongs" way back when. To be honest, though, hookahs have been around for thousands of years, so maybe the bong is the less fancier sounding and with less fancy apparatus.)

♫ ♫ ♫ ♫

Moving on, with progress must also come change. This is an uncomfortable thought to those in power, but those who do not heed this truism are bound

Introduction

to learn why nations fail. Change does not necessarily bring progress, but progress will always bring change. Nations themselves have serious beefs, as we see with what is happening with Russia and Ukraine, Ethiopia and Tigray, Ethiopia and Eritrea, Israel and Palestine, and French Cameroun and British Southern Cameroons (now known as "Ambazonia"). Those are international beefs involving the illegal use of phosphorus during their respective conflicts (as Israel Ethiopia and French Cameroun have been credibly accused of doing within the past seven years), and cluster munitions (allegedly employed by both the Russians and the Ukrainians).

Then there are the national beefs, which are primarily (or proclaimed to be) "internecine," usually involving an increasingly tyrannical government seeking to thoroughly dominate the Average Joe. The Average Joe just seeks to be able to provide for himself and his family without the government concocting some yearly crises, the result of which is an ever-rising trillion-dollar American debt ceiling. These are usually accompanied by Big Pharma's mandates to inject the people with experimental MRNA vaccines that have caused millions of "sheeple" (people who are as brainless and as easily led as sheep) to develop many various and hitherto unseen medical complications.

Compared to all the above, music rivalries seem like peanuts, one would think. But even on this smaller stage, lives have still been lost. The United States is a perfect example of this internecine national strife. As stated above, The Culture survived everything the U.S. government threw at us: from worldwide displacements, to slavery, to unfair, criminal, and recurring disenfranchisement, to terrorism, to land (and other assets) seizures, to Jim Crow, to the Ku Klux Klan, to the Civil Rights era, to the suffragette movement, to the Rockefeller Drug Laws, and finally, to the War on Drugs. Black people also survived the poisonous drugs introduced into our communities, for the most part. The real war now is that which Black people in America *know* is being fought: the War on Blacks. And it seems as if the entire world is in on it. But the world loves our music, among other cultural innovations. It just does not love *us*, the creators behind said "cultural innovations."

We also survived the weaponization of the institution of what was finally decriminalized and is now seen as a recreational drug. Literally thousands of times I have seen Black people and White people casually light up blunts (for those who still might not know what a "blunt" is, it is marijuana rolled in the the outer leaf of a cigar) outside, or in the club, or at the park, or at some such other gathering. I have never, *ever* seen anyone shooting up dope (heroin) at a URL show or a Jay-Z concert. In thousands of rap, hip-hop, and R&B songs, people are described as, and can be *seen*, smoking weed or otherwise glorifying the use of marijuana - I have never seen heroin, crack, or even cocaine painted in the same light and with the same levity as weed.

Let the reader ask himself/herself why this is so.

When "they" started realizing that it was not marijuana breaking up families, but rather dope and crack, cocaine and methamphetamines, they surmised that marijuana had to be decriminalized. Opiates were -*are*- the newest targets in the War on Drugs, and fentanyl. Yes, Black people sell (and use) these newer, deadlier, drugs, but nowadays a much higher percentage of White people (primarily White Americans) are both drug dealers and drug users.

It reminds me of what Dave Chappelle said about Ohio's heroin crisis: "This opioid crisis is a crisis, I see it every day, it's as bad as they say. It's ruining lives, it's destroying families. Sadly, you know what it reminds me of, seeing it? Reminds me of us. These White folks look exactly like us, during the crack epidemic. Ya know, it's really crazy to see. And all this shit they talking about on the news about how divided the nation is, I don't believe it, I feel like now, niggas - we're getting a real good look at each other. 'Cause why? Because I even have insight into how the White community must have felt watching the Black community go through the scourge of crack... Because I don't care, either... Hang in there, Whites... 'Just say no,' what's so hard about that?... Remember when y'all said that to us? But it's okay; there's no grudges, now you finally got it right. Once it started happening to your kids, you realized it's a health crisis. These people are sick. They are not criminals, they are sick!" I know for a fact that Gen X vividly remembers those thoroughly ineffectual "Just Say No" commercials that did *nothing* to help anyone break their addiction.

Not strangely enough, trauma bonded many White people to Black people. Having shared the worst of what drug addiction (*hard* drug addiction) did to Black folk, Whites who experienced the same thing, or who had a family member or friend go through the same thing, now felt our pain. And that led to a "cultural osmosis," of sorts.

Which included music.

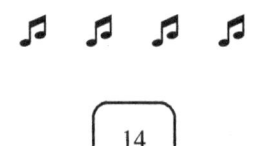

♪ ♪ ♪ ♪

Introduction

The majority of White people who have understood The Culture a bit more than other White people are poor. They know our pain. And yet, bafflingly, so many of them still use the "n" word against us so glibly. It is a shocking phenomenon. The worldwide appreciation of hip-hop and battle rap came from different people identifying with certain familiar struggles and/or idiosyncrasies of The Culture. Shared experiences normally create bonds between fans and their stars. But if you identify with me, a Black man, and can still call me or another Black person the "n" word, there is a disconnect somewhere.

Rounding off, to this day, breakdancing battles still exist in different musical genres, but the focus of this book is to explore notable *rivalries* in hip-hop and how they made us Gen X'ers feel at the time, as the years passed in relation to subsequent beefs, and now.

Thus, without further ado, let us anon.

B. Honorable Mentions

This book would not be complete without its honorable mentions. First and foremost, I would like to thank NWA, as a group, for having the brazen audacity to create *"Fuck The Police."* Until House of Pain, no White person had ever attacked the police authorities on a song. But an entire song dedicated to exposing, shaming, and excoriating crooked police officers and calling them out on their brutality towards people of color (primarily Black folks), versus, *"I never eat a pig 'cause a pig is a cop"*? That doesn't even out at all.

NWA, as violent as some (maybe many) saw the group to be, was an unexpected middle finger to *them* (the ubiquitous ones). Conscious rap came before, and ultimately gave ground to, gangster rap. The Culture was reeling and trying to regroup from the HIV and crack epidemics. There were "conscious" Black youth who generally would not smoke crack or do dope (heroin), sometimes would not even touch weed. They were frustrated with and angry at the poverty in which they were being raised, as well as the daily harassment and torturous racism of primarily White police officers, which even self-styled "trailer park trash" would rarely encounter.

With their intelligence and righteous indignation, this new, disgruntled era of conscious youth gleefully bumped their radios and sound systems to *"Fuck The Police,"* thanking NWA for publicly voicing their discontent with the prevailing zeitgeist, and not just as seen through the eyes of African-Americans. I am reminded of a jewel of a book I read some time ago and on which I recently happened to get my hands. In chapter 4 of the book, the authors write, "The Black Death is a vivid example of a critical juncture, a major event or confluence of factors disrupting the existing economic or political balance in society. A critical juncture is a double-edged sword that can cause a sharp turn in the trajectory of a nation."

The emergence of NWA was, to me, such an unforeseen "critical juncture" that inarguably caused "a sharp turn in the trajectory" of the United States. Black folk were not going to be cowed any longer, and empowerment was in the air. Gangster rap was liberating, as the youth were now talking big shit, openly, to authorities who regularly abused their policing powers. Yes, Kool Moe Dee, X-Clan, and Public Enemy were exposing the powers that be in a "conscious" manner, and even coming close to, or straight trampling

Introduction

over, the line of disrespect of those powers, but NWA was screaming it from the tops of skyscrapers. This critical juncture must also take into account the theory that gangster rap was deliberately installed into society in order to make the (Black) youth more violent, replacing the more race-uplifting and almost universally binding conscious rap movement.

In any event, thank you, NWA.

Let us remember that the Central Park 5 would be wrongfully convicted of a heinous crime they did not commit (with Donald Trump trumpeting for the death penalty) the year after *"Fuck The Police"* was released. Also, Rodney King would be savaged a little over two years later, leading to the Los Angeles riots after the four White police officers that beat him were acquitted by a mostly White jury. Black folk were standing in solidarity nationwide, condemning and resisting the overt racism and homicidal inclinations of the Los Angeles Police Department (L.A.P.D.) *and* the New York Police Department (N.Y.P.D.).

Thanks are also in order to Mr. Gilbert Scott-Heron and his most famous song, *"The Revolution Will Not Be Televised"* (1970). Considered to be the "father of rap," he was also a musician, a novelist, and a poet. Every time I hear that song, I am somehow, some way, encouraged and empowered. Hope does, indeed, spring forth eternal. Thank you, sir. (And Kendrick made sure that the revolution was both televised AND live.)

Let us also exhibit our appreciation to Kool Herc, real name Clive Campbell, who emigrated from Jamaica around 1969 and was one of the first to start hip-hop in the Bronx, New York, one of the first (if not *the* first) to start turning tables while rapping over the beat. Thank you, sir, for putting deejays on the map, as well as propagating emceeing in the hip-hop genre. All deejays all across the world need to thank this man, as many of the ways in which they deejay came from his origination of the art and experimentation with the equipment and how it could be finessed.

The term "MC" in hip-hop is derived from "Master of Ceremonies," a person who, usually at a party or other such social function, holds a microphone in their hand as they direct and coordinate the said function. The person credited as being the first *recorded* MC, however, goes by the name "Coke La Rock," aka Coco La Rock. I would be remiss in my duties as a novelist and hip-hop aficionado if I did not also mention and show appreciation to: Rufus Thomas, Jr., Africa Bambaata (man to man, you got a lotta shit with you, brother, and eventually, all that shit is gonna be exposed, but at least you weren't completely useless), Curtis Blow, KRS ONE (stop supporting known rapists, king - it's not a good look and your own reputation could be severely damaged), Heavy D, Kid n Play, Grandmaster Flash, Slick Rick, Doug E Fresh, MC Lyte, Kool Moe Dee, Public Enemy, Big Daddy Kane, Melle Mel, Too Short, Special Ed, Roxanne Shante, Run DMC, Heather B, Spoonie Gee, Scarface, Lovebug Starski, LL Cool J, Marley Marl, Dana Dane, Kool G Rap, Nikki D, DJ Premier (aka "Premo"), DJ Polo, Screamin' Jay Hawkins, Linton Kwesi Johnson, and last, but definitely not least, Biz Markie and Miss Melodie (rest in peace to all who have thus far passed on). There is not enough space for me to name all of the artists who pioneered rap and hip-hop. But please know that you are all appreciated and have left indelible marks in The Culture, which has evolved in so many ways to what it is today because of you. Thank you all, most sincerely and gratefully.

Also, a certain group from as far back as 1934 practiced and, more importantly, *performed* the spoken word, in rhythm and sync, so they can be called rappers too - the group was known as the Golden Gate Quartet. Yet another group, The Jubalaires, also vocalized poetry in singsong fashion, and was founded in 1936. The late, great Pimeat Markham came along in 1968 with more advanced spoken word lyricism, followed by King Tim III in 1979. Legends, and far ahead of their time, all.

♬ ♬ ♬ ♬

Thank you all so much for beginning and continuing a style of music often imitated (but never duplicated) everywhere music can reach. Hip-hop has flourished and become a vessel by which so many Black (and, apparently, non-Black) people have been lifted out of poverty and duress, or saved from a life of the doldrums. But what good is it if I leave the 'hood and forget about or do not come back for others? This door was opened by others - it would only be right if I opened it further or provided another door entirely for others who are caught in the recurring cycle of poverty and violence with no way out.

Now *that* would be a legacy worthy of anyone who sees themselves as some sort of "star" or "superstar." Now, to be fair, some of the above-

Introduction

mentioned hip-hop pioneers got some shit on them, and some of that shit is nasty indeed. This book deals primarily with hip-hop rivalries, yes, but we will also touch on the idiosyncrasies (outré or otherwise) of the superstars within these pages. On behalf of The Culture, I would like to take this opportunity to apologize to anyone and everyone wrongly or wrongfully hurt, assaulted, or otherwise adversely affected by the above-mentioned pioneers and other stars to be ever and anon discussed. Except if you're a racist. Or a Nazi... Because fuck Nazis. If the shoe fits...

On to the next one.

C. The Buildup

From the time that skilled African craftsmen, tradesmen, hunters, masons, doctors, sailors, carpenters, chefs, herbalists, generals, metal workers, princes, chiefs, bakers, magistrates, farmers, arbiters, warriors, engineers, metallurgists, concubines, textile experts, and kings (to name a few), who were many of The Culture's forefathers and foremothers, began being forced to work for free on American soil, the air used to be filled with what we today call "spirituals," woefully lyrical songs, almost enchantments, in which one could feel the longing to return back to their homeland. I believe the exact word is "hiraeth" - a spiritual longing for a home that maybe never was (and which many of their progeny would come to believe never was). Nostalgia for ancient places to which we cannot return. It is an echo of the lost places of our soul's past and our grief for them. It is in the wind, and the rocks, and the waves. It is nowhere and it is everywhere.

Hiraeth is a Welsh word, and I don't know from exactly where I got that particular definition, but it fits perfectly the emotional tonality of early African-American spirituals. Up to this day, many Black people in America are afflicted by this, whether or not they wish to face such a truth. However, the United States is now also their heritage, as their blood and flesh is part of the soil of that landmass. But their spirits long for Mama Africa, too. Truth be told, many of the natives of the United States were dark-skinned as well, so it's a fact that Black people are usually indigenous to all lands where man has explored.

These abovesaid spirituals would later on meld into and with gospel songs. From gospel would come bebop and ragtime, the latter forming into soul jazz, from which we get jazz. The blues emerged from the work songs our ancestors sang in the cotton fields and around cookfires at night. From jazz would come funk music and, in addition to bebop and soul (another offshoot of gospel music), the Rhythm and Blues genre ("R&B") would rise up. As a matter of fact, rock-and-roll came from African-American music; blending with jazz, gospel, country music (of African-American origin as well), and rhythm and blues, rock-and-roll was brought to life by the late greats Chuck Berry and Rosetta Thorpe, known as the "Godmother of Rock and Roll."

It was a White man by the name of DJ Alan Freed who first coined the term "rock-and-roll," but its definition, the meat and potatoes of rock-and-roll, were provided by the superfluous talents of Rosetta Thorpe, Little Richard, Etta

Introduction

James, LaVern Baker, Fats Domino, and Bo Diddley. (The last two could also do gospel, jazz, and blues.) In the context of music rivalry, of course it existed, even back then, but it was usually good-natured and muted, as Black artists had the pestilence of racism with which to contend. Efforts were always made to uplift the collective through the individual's contributions, as Harry Belafonte, Nat King Cole, and others, succeeded at doing, improving the lot and lives of their people all over the world, financing social justice movements and the like.

African-Americans have contributed heavily to the evolution of the world, not just Black people in general. Due to their contributions, the plight of Black families in White America was filmed and broadcast to the world. They were able to travel internationally and brought their own experiences to share with their densely Caucasian fans. This garnered the strengthening of The Culture and a steadily hardening resolve that the age of slavery was over, and Black people wanted - nay, *demanded* - a seat at the table and "a piece of the pie" - again, like The Jeffersons.

For a large (though not the most) part, and on behalf of Black people in the United States, I can report an honest "(somewhat) Mission Accomplished" to The Culture here in the Motherland. But there is still a tremendous amount of work to be done because the existing power structure is loath to willingly set a place for us at the table. Attempts to set up our own table have resulted in violent opposition and physical attacks on Black businesses and other such holdings, such as the destruction of Black Wall Street in Philadelphia in the 1980s. The United States government literally bombed a thriving African-American community in order to quell what it saw as a threat to the Caucasian American order. Let's also not forget the complete destruction of another thriving Black community located in Tulsa, Oklahoma in 1921.

In the 1990s, there was a term popularized to denote the slang used by Black people. That term was "Ebonics." It encompassed the myriads of ways Blacks have addressed each other, linguistically and grammatically, from New York to California, and from Wyoming to Mississippi. In my travels I have noticed how endemic to a geographical region a certain manner of speech can be. People from the East Coast, generally, and people from New York, in particular, see almost anything foreign, strange or out of the ordinary as "abnormal" or even *inferior*. It's just facts, I lived there. Not that New York or East Coast residents are xenophobically snobby, but you gotta have tough skin to be over there.

Hip-Hop Rivalries: East Coast Versus West Coast

Strangely and embarrassingly enough, this view is shared by some Blacks, racist Whites, Chinese, Indians, et al. - it is quite a bizarre phenomenon that we, as a people, and having been subjected to the worst depredations xenophobia has produced, will now have the hypocritical gall to turn around and sneer at anyone of our own color who perhaps slurs her words a bit, or pronounces "there" as "thurr," "here" as "hurr," and the like. (Spectacularly huge shout-out to Glorilla: stay authentic, stay **you**! Stay "burrtiful." Shout-out to @officialdeedess, too.) The Culture on the East Coast knows itself to be more and "better educated," more gifted, richer, more fashionable, and more in tune with the sociopolitical zeitgeist than The Culture on the West Coast and our people down South and in Canada.

However, because of artists like Ice Cube, Eazy-E, Snoop Dogg, Master P, DJ Quik, Too Short, Bone, Thugs, and Harmony, T.I., Ludacris, Lil' Wayne, Juvenal, and Mystikal, our respect for rappers from those places increased exponentially. Hip-hop has made it possible for anyone who can "spit" (Ebonics for *rap*) fluently and cogently to become wealthy. Some rappers, however, like Fetty Wap, were not content with the dividends their music was paying and decided to continue living the lives they had been living before their rhyming skills brought them fame and fortune. Free Fetty, free Thugga, and free Meech. Free Pooh Shiesty and Tsu Surf, too.

(At the time of one of the final edits of this book, I have learned that Big Meech is out of prison and in a halfway house. Welcome home, big homie. During one of the final revisions of this book, it was announced on Thursday, 31 October, 2024, at approximately 23:52 [11:52p.m.], by Willie D on his YouTube show ["No Mo Talk"]: "Young Thug Freed From Prison After Pleading Guilty in YSL RICO Trial." Allegedly, the State of Georgia will have Thugga on a hefty amount of time on probation, and he pleaded no contest to conspiracy to violate the RICO Act. This book is set to be published in 2025, but please allow us to say, "Welcome home, Thugga.")

♪ ♪ ♪ ♪

There was an African-American social psychologist called Robert Lee Williams II (the irony of that name belonging to a Black man should not

Introduction

be lost) who originally coined the word "Ebonics" in 1973. The word has been around for some time; it itself has been relegated to the stratum it described. Mr. Williams described Ebonics as "...the linguistic and paralinguistic features which on a concentric continuum represent the communicative competence of the West African, Caribbean, and United States idioms, patois, argots, ideolects, and social forces of Black people... Ebonics derives its form from ebony (black) and phonics (sound, study of sound) and refers to the study of the language of Black people in all its cultural uniqueness."

Ebonics is not *just* slang. It was originally a method of communication among Black people in such a way that neither "Massa" (the slavemaster) nor other Whites would be able to understand. It has now developed into a worldwide movement, used by so many non-African-Americans on a daily basis. "Ebonics pronunciation includes features like the omission of the final consonant in words like 'past' (pas') and 'hand' (han'), the pronunciation of the th in 'bath' as t (bat) or f (baf), and the pronunciation of the vowel in words like 'my' and 'ride' as a long ah (mah, rahd). Some of these occur in vernacular White English, too, especially in the South, but in general they occur more frequently in Ebonics."

It is also submitted that some "Ebonics pronunciations are more unique, for instance, dropping b, d, or g at the beginning of auxiliary verbs like 'don't' and 'gonna,' yielding 'Ah 'on know' for 'I don't know' and ama do it for 'I'm going to do it.'" Black people ourselves seem to automatically know the rules to our own jargon, despite the region. Although English is not the native tongue of any Black person on this planet, we were forced to learn the language of our oppressors and slavers in order to universally communicate with one another.

We created our own *dialects* of English, which has confused so many White people to this day. But take a look at how White Texans talk as compared to White Louisianans - totally different drawls. Blacks in the United States would automatically attribute racism, incest, and retardation to either drawl, but in our ears, particularly the ears of a Black person from the East Coast, the Louisiana drawl is more unintelligible than the high, dry, and extremely nasally (but more phonetically comprehensible) Texas *twang*.

Now, let's take a *lyrical* look at what Ebonics is. In the song *"Ebonics,"* featuring Big L. (Digging in the Crates), he gives analogies of what certain everyday people, places, and things are called in Ebonics: *"...the linguistic and paralinguistic features which on a concentric continuum represent the communicative competence of the West African, Caribbean, and United States idioms, patois, argots, ideolects, and social forces of Black people... Ebonics derives its form from ebony (black) and phonics (sound, study of sound) and refers to the study of the language of Black people in all its cultural uniqueness."* [Author's emphasis] If this definition goes above the heads of some people, just call it "Blackspeak," or Black slang. And yes, as opposed to "Whitespeak," or White slang.

Big L skillfully breaks down what White American culture deems is "proper" or "normal" (you can call this "Whitespeak") as compared to, or *translated into*, Blackspeak. For example, weed smoke (or weed [marijuana]) in Blackspeak is known by many terms, one of which is "lah," and one kilogram of cocaine is a "pie." Payphones turn into "jacks" in Blackspeak, a razorblade is an "ox," getting shot meant you got "bucked," and if you got punched, it was called a "snuff." This was everyday language to Black people but it mystified many White people, and The Culture was unique, set apart, in that regard. Sure, some of Ebonics (a negligible percentage) incorporated what Massa and his descendants forced into the literary and phonetic syllabi of that which Black people were eventually taught. Some "White slang," so to speak, leaked minutely into Ebonics; it was inevitable.

Other examples of Ebonics are: heroin being "dope," homes being "cribs," condoms being "'Jimmy' hats," robberies being "juxes," a train (or system of trains) being the "iron horse," jealous being "jelly," and a cellphone being a "celly." Now, some terms or words in Ebonics can mean two different things, though rarely at the same time, as is the case with most words in the English language. For example, as a cellphone becomes a "celly" in Ebonics, so too does one's *cellmate* in prison become one's "celly." This is also known as a *homonym* - that is, two words that have the same spelling and even the same pronunciation, but with different definitions.

Also, anywhere there is a word that phonetically seems to end with "in'" (such as "bleedin'," "stealin'," "dealin'," "feelin'," etc.), the apostrophe usually means it has replaced a "g." Oftentimes in Ebonics the "g" is not pronounced. Big L was one of the greatest lyricists I had heard in a while and I was waiting to see the success he would attain in the industry.

Introduction

Tragically, he was killed in a shootout in Harlem gunned down, really. His killers were allegedly looking for his brother. The wittiness, grittiness, and apparent ease with which Big L could weave words was praiseworthy and a delight to behold. He was a true wordsmith, in the vein of Nas and with the determinative feel of Mase back when the latter was called "Mase Murder." His analogies, similes, and metaphors are clear as day and the reality of his poverty, and the probity inherent in his delivery, permeated his rhymes. Some of the Ebonics terms are really old school and I wonder if the youth of today will not have trouble understanding it. Well, they are greater than the Android Generation - if they want to find something out, they will.

I noticed that Big L also used some jail terminology in his breakdown of/in *Ebonics*. This is definitely Ebonics as well, but make no mistake, the Ebonics of jail and prison culture *can* be vastly different than the Ebonics used among Black folks outside of jail and prison. But I have a problem with the first verse of the second stanza. Big L says, *"A burglary is a juk"* when, in all actuality, a *robbery* is a juk (or "jux"). When you "juk" (or jux) someone, you are robbing them of some valuable(s). A burglary could, perhaps, *technically*, be considered a juk, but I have never heard that terminology apply to such a soft juk.

You did damn good, young king. Thank you for your artistic contributions to the world and to The Culture. Rest in peace.

♪ ♪ ♪ ♪

To revisit "Black slang" and "White slang," *ubi supra*, an interesting phenomenon seems to have occured within these two cultural environments. Some people on social media noted that White slang is Black slang in reverse. I say White slang is Black slang in reverse since White people had their language and internecine slang from England and in America before Black people were kidnapped and forcefully brought around. For example:

- (White slang) You better not. (Black slang) I wish you would.
- (White slang) Say no more. (Black slang) Say less.
- (White slang) It's been a while. (Black slang) It's been a minute.
- (White slang) Deal. (Black slang) Bet.
- (White slang) Swing by. (Black slang) Pull up.

- (White slang) You got the right one, buddy.   (Black slang) I ain't the one.
- (White slang) Hey, let's go.   (Black slang) We gone.
- (White slang) He's a cool cat.   (Black slang) That's my dog.

Thank you to @cadenmcdonald on Instagram and a few others whose information I could not get. It seems amusing, *prima facie*, but I thought about it some more and realized that the nuances of the raciolinguistic peculiarity comprising of and emanating from the varying dialectical components of Ebonics (to be discussed at some length in the next subchapter) could have likely evolved *instinctually*, as a way of *protecting ourselves*. This could have just been something so primal and innate in Black people that automatically steered our cultural methodologies diametrically opposite to those of our former so-called "colonizers."

And now, all these years later, here we are, still resilient enough to build fortunes and establish specific and distinct endemic geographical linguistic dialects after our near-wholesale destruction, after 400 years of blood, sweat, tears, brutality, homicide, and a hodgepodge of other indignities and evils being forced upon us. The only difference among Blacks in the U.S., Blacks in Brazil, Blacks in Colombia, and Blacks everywhere else is where the ships dropped us off from Africa during the Transatlantic Slave Trade. (And we have not forgotten about the Arab Slave Trade, either - including the Trans-Saharan Slave Trade and the Red Sea Slave Trade - their time is also coming.)

Without a doubt, reparations are in order for African countries from which significant amounts of the population (and natural resources) were forcibly taken, and certainly for our brothers and sisters in the United States. It's only right. Nobody tells the Khazarians to forget about the Holocaust. Nobody tells the Japanese to forget about their internment. Nobody tells the Native Americans to forget about the genocide visited upon them. Thus, neither shall any person or nation intimate that Black people *worldwide* should just forget about the atrocities that the greatest Belgian barbarian visited upon our people in the Congo. Nor shall we ever forget the hundreds of years Great Britain raped our lands for their natural resources and their peoples. Nor shall anyone dare tell us to forget the White American barbarism shoved down our collective throats during America's nastiest and most shameful years.

Introduction

Until there are reparations, or until there are no more Black people on Earth, all of those nations (especially Portugal, Belgium, Argentina, the United States, Spain, and England) that participated in slavery should be forced to remember their past crimes against humanity; they should all pay reparations to the approximate African landmasses from which they harvested human souls, gold, silver, diamonds, and other valuables; and they should have recurrent social sensitivity training sessions on this topic.

That which came before culminated in the present deleterious state of affairs. As human beings who have gravely and maliciously hurt other human beings, *consciously*, we must choose to be better and to *do* better. Apologies are inutile without substantive action in accompaniment to the recognition of the whilom (and even *ongoing*) said grave and malicious hurts: this is called *accountability* and *responsibility*.

In the words of the late, great Stan Lee: Excelsior!

1
The Backdrop and AAVE

The raciolinguistic peculiarity of varying dialectical assignments must, in my opinion, take geographical factors into account. The United States was colonized predominantly by British settlers: criminals, entrepreneurs, adventurers, etc., all of whom were fleeing the persecution and oppression of their king. It is, by extension, an English nation. However, the English spoken in New York is not quite the same *dialect* of English as that spoken in Nebraska, or California, or London. Mexico, Cuba, the Dominican Republic, Puerto Rico, and some other South and Central American countries all speak "Spanish," because they were conquered by them. But the Spanish spoken in Puerto Rico is not the same Spanish as that spoken in the Dominican Republic, although strangely enough, those Spanish *dialects* are more similar to one another than to their parent tongue.

The colonizer comes with his iron fist, deceives and enslaves much (if not, most or all) of the indigenous population, oppresses the said population, gives them his language, religion, and beliefs to learn and assimilate, and goes about his merry way (taking with him all the gold and diamonds he could steal), thinking all is well, when it is not. Such imperialistic designs were instituted all over the world, until the enslaved indigenes vomited out their oppressors. Such is the case with African-American Vernacular English ("A.A.V.E."), just a more flowery and more sociopolitically acceptable way (ostensibly) of saying "Ebonics." Such a coincidence, how both terms were coined contemporaneously. Ebonics, though, is regarded as the "ghetto" way of saying A.A.V.E. From further analyses, however, I have concluded that Ebonics is the more appropriate term for defining "the totality of dialectical linguistics" African-Americans created and use.

The Backdrop and AAVE

The A.A.V.E.'s vocabulary includes normal English words that may have the exact opposite meaning than the words themselves. For example, a "blade" may be understood to be something like a *razorblade*, but A.A.V.E. will describe it to be a "knife," or, in prison terms, a blade can be a homosexual male. (Those homonyms again.) Something that is "bad" is actually very good (like, damn, that chick is *bad*, meaning the woman is very pretty or pleasantly and amply endowed). "Paper" or "moolah" is money and to "murk" or "body" means to kill. With my grammarian insight, I must also add that, whereas A.A.V.E. concerns itself with the words and terms of English, Ebonics comprises not just words and terms but how they are used and the rules *behind* how they are used. Thus, to me, "Ebonics" is the more apropos appelation, but A.A.V.E. can still be used, just not exclusively.

In the music industry, success is based on a variety of factors: the artist's appeal, dope bars, dope beats, good diction, enunciation, and delivery, to name what I see as some of the most important points. A rapper can be gifted at writing rhymes but suck at rapping, actually *vocalizing*, those same rhymes (also known as "bars"). Shout-out to Mad Skillz and all the other super dope ghostwriters who sacrificed their own careers as rappers in order to propel others to superstardom (which, granted, still gets them *paid*).

But, in this age of seemingly moribund commercial rap, mumble rappers have become the next big thing. Aficionados of real rap and hip-hop pray fervently that this trend of unintelligible rhyming ("mumbling"), or puerile diction, passes quickly. I am one of the first to offer up such prayers, not only for the extinction of mumble rap, but for quality bars over banging beats that will make me bump my head and talk about issues pertinent to The Culture. Rap and hip-hop are devolving into a fentanyl-laden and pill-popping morass, especially the pills, and most especially with the newest drill music coming out of the South and mid-West. Indeed, some of those rappers have some middling skill, but many do not appear to be too bright, as they are getting arrested for rhyming about murders they and others committed. Truly gifted young men who cannot hold water in their songs. (As I rewrite and edit this after experiencing Kendrick Lamar wallop Drake, I am greatly encouraged that rap and hip-hop are alive and well, and there is hope for these genres of music in the future.)

In any event, as A.A.V.E. developed, and due in very large part to our music, the world was so influenced by it that even the way African-American rappers *deliver* bars is copied by rappers in Nigeria, Cambodia, and the U.K. Flows, accents, cadences, acts, and other idiosyncrasies are being mimicked and, where possible, slang as well. Emancipation and freedom of expression are very important in any society. In many rap battles, when a rapper pronounces (or *starts* pronouncing) words in a certain way, the audience automatically knows that a punchline or scheme is underway, or some type of amusing skit.

Other times, rappers will overtly enunciate words or phrases a certain way in order to deliver impending double or even triple entendres. For instance, Jay-Z says in his song *"La La La (Excuse Me Again)"*: *"This ain't Chris Rock, bitch, it's the Roc, bitch, and I'm a franchise like a Houston Rocket: Yao Ming!"* Witty, and punny. Jay's pronunciation of "Yao Ming" could confuse virgin listeners into believing they heard "ya mean?" Or "y'nahmean?" They both sound like Ebonics for "you know what I mean?" but Jay makes it sound like the basketball star's name, which is appropriate as he ends the couplet with reference to Yao Ming's former basketball team, the Houston Rockets. Only the best rappers know how to craft such entertaining verses, which are, properly speaking, "equivokes," that is, *puns*.

♪ ♪ ♪ ♪

CAUTION: The following part of this section of the book involves use of the "n" word. The reader may skip this part if offended by "nigga" or "nigger." However, I plead with the reader to bear with its usage anywhere in this book, but primarily here, since it is such a *poignant* facet of The Culture, tied up deeply with White America, for educational purposes. From my socio-historical studies, I noticed that racist and prejudice words and/or phrases ascribed to Blacks or other people of color in various lands, primarily by White people, let us not forget, were later adopted by those same oppressed groups of people and used as terms of endearment, sometimes cynically, most times not, but definitely tongue in cheek. These may be referred to as exonyms (also known as "xenonyms").

I have seen Indians call each other "coolie" jokingly, and I have heard Black South Africans refer to each other as "kaffir." I have even heard some Italians call each other "wop" or "moolie," or "guinea"! And it was not just one age group, nor any specific demographic, within the Indians or Italians

The Backdrop and AAVE

(although it appeared more prevalent among the more youthful). As an African man raised in the United States, I have definitely experienced racism and I also use "nigga" as a term of endearment. The word "nigga," Ebonically speaking, is a term of endearment among most young African-Americans, even among many of the middle-aged and elderly Blacks in the Americas.

Derived (and [perhaps *not*] completely exclusive) from the racial slur "nigger," *nigga* is also used as an exclamation, an expression of disbelief or surprise, even a congratulatory utterance. Context (and racial designation) is absolutely crucial. Blacks can use this term when addressing each other, and in reference to (other) people, places, and things. But woe betide any *White* person using "nigga." We do not want to hear it because in our minds, White people are still calling us *nigger*. (After all, are they still not insulting us in such a fashion publicly?) Now that we have taken the same pejorative, transitioned it, and made it our secret/not-so-secret term of endearment (exonym), to then have the slavemaster or his descendants also be able to use that "nigga" is like reopening a barely scabbed-over wound and rubbing salt in it. That is unacceptable and morally degenerate.

And secretly/not-so-secretly, Black people get a kick out of seeing so many White people so uncomfortable as concerns use of that word; at least, *some* White folks appear to be uncomfortable. Others do not care; but The Culture has ways of discerning this. It is *verboten*, unacceptable, dejecting, deplorable, unaccepted, unwelcome, and just plain stupid for Whites to recite rap lyrics, spewing "nigga" left and right! If a White person would not normally use "nigga" or "nigger," why would they sing it in a song? If a White person would not use "nigger" in everyday conversation, why would they use *nigga*, which, although distinct from (the "hard 'r'") *nigger*, still has its roots therein?

I have never, in my entire life, heard a Black person call a Jew a "kike," or call an Indian a "coolie" (let alone out of spite), but Gandhi abused Black people verbally, called us all sorts of pejoratives, including the word "kaffir"! Even in battle raps, Black people, *for the most part*, will not use racial slurs, even if the people whom we are addressing have intra-ethnographically transitioned slurs (their erstwhile slavemasters used to debase them with) into euphemisms. Both "nigga" and "nigger" should be considered *disphomisms* and kryptonite to White people. Even while being exonyms to Black people.

Then, in many Black neighborhoods across the United States, we are presented with a culturally ambiguous being: The Neighborhood White Boy, the one always hanging out with Black guys. If he is wise, he too should never use either of the "n" words, euphemistically or disphomistically. It kicks up something really primordial in our DNA. I have even heard some White (and Black!) people say, "It's just a word." No, it is not "just a word"! *Nigger* has been used malignantly, demeaningly, incitefully, and animalistically over a period of *centuries*, perhaps millennia. Its use was usually accompanied with beatings; rapes; dismemberment; humiliations; mutilations; maimings; appliances of physical, mental, and emotional degradation; lynchings, *ad nauseam*! The trauma of all of those depredations is passed down through generations (who also witness and are victims of this viciousness). It becomes generational and is literally *in the blood*.

In **our** blood, specifically.

Concurrently, the inherent racism and prejudice of so many White people who indulged in those heinous acts is also generational - it is, quite literally, *in their blood*, too. Which is why so many of their descendants see nothing wrong with saying either of the "n" words. It matters not if you grew up around Black people - if you are Chinese, Indian, Arab, Mongolian, or generally speaking (and specifically, if you yourself *identify as*) Caucasian, you should not be using the "n" word, at all.

The roots of the word "nigger" allegedly lie in the word "Niger," as in the Niger River, but this is somewhat disingenuous, as the root word goes back almost two thousand years before the word "Niger" even existed. The root word for "nigger" comes from the Latin *niger*, meaning "black" or "*dark*."

In the app Quora, it is said, "The word 'Niger' does come from the Latin word 'niger,' which means 'black.' However, *the use of the word* 'Niger' to refer specifically to the Niger River is a relatively recent development. The name 'Niger' for the river is believed to have been first used by European explorers in the 1800's." [Author's italics] It goes on further to state, "It's worth noting that the Latin language was not always standardized, and different regions and cultures may have had different ways of referring to the same thing. Additionally, many historical records from ancient civilizations have been lost to time, so it's possible that the word 'niger' was used *in reference to* the Niger River by the local peoples, but these records have not been preserved." Possible... but unlikely.

The Backdrop and AAVE

As we go exploring the roots of the word "nigger," let us slightly divert to another similar raciolinguistic pejorative: *negro*. "In the English language, the word **negro** (or sometimes **negress** for a female) is a term historically used to denote persons to be of Black African heritage. The word *negro* means the color Black in both Spanish and in Portuguese (from Latin *niger*), where English took it from. The word can be construed as offensive, inoffensive, or completely neutral, largely depending on the region or country where it is used, as well as the context in which it is applied." Both *nigger* and *negro*, ostensibly, come from the same root word in Latin: *niger*, meaning "black" or "dark." But the word *negro* is far older in origin than *niger*. As a matter of fact, after reading the following compilation of excerpts, the reader will come to realize that the Latin *niger* was likely another pseudonym that developed from the Greek word *necro* (meaning *dead*).

Greece and Greek preceded Rome and Latin by several hundred years. Egypt preceded both by several *thousands* of years. "The name that you respond to determines the amount of your self worth. Similarly, the way a group of people collectively respond to a name can have devastating effects on their lives, particularly if they did not choose the name. Asians come from Asia and have pride in the Asian race. Europeans come from Europe and have pride in Europe accomplishments. Negroes, I am to assume, come from negroland - a mythical country with an uncertain past and an even more uncertain future." The author goes on to denote "negroland" (from which, we are to cheekily assume, negroes come) as a mythical place. He questions whencefrom originated this ostensible myth of the negro. We are then told that comprehending the origins and/or (the definition of) the negro will lead us to comprehending the negro.

♪ ♪ ♪ ♪

"The word negro is Spanish for black. The Spanish language comes from Latin, which has its origins in Classical Greek. The word negro, in Greek, is derived from the root word necro, meaning dead. What was once referred to as a physical condition is now regarded as an appropriate state of mind for millions of Africans. Historically when the Greeks first traveled to Africa 2,500 years ago, the Egyptian civilization was already ancient. The Great

Pyramid was over 3,000 years old and the sphinx was even older. Writing, science, medicine and religion were already a part of the civilization and had reached their zenith. The Greeks came to Africa as students to sit at the feet of the masters, and to discover what Africans already knew. In any student/teacher relationship the teacher can only teach as much as the student is capable of understanding."

Other Africans (and not just Egyptians) "understood that life existed beyond the grave. Ancestral worship is a way of acknowledging the lives of the people who have come before you, and their ability to offer guidance and direction to the living. Temples were designed as places where the ancestors could be honored and holidays (Holy Days) were the days designated to do so. The Egyptians had hundreds of temples and hundreds of Holy Days to worship their ancestors. The Greeks thought the Africans had a preoccupation with death. The act of ancestral worship became known as necromancy or communication with the dead. The root word necro means dead. Another word for necromancy is magic - that Old Black Magic which was practiced in Ancient Africa. When the Greeks returned to Europe, they took their distorted beliefs with them and the word negro evolved out of this great misunderstanding."

Furthermore, the author details how, only a couple of hundred years after the Greeks came to Egypt as students, their descendants returned as conquerors. These so-called "conquerors" razed and burned libraries, temples, and entire cities to the ground, deceitfully claiming African sciences as their own. Slavery began soon afterwards, and with its birth came the need to debase Africans in order to "prove" to them and their later descendants that they were of little worth and use. Stolen legacy. From there the negro can be said to have been "a race of dead people with a dead history and no hope for resurrection as long as they remained ignorant of their past."

Everyone knows that it was *verboten* for Black ("negro") slaves to be literate. Being literate meant the negro could read and learn and free himself with such skills, which were refused and forbidden to him. But progress cannot be withheld, only stalled. Despite all odds, Blacks educated ourselves and, with the recognition of the evolution of human rights, we restructuctured and reclassified ourselves. From Negro, to Colored, to Black, to African-American, the endonyms have only become more unique as our self-awareness has increased. "Knowledge of self is the key to unlocking the door to the future."

African sciences were purloined and repackaged to fit the narrative of what would be the millenia-long deception of the world into believing that Caucasians were somehow the perfecters of relatively contemporary civilizations. During these horrendous and deceitful millenia, the Caucasian ruling orders would denigrate and in so many ways belittle the selfsame source from which their civilizations had learned and then turned around to ruthlessly plunder. The irony is galling!

In addition to all of that: "Socially and politically, black implies *'Civiliter Mortuus,'* which means *'Dead in the eyes of Law.'* Black American is not a Nationality nor is it a Nation; therefore, 'black' has no political interests nor powers in the Free National Constitution that was prepared for all Free National Beings." [Author's emphases] We (Black people) were not even considered *alive*, let alone whole human beings, by White America, whose founding fathers created the "Three-Fifths Clause" of the United States Constitution in 1787. This Three-Fifths Clause was, indeed, for taxation and representation, and it disenfranchised Blacks from being able to vote.

Of course, the Slave States benefitted the most, being able to count each enslaved Black slave as, literally, *three-fifths* of being able to even *be* human. The interconnectedness of a vast melange of factors instituted to strip Blacks of their identity began *thousands* of years ago, beginning with the attempted Hellenization of African grandeur. This was followed by the wholesale pillaging of our ancestral worship sites (what Whites call "cemeteries" or "graveyards" today); this was again followed by the plundering of our natural resources, and our most precious resource: **us**. It continued with resource-hungry individuals (the majority of whom were White) carving up Africa like cake and ruling like robber barons. (And let us not forget that White people have been literally eating Black people for thousands of years.)

Nigger, then, ultimately comes from *negro*, the root word of which, "necro," is defined as being *dead* or *inanimate*. However, that delineation is *rejected* as being the implicit true state of being of The Culture, for long before the denizens of the Caucasus Mountains bred enough and in such numbers as to eventually venture forth and become world powers, Kemet, Sumeria, Akkadia, and Babylonia - all Black civilizations - had flourished and waned severally. So "nigger" might mean something dead or dark to the

White man, but that appellation is a comparatively recent construct, created to keep the powers that be in positions of seeming authority. However, once that vaunted and friable authority begins crumbling, there is no coming back (as we can see from the increasing pro-Palestinian rallies on college campuses across the United States).

The saying goes that "what's understood doesn't need to be explained," but I would like to give one example of the devolution of White supremacy - the appropriation of a malignant designation ascribed to all non-Whites, (and) its sociolinguistic mutation and subsequent ascription to a particular social (even societal) bracket impenetrable to White supremacy (save by rape or fear mongering). But now, neo-White supremacy asks Black people, "It's okay if I say the 'n' word if it's in a song, right?" No, my unwitting pawn of White supremacy, or Mr. White Supremacist himself, it is, in fact, *not* okay to recite "nigga" or "nigger" in rap songs. And why is it that so many racist Whites cover their faces when out and about? Why do they wear masks and white hoods when trying to intimidate the non-White population? Because they know, intrinsically, that what they're doing is WRONG! Otherwise there would be no need to cover their faces - they would proudly commit the evils they commit.

This incredible sense of entitlement held by so many White people is the glaring legacy of the casual racism practiced by their ancestors - so now the progeny of that evil epoch seeks to infiltrate The Culture with such a detestable (and **racist**) allowance. They are so privileged that they have the privilege of not even *seeing* that privilege. Make no mistake - if you are a White person and you have said, and (continue to) say "nigga" or "nigger," while singing a rap song or not, *you are a racist*. And if you do not see anything wrong with that, go ahead and *embrace* your animality. I do not know if anyone else sees the danger, but just imagine if The Culture somehow, some way, goes mad and all Black people simultaneously give all White people a pass to say "nigger" or "nigga" **only** in songs - do we really think it will stop there?

No, it will not! White people will start unabashedly dropping *nigga* in everyday conversations, which, to me and the majority of Blacks concerned, is unacceptable. Or imagine White people singing songs with prominent use of *nigga*! Furthermore, envision, if you will, White people *and other non-Blacks* singing out *nigga* in a convertible or other such open-air vehicle... in Brownsville, Brooklyn, or Chicago's south side, or in New Orleans, or

The Backdrop and AAVE

Compton, or Los Angeles, etc.? I have zero doubts they could easily lose their lives - and for what? Hateful and racist words they could have merely avoided using. Also, any Black person telling their White friends that it is all right to say *nigga* or *nigger* around them - you, too, are an unwitting automaton controlled by White supremacy, and a sellout. Stop it! It's *not* okay for White people to say those racially insensitive epithets! As offended, hurt, or uncomfortable as White people may feel reading this, it is truth, and if you feel *offended* that Black people do not want you calling us nigga or nigger, *ask yourself why*. You just might find out that you are a racist.

When I discovered the older root meaning of negro many years ago, I found myself loathing the word more than its misshapen, but also hugely powerful and almost equally loathsome mutant offspring: nigger. We conclude this relatively brief, painful, and terribly sensitive expatiation on this charged subject by remembering the words of Randall Kennedy, Professor of Law, Harvard University: "The word 'nigger' is a key term in American culture. It is a profoundly hurtful racist slur meant to stigmatize African-Americans; on occasion, it also has been used against members of other racial or ethnic groups, including Chinese, other Asians, East Indians, Arabs and darker-skinned people. It has been an important feature of many of the worst episodes of bigotry in American history. It has accompanied innumerable lynchings, beatings, acts of arson, and other racially motivated attacks upon blacks."

How many times has it "been featured in countless jokes and cartoons that both reflect and encourage the disparagement of blacks. It is the signature phrase of racial prejudice. To understand fully, however, the depths and intensities, quirks and complexities of American race relations, it is necessary to know in detail the many ways in which racist bigotry has manifested itself, been appealed to, and been resisted. The term 'nigger' is, in most contexts, a cultural obscenity." I myself contend that the latter part of Dr. Kennedy's astute description of *nigger*, in that the term *nigger* (not *nigga*) is in all contexts a cultural obscenity, predominantly and primarily when spoken by White people.

Yes, even in pedagogical environments, White people (which includes, but is certainly not limited to, the Chinese, Japanese, Taiwanese, all European Caucasian, all White Canadian, all White Australian, all non-Black White North American, White Puerto Rican, White Central American and White

South American, etc.) - even in pedagogical settings, White people can not, *should* not, say the "n" word, in any of its iterations. Conversely, people of color *can* say the "n" word in all of its iterations - it is a reminder to us of the midden heap from which the word came, the exonym that binds us people of color together in our shared grief, outrage, and *wisdom*. White supremacy in the world in general and in the United States in particular cannot be dismantled without first criminalizing use of the "n" word (in all its iterations) by non-people of color (if one of your parents or grandparents is not fully Black, along with a Caucasian co-parent, yes, it should apply to you, too).

Melanin can be diluted out of a Black family by the third generation. For example, if my mother were White and my *father* was clearly a Mulatto, I would be considered Black, no doubt about it. But if I have a child with a White person, it just means my child has Black in their family, *not* that the child is Black. The birth certificate of the child could indeed state the child as being White and, because of its watered-down phenotype, it would never be disputed. And that child could never say *nigger* or *nigga* "safely" because, for all intents and purposes, they are, in fact, (predominantly) Caucasian, and that occuring within just a couple of generations. In a few rap battles, White people have been punched in their face or booed offstage for saying *nigga*. A certain Caucasian battle rapper tried to be slick and thought no one would do anything, but he got a rude awakening that night.

♪ ♪ ♪ ♪

There have been so many other White people who apologized after using the "n" word who knew exactly what they were saying and doing at the time - they only apologized, after all, because they got caught, just like so many criminals after breaking the law. The utterance of the word, *publicly*, has become so taboo that, on 12 October, 2007, when Nas announced his upcoming album name to be "*NIGGER*," even Congress (allegedly) and other political personages threatened him and he was forced to change the name of the album to "*Untitled*." Either that or Def Jam was going to drop him because of the highly controversial album title. Credence is given both allegations because, on 19 May, 2008, a Def Jam representative announced that the album title name would be changed to "*Untitled.*"

The Backdrop and AAVE

This just goes to show how repugnant *nigger* is to many of today's White American population and their Savior Complex. That, and the fact that very few people want a civil war or a race war. Among African-Americans, the word "nigga" is ostensibly flailed about, but, we bleed each time we say it, subconsciously always reminded of the United States's checkered and violent past, and present. In spite of devastating odds, we turned that hated and despicable dysphemism into an intraracial euphemism, an exonym. In case White people were wondering, the *orthophemism* is "African-American," or even "Black," or "Black people." Now, as far as Eminem is concerned, let us just say early on that he *could have been* a proverbial "rap god," but, as we shall later on dissect and discuss, his early racist *faux pas* cannot be easily forgotten or hashed over.

We recognize Eminem to be a good rapper, no doubt, but he can never be a rap god, no matter how long, how fast, or how originally geeky he rhymes on a track. In addition, he can never be *the* rap god of a genre of music created, fashioned, popularized, and monetized by Black folks. We will be going down the rabbit hole of who and what Mr. Mathers is later, but it must be stated as a premise that no White person could ever be the "God of Rap" or the "King of Hip-Hop." This is because:

1. Nas, Jay-Z, Redman, Yeezy, Kendrick Lamar, Method Man, Weezy, Jadakiss, and quite a few other heavy hitters, are still around;
2. The use of the "n" word, inadvertently or otherwise; and
3. *Because they're White.*

So many White people are always so tempted to say *nigga* and most Black Americans kind of telepathically *know* that their White associates have, at one point or another, said the "n" word, be it in general conversation or in the mirror with themselves. Just for one second imagine the absurdity of a racist White "rap god" who repeatedly raps the "n" word. It is simply unrealistic for any Caucasian, no matter how talented, to aspire to such a lofty and unobtainable echelon while having rhymed racist lyrics. What Nas said, about not being mad at Eminem because - whatever! is all good for the cameras, but behind the scenes, in real life, as we all know, it is an entirely different story.

2
What's Beef?

A. Tupac Shakur vs. The Notorious B.I.G. (aka "Biggie")

In 1781, there was a failed rebellion against the Spanish in Peru. The descendant of the last Incan ruler at the time was captured, tried, tortured, and executed by the inimical Spanish so-called "colonizers" for his role in said revolt. One hundred and ninety two years later, the parents of a certain African-American man child would change his name abruptly in order to honor the aforesaid Incan descendant (whose name was **Tupac Amaru Shakur II**). The precocious man child had originally been named "Lesane Parish Crooks" when he was born on 16 June, 1971, but a year later, his name was changed to Tupac Amaru II. Most of the world now knows him as Tupac Shakur, or Tupac, or just "'Pac."

Tupac was born on the Upper East Side in Upper Manhattan, East Harlem, New York City. His parents are Afeni Shakur (nee Alice Faye Williams), a whilom Black Panther, and Billy Garland. Tupac grew up partially in East Harlem (also known as "Spanish Harlem" because of the high concentration of Hispanics living in those environs) until his family moved to Baltimore, Maryland in 1984. During his high school years in Baltimore (primarily the Baltimore School for the Arts), he came to know and become lifelong friends (and allegedly, later on, lovers) with Mrs. Jada Pinkett Smith. Their burgeoning friendship at that time was cut short when Tupac's family again moved to Oakland, California in 1988. Throughout his life, Tupac would often be seen in those three cities (New York, Baltimore, and Oakland). His love for them was evident even in his music as he would later on shoot videos in those same cities.

It was between 1984 and 1988 that Tupac really began, for his age, "showing his ass" (Ebonics for *showing off*). He was 13 years old when he first got to Baltimore, one of the most poverty-stricken cities in the United States. Still, he managed to attend the Baltimore School for the Arts (after attending two other high schools) and cultivate what would become a strong foundational basis for his later revolutionary and thought-provoking lyricism. How dare anyone in today's hip-hop *mise-en-scène* question the lyrical ability of Tupac!

In the song *"Dear Mama,"* Tupac details in the first stanza how he and his mother always had problems when he was younger and how, even though he was kicked out of the house, no one could ever replace her. Crying together with his baby sister because of their poverty, they would find a way to put the blame on their mother for everything wrong in their lives. He raps about getting into trouble by running from police, how his mother would catch up to and beat him, and about how he finally understood that, after it was all said and done, for everything his mother did for him and his sister, "there's no way I could pay you back." But the plan was to show her that he understood the sacrifices she made for him and how much she was appreciated, as he closed each stanza with those same reflections.

That's just the first stanza of Tupac's moving, very well-written, emotionally apropos, and focused tribute to his mother. As the lead single for the album *Me Against The World*, released on 21 February, 1995, it peaked at Number 9 and became Tupac's first entry into the Top Ten of the Billboard 100. (The Billboard Hot 100 is a type of "chart" that ranks the most popular songs in the United States. Billboard Weekly publishes it on a weekly basis.) The delinquency and dissatisfaction at life in general, and at times with his mother, began and burgeoned during his time in Baltimore. The Baltimore School for the Arts was, and remains, an excellent environment, and one in which he began honing his poetical skills. The year in which he claims to have begun "slingin' rock" (Ebonics for *selling crack*) and got kicked out of the house was approximately 1988, around when he turned 17.

Ms. Afeni Shakur, although alleged to having indulged in crack (also noted in the first stanza of *"Dear Mama"*), God rest her soul, always put the welfare of her children first. Seeing her son heading astray fast, she moved the family once again, this time to Oakland: one would say from the frying pan into the fire. Tupac Shakur was *born* for stardom, and his light still shines bright, and his love for his people was clear and palpable from the beginning. In his brief adult lifetime, Tupac was a rapper, an actor, a model, and most definitely a poet. He remains, to this day, one of hip-hop's greatest social media icons. From childhood, the limelight called to him, and he answered confidently, starring in a certain nostalgic production of "A Raisin in the Sun" with the 127th Street Ensemble in his more innocent and much younger days in Harlem. For those who might not know, "A Raisin in the Sun" is a spot-on drama and three-act play by Lorraine Hansberry, who describes the struggles of a Black family, the Youngers, in the 1950s. It got its name from the Langston Hughes poem "Harlem" and debuted on Broadway in 1959.

Indeed, Tupac Shakur was taken away too soon from the world, not just the hip-hop community. At the age of 20, he had already featured in two albums by Digital Underground and released his own album at the end of that same year, *as well as* starring in TV roles and large movies. The most impressive thing was how he was able to juggle all of these responsibilities and *still* have time for beef!

The Culture deeply enjoyed all the movies in which Tupac starred: from the iconic and classic "Juice" in 1992, to "Poetic Justice" in 1993, to "Gang Related", a posthumous movie that was released in 1997. (He also guest starred in several other movies and t.v. shows.) It was such a pleasure watching him on the big screen - it was his *destiny* to be famous. He brought a certain *panache* to his roles, but one particular role in which I, personally, will always remember him in as striking the perfect balance between "thug life" and being "soft" was his character Lucky in "Poetic Justice." Speaking of which, whether a PR stunt or an actuality, no one but Janet Jackson and God know whether or not she asked Tupac to take an H.I.V. test before an intimate scene in the movie. What we *do* know is that Tupac "fumbled the bag" (Ebonics for *messed up*, usually *big time*) on "shooting his shot" (Ebonics for [usually] *initial courtship*) with Janet because he foolishly shot his shot, somewhat simultaneously, with one of Janet's dancers!

What a terrific *fumble*!

However, with the entire *world* showing him love, Tupac bounced back from that fumble before the film was even finished. As time went on, other

What's Beef?

rappers emerged, trying to give Tupac a run for his money. One of the said rappers had also been making a buzz for himself back home in New York. On 16 February, 1993, Tupac released his second studio album, *Strictly for my N.I.G.G.A.Z.* Hip-hop was in full swing, in what this author concurs to have been part of rap's Golden Age. Lyricists like Nas, Redman, Wu-Tang, Das Efx, Ice Cube, and NWA were among the relatively few and upcoming artists enjoying great fame, and some fortune, at the time.

But also coming up were Dr. Dre and Snoop Dogg, whose hit single, *"Nuthin' but a G Thang"* peaked at Number 2 on the charts; Onyx's *"Slam"* had taken over New York but only peaked at (a still fair) Number 4, tying with Salt n Pepa's *"Shoop"*; surprisingly, Arrested Development's *"Mr. Wendel"* peaked at a still decent Number 6. A Tribe Called Quest, Queen Latifah and her proteges in Naughty by Nature, Cypress Hill, Lost Boyz, and *some others* appeared to be "doing their numbers" (Ebonics for *making enough, and more, money*), and making their rounds, becoming more famous. Rhythm and Blues was also doing its numbers: Whitney Houston took home 11 awards at that year's Billboard Music Awards from her soundtrack for "The Bodyguard," a very successful movie in which she starred opposite Kevin Costner.

Incidentally, Chance the Rapper was born that year. As were Ariana Grande, Metro Boomin, PARTYNEXTDOOR, Vic Mensa, Vince Staples, Tinashe, Meghan Trainor, Keke Palmer, Gunna, Bryson Tiller, Zayn, Pete Davidson, Amber Mark, Famous Dex, and Stormzy. Wild! I remember it like it was yesterday. Cellphones were not really a thing, except for the hustlers and the gangsters and some Wall Street shleps. Most of us were still on our desktops or pagers, and payphones. For a dollar I could buy a four-cookie pack of chocolate-chocolate or chocolate chip cookies, a heavy bag of Fritos or Doritos, a five-stick pack of Spearmint or Doublemint (or 5 Bazooka Joe pieces that could crack a tooth at the first bite), and a quarter water. I do not know if these things are even still in rotation, but they were fun times for Gen X. A dollar went a long way back then, but Baby Boomers were complaining about inflation and the rising cost of living. Strange - it is kind of like the same way Gen X now complains about inflation and the rising cost of living, while criticizing Gen Z and their, quite frankly, herculean efforts at merely existing in this price-gouged world.

To Generation X, the mid to late 1980s and the 1990s (and early 2000s) were the best years of our lives, or ever in existence. The air just seemed fresher, and the food and music was still organic and original, respectively. Racism existed and was being addressed in a wholesome manner by wholesome leaders of The Culture. Somehow, life was just *better*. Perhaps it is because I was raised with something of a silver spoon in my mouth, but the 'hood and the streets were calling me, too; their appeal, especially, lived vicariously through our rap artists, of whose album releases I and others kept abreast. Basically, I was a "good kid" whom the streets turned into a gangster. My only regret in life is that maybe, had I taken the straight and narrow path in life, I would have touched more lives than I feel I have at my age. But I am still young and there is still time to do a massive amount of more good for The Culture.

Tupac Shakur was a revolutionary and a gangster, and everybody knew it. There was no fake shit in him, and he would not let anyone or anything fake come around him without exposing it. Christopher Wallace, also known as "The Notorious 'B.I.G.,'" "B.I.G.," or "Biggie," was also a gangster. From everything I know and have learned further of Tupac and Biggie, the latter looked up to the former, as they were both of an age and had met on the set of *Poetic Justice* when Tupac was bumping Biggie's newest hit at the time, *"Party and Bullshit."* The proximity both of them shared increased Biggie's visibility on the rap scene. They were like brothers, and Biggie would crash at Tupac's crib whenever he was in Los Angeles.

"Biggie looked like he was wearing the same pair of Timberlands for a year [while] 'Pac was staying at the Waldorf-Astoria and buying Rolexes and dating Madonna." Those are the words of *Outlawz* member "E.D.I. Mean" (even names can be puns in hip-hop: "E.D.I. Mean," a homophonic play on *Idi Amin*, the former president of Uganda). E.D.I. Mean also stated how Biggie was not happy in his recording career with Sean "P Diddy" Combs. Allegedly, Biggie went so far as to ask Tupac to be his manager, but the latter, in what I deem to be another monumental career fumble on his part, refused, urging Biggie to stay with Bad Boy and Diddy, as the latter would make Biggie a star. Tupac was shooting the movie *Above The Rim* in New York and crossed paths with some well-known gangsters (Jacques "Haitian Jack" Agnant, Walter "King Tut" Johnson, and Jimmy Bosemond, more popularly known as "Jimmy Henchman," or "Jimmy *The* Henchman"). Biggie supposedly warned Tupac to stay away from them but 'Pac, his elder, who was also from New York, was not keen to hear that.

What's Beef?

It was on 22 March, 1994, that the *Above The Rim* soundtrack "dropped" (Ebonics for *was released*), with the double platinum hit banger single *"Regulate,"* by Warren G and Nate Dogg. Snoop Dogg, Tha Dogg Pound, Treach from Naughty by Nature, as well as Tupac and some others, featured on the album. In the meantime, Biggie and Tupac were doing tours and shows, but Biggie still lagged behind 'Pac. However, that would change and Biggie would blow up on the hip-hop scene with his hit singles *"Big Poppa"* and *"One More Chance/Stay with Me [the remix]"*; Biggie's debut album, and classic, *Ready to Die,* dropped and would go platinum about a year later. Almost two weeks after *Ready to Die* was released, Tupac dropped *Thug Life: Volume 1,* another successful banger. Celebrations of each other's success were short-lived, however, as Tupac and Biggie were destined to clash again when, on 24 November, 1994, Tupac went to Quad Studios to lay down some verses for Little Shawn, one of Jimmy Henchman's clients, with whom he, Biggie, and Diddy were to have gotten together.

A few no-good unsavory types tried to rob Tupac in the lobby but he fought back. For his courage, he was served five bullets. One of the robber unsavories, Dexter Isaac, serving life for murder, confessed in 2011 to the hip-hop/rap magazine XXL that he had been paid $2500 to rob and shoot Tupac. His employer? Allegedly, none other than Jimmy Henchman himself, which, *prima facie*, seems quite strange, as Tupac *and* Biggie were to have dropped some bars for Henchman's artist. The lifer's confession came seventeen years too late, as this murder attempt on Tupac would ignite one of the most bitter hip-hop rivalries in history. "In 1994, James Bosemund hired me to rob Tupac Shakur. He gave me $2500, plus all the jewelry I took, except for one ring, which he took for himself."

The whole New York was abuzz with surprise and no mean concern for Tupac. No matter that he repped (Ebonics for *represented*) "West Side," 'Pac was still a son of New York, a man of that soil, and we still loved and cherished him as such. And he was not just a New Yorker, but a "Harlemite" (native of Harlem) by birth. The nascent beef was exciting for us New Yorkers, but also a bit confusing. To this day the sub-borough of Harlem secretly hates Brooklyn because of this (Biggie was from Brooklyn). In any case, Tupac was incarcerated and sentenced for something he did not do mere *months* after he was shot. Somehow, though, I do believe this imprisonment preserved his life a lot longer than if he had convalesced on the outside, where he would have been more vulnerable and in his debilitated state. On 20 February, 1995, Biggie released *"Who Shot Ya,"* seemingly a diss song directly aimed at Tupac, who already believed the former and Diddy had set him up for the robbery and attempted murder. The song made Tupac extremely angry, and rightfully so. (Incidentally, Diddy is also being investigated for his role in the shooting and subsequent murder of Tupac.)

Even though Biggie and his entourage denied that *"Who Shot Ya"* was meant for Tupac, due to the quite unfavorable *timing* of the song's release, one can hardly fault Tupac for believing contrariwise to Bad Boy's averrals of innocence. A hip-hop/rap magazine called VIBE published *"Tupac talks Hit Em Up [vs] Who Shot Ya"* (Part 2, VIBE): "Niggas been talking shit all while I'm in jail. 'Who Shot Ya?' LL got a song 'I Shot Ya.' Even if it ain't about me, nigga, you should be like, I'm not putting it out 'cause he might think it's about him." That was real talk. Biggie and Diddy seemed to know *exactly* what they were doing when they released that track.

We are going to look into *"Who Shot Ya"* to see exactly what infuriated Tupac. Analyzing this song now, all these years later, I have to say that, although nothing *specifically* referred to Tupac (save for the glaring song title), again, it was more the *timing* and title of the release of the song than anything else that made Biggie an instant enemy of Tupac. The song, as claimed by Diddy and even Biggie himself, likely *was* written before Tupac got shot, but one could also argue that the songmaker knew beforehand about Tupac's future shooting and either set it up, helped to set it up, or adopted a *"laissez-faire"* attitude when finding out about it. Biggie should not have released it *at that time* - after all, the shooting had just occurred a couple of months back. Plus, Tupac was still healing up and going through his court travails, culminating in a sentence of 18 months to 4½ years in the custody of the New York State Department of Correctional Services (NYS - DOCCS). Tupac was in Clinton Correctional Facility one week later and Biggie dropped *"Who Shot Ya."*

For me, personally, it was a weak but cunning move in that it exposed Biggie's wariness when Tupac was around, yet how much freer he felt when Tupac was "up north" (Ebonics for *serving prison time*). It is my contention that Biggie even feared Tupac; after all, the latter's influence was undeniable and already huge, his rizz intimidating (how do you even compare to someone who dated one of the music world's greatest icons, and kissed another in a film in which both acted?), and he was well on his way to becoming a master lyricist.

And then came the fuel to the fire. The big homie Suge Knight bravely went onstage at the 1995 Source Awards and *clearly* disrespected Diddy, and the East Coast. Say what you want about Suge Knight, but it took a set of balls the size and strength of football helmets for him to have done what he did, and he was speaking for the entire West Coast, which was feeling slighted and looked down upon, or straight-up overlooked, at the time. Suge effectively united the West Coast behind him even *more* with that move. The next month, "Big Jake" (Jai Hassan-Jamal Robles), who was employed by Death Row, was shot after a Jermain Dupri party. He died a couple of weeks later while hospitalized. Allegedly, Diddy's erstwhile bodyguard, Anthony "Wolf" Jones (rumored to be the real father of Diddy's son, Justin Dior Combs), was the culprit behind that hit.

One of Tupac's entourage, Stretch, who had been with him at the Quad Studios shooting but whom Tupac suspected of knowing about the shooting beforehand, was, ironically, himself "stretched out" (Ebonics for *killed*) just after being dropped off by Nas one evening. He had been working on Nas's *It Was Written* album at the time of his murder. That day oh-so-coincidentally happened to be one year to the day of the Quad Studios shooting. The beef escalated when Snoop Dogg and Tha Dogg Pound came to New York in December of that same year to film their video *"New York, New York,"* but nobody was hurt. Suge bailed out Tupac on a 1½ million dollars bond on 12 October, 1995, as he had just agreed to sign with Death Row.

♪ ♪ ♪ ♪

Things cooled off for a few months, until Tupac and Biggie came *vis-a-vis* with one another for the first time since around the time the former had been shot. Brief but bitter words were traded but security for both Death Row and Bad Boy handled the unexpected meeting professionally, keeping the camps apart. Biggie was later said to have called Tupac's reaction to him that night an act, being that of the vengeful character "Bishop," whom Tupac had played in the classic and memorable movie *Juice*. Well, I don't know about that, but I do know that Tupac appeared to be living life highly as his second Billboard chart-topping album, *All Eyez on Me*, was released in February, 1996 (the first in a long line of his chart toppers was *Me Against the World*).

Tupac was all the rage, and he kept himself in the limelight, dropping *"Hit Em Up"* in response to *"Who Shot Ya,"* and attacking Mobb Deep (rest in peace to Prodigy and a huge shout-out and salute to the big homie Havoc). That was on 4 June, 1996. Exactly three weeks later, the newest and a fast-rising artist on the scene, Shawn Carter, released one of the greatest rap albums ever to exist in any universe: *Reasonable Doubt*. I remember buying this CD and, anytime me and some of my friends rented a New Ways or New Harlem "system," I would bring that album. (A "system" was a tricked-out luxury car or, in our case, usually a tricked-out behemoth of an SUV that could be heard from several blocks away in which we rode around, looking for beef or just smoking massive amounts of haze or 'dro, also known as "piff" back then.) Shout-out to 75, 95, and 500. Shout-out to O'Jay's, too.

My childhood friends were not up on Hov yet and were surprised by his nimble and thought-provoking wordplay. I must digress briefly and address something of import to me. Right now, the *#MeToo* movement is on a rampage and Diddy is its biggest and juiciest target. Allegedly, LL Cool J, MC Lyte, Vin Diesel, and Axel Rose (of Guns 'n Roses fame, whose album *Use Your Illusion 1* is an eternal classic) - all of them are its targets. Black people have seen and are acutely aware of the disparity in the pursuance and prosecution of Caucasian and African-American *alleged* "offenders." ("Alleged" because, of course, one is presumed innocent until proven guilty.) The Culture in no way condones sexual abuse; we do not condone *any* kind of abuse. Speaking for myself, *personally*, I do not condone sexual abuse, child abuse, animal abuse, etc.

However, The Culture has noticed how the criminal justice system *pounds* on alleged Black offenders, degrading them and stripping them of any dignity. Meanwhile, those on the Epstein flight log list are still being allowed to gallivant about despite having frequented environs where sexual abuse of women and minors of either gender was the norm. Please make it make sense. *Minors*, for Christ's sake! What's good for the goose must also be good for the gander. *Expose, ridicule,* and *bankrupt* all pedophiles and rapists, *not just* alleged African-American perps. I say this because I am seeing it happen more and more in the hip-hop/rap/R&B industries, and I must speak to the truth of an ugly undercurrent: the more African-

What's Beef?

Americans are disproportionately prosecuted but non-Blacks are getting wrist slaps or not even getting prosecuted, the more unsympathetic and numb The Culture will become to what crocodile (or should I say *kangaroo*) courts are, apparently, trying to emphasize: "All Lives Matter." Yes, we know, all lives matter, but Black Lives Matter, too. Not "more," but *too*, as in "also." And especially at this critical juncture in history. (This is because "all" lives have NOT mattered in the United States, especially Black lives and those of the indigenous peoples of the Americas. Up until the very day these words are being penned!) I'll be addressing this issue later on.

Since we were on the topic of Shawn Carter and *Reasonable Doubt*, some extremely nasty rumors about him are surfacing, such as him having groomed Aaliyah, Foxy Brown, and Rihanna. I do not know if any of that has any veracity to it, but without a doubt, before Cancel Culture comes for Jay-Z, allow me to formally give him his flowers, *musically* speaking, on *Reasonable Doubt*, *Hard Knock Life*, and so many other other albums. But *Reasonable Doubt*? Absolutely *superb* and one of the most underrated albums, ever.

For now, though, let's take a look at *"Hit Em Up"* and see how Tupac giftwrapped Biggie at this stage of their beef. Tupac's verbal assault on Bad Boy in general and his vitriolic *ad hominems* on Biggie in particular were masterful and surely hurtful. If I were Biggie hearing this I know *I* would have been hurt. After the first stanza (accompanied by goading and fiery ad-libs), one would reasonably conclude that the hate Tupac had for Biggie was *visceral*. Of course, *"Hit Em Up"* was not the only diss track on which Tupac slayed Biggie. Furthermore, Tupac's man Hussein Fatal continued the verbal attack in like fashion, coining a term Nas would later on popularize and use as the title of a song that is, to this day, in humorous reference to someone who did not mean to kill someone else: an *"accident murderer."*

Tupac's first verse, however tough, was just a warm-up to his second verse (after Hussein Fatal), although what else could someone say who early on stated that your click ("clique") wasn't shit and that he had fucked your wife was beyond me. But Tupac was a talented evil rap genius.

Without a doubt, on top of sleeping with (or even *claiming* to have slept with) R&B songstress Faith Evans (Biggie's wife at the time), Tupac revealed (in the third stanza) how "bummy" Biggie had been (practically homeless at some points), and how he (Tupac) survived the hit he thought Biggie and/or Diddy had contracted at Quad Studios. No lie, these words had to have been sore to Biggie. You see, growing up in New York City, one thing I learned was that, if someone continually accused me of something I did not do, *eventually*, the thought would come into my head that *I might as well do it*. Imagine Biggie's thought process at this point, being a rising international rap star, and how he might have gritted his teeth while listening to *"Hit Em Up,"* just as hard as Eazy-E and Dr. Dre gritted theirs when they heard *"No Vaseline."* Tupac was "sonning" him, making him look like his li'l nigga, a punk, *internationally*. There was also the undercurrent of Tupac heavily into the Westside, despite being from New York, so it was as if the West Coast was also sonning the East Coast!

♪ ♪ ♪ ♪

There were so many facets to this beef that had extended between and along thousands of contiguous United States miles. Kadafi, a rapper originally from New Jersey who joined the West Coast-based rap group The Outlawz, was next to feature on *"Hit Em Up,"* taking shots at Junior M.A.F.I.A. in the same vitriolic vein as Tupac and Hassan Fatal. His feature was followed by that of E.D.I. Mean, who also rained disses and metaphorical jokes on Biggie and Co., one such being when he said Bad Boy was *"softer than Alizé with a chaser."* Alizé is a type of French cognac and vodka mix drink that, combined with its various fruity and exotic flavors, is itself "like a chaser." (For those who don't know, a chaser is a soft drink, often, but not always, mildly alcoholic, taken after hard alcoholic drinks. For example, whiskey is a hard liquor that can be "chased" with Coca-Cola. Lemonade is also a chaser.) Thus, E.D.I. Mean was saying Bad Boy was softer than a soft drink. At the end of *"Hit Em Up,"* Tupac goes on an outro rant that sometimes rhymed in its freestyle-*like* delivery over the beat, which, we must note, is the same beat used by Biggie in his song with Li'l Kim and Junior M.A.F.I.A. in their *"Get Money"* video. The beat itself is sampled from Sylvia Striplin's 1981 song *"You Can't Turn Me Away."*

Tupac says (in part): *"Now tell me who won? I see them, they run [laughs]. They don't wanna see us. Whole Junior M.A.F.I.A. clique dressin' up tryna be us. How the fuck they gonna be the mob when we always on our job? We millionaires. Killing ain't fair but somebody gotta do it."* (These are ad-libs, not lyrics, to the actual song.) There was something about this part

What's Beef?

that I have to point out - throughout the entire song, no one said anything to or about Mobb Deep. But at the very end, Tupac addresses them and others, directly. It was as if Prodigy and Havoc were a "P.S." or *"Nota Bene"* Tupac brusquely addressed at the end of this shellacking of Bad Boy. Please file this in a mental cabinet as we will once again come across this battle *tactic*.

"*Oh yeah, Mobb Deep, you wanna fuck with us? You little young ass muthafuckas! Don't one of you niggas got sickle cell or something?*" Tupac had no shame in hitting below the belt - Prodigy did, in fact, suffer from sickle cell anemia, the complications of which illness were related to his death on 20 June, 2017, also coincidentally in Las Vegas. File this below-the-belt *tactic* for later perusal as well. Tupac may not have known that he was creating and opening the doors to ruthless types of battle rap tactics still controversially used in hip-hop/rap battles today.

After listening to the rest of Tupac's outro ad-libs, slower, I must admit, there was no doubt somebody was going to try to kill him. Phew! His mouth was *foul*! He told Bad Boy they would get heart attacks and seizures if they kept beefing with him, that he was going to kill "all of [them] muthafuckas." Everybody caught a "Fuck you!" and a "Die slow!" His language was incendiary, very harsh, threatening, galling, worrying, and I am certain it was to incite a reaction out of Bad Boy. However, some people's reactions can be fatal. Imagine working for Bad Boy and you hear Tupac and some other West Coast rappers telling the world that they were going to kill you. I daresay those words could be looked at as credible threats. There was simply too much hate spewing out of Tupac.

Of course, we *should* take into account that this was because Tupac felt he had been set up, and he *had* been set up, and shot. By those he considered friends. He felt betrayed on almost all sides. And so, he lashed out, but without restraint.

Tupac was not known for shying away from confrontation or controversy. However, those were *highly* disrespectful words, and spoken with *passion*. Although Tupac lived Thug Life, even thugs know that they are not free from the consequences of their words and actions. But you know something? Perhaps he *did* know the consequences and was ready to face them when they came. Yes, I do believe that was the case, because even with his dying breath, he did not snitch on the unsavory who killed him. I also believe that, if Biggie could have spoken the names of his killers, he too would have stayed quiet as to who *those* unsavories were. They both lived Thug Life, but misconceptions, untruths, and whispered innuendos destroyed what could have been a powerful and dynastic union of masterful lyricism.

♪ ♪ ♪ ♪

Now, as for how and why Shawn Carter was drawn into the beef between Tupac and Biggie: Jay-Z is from Brooklyn, as was Biggie, and although they were not from the same projects (Jay-Z is from Marcy Projects and Biggie was from Bedford-Stuyvesant Projects), at *some* point, given their rise in the game, they would have linked up. After *"Hit Em Up"* (released on 4 June, 1996, let us remember), Jay-Z released *Reasonable Doubt*, on which album there is a song entitled *"Brooklyn's Finest."* Biggie featured on that song and rapped brilliantly. The scheme was about he and "Gutter" having "two spots" (two locations where they sold drugs), where he describes them selling the "two-for-five dollar hits: the blue tops." Bigs continues by letting us know the code for when those spots were "getting too hot" (meaning, garnering too much [unwanted] attention), which was "Gotta go, Coolio."

Biggie balanced words and put them together into visible scenery so vivid that even now most of his skills are a pleasure to listen to. After the spot got "too hot," he drops the punchline of the scheme: "If Faith have twins she probably have Tupac's... Get it? Two... Pacs!" As soon as real hip-hop heads heard "two spots," we knew this rhyme scheme would involve "Tupac" somewhere, and Biggie did NOT disappoint. For those who may still not understand the wittiness of this double entendre equivoke, Biggie was saying that if, in fact, Faith Evans (his wife, who was pregnant at the time, and with whom Tupac claimed he had already allegedly slept [nasty work, yes, but Faith used to sleep around with many men back when]) - if Faith had slept with Tupac and she did have twins, they would, of course, be "Tupac's": twins, hence, *two* 'Pacs, as well as Tupac's. The pun on the name "Tupac" ("Tupac's" and "two 'Pacs") is a marvelous and highly enjoyable double entendre and, as Faith was about four or five months pregnant at this time, it was perfect timing (although I doubt Faith would call it that, nor in any demure tone).

Faith is an accomplished R&B artist herself who, in my opinion, could have been much more popular, had she earlier focused on a career

What's Beef?

distinct from Biggie's, given Bad Boy's desuetudinous influence. She was, and remains, a great singer. Her and Biggie's son, CJ Wallace, was born in October, 1996. He is now an actor and entrepreneur running his own cannabis company. And that was how Biggie's feature on *"Brooklyn's Finest"* drew Jay-Z into the Tupac/Biggie beef.

Before we continue, something needs to be addressed that just came to mind. I do believe *"Who Shot Ya"* was released as a diss to 'Pac, yes, but I believe it was also made for Wu-Tang Clan, specifically Ghostface Killa and Raekwon. Peep game (Ebonics for *let me tell you what happened*): allegedly, *"Who Shot Ya"* was written or recorded before the Quad Studios shooting, right? But it was still recorded *after* Ghostface Killa and Raekwon released *Only Built For Cuban Links* on 1 August, 1995; known also as *The Purple Tape*, it, too, is one of the greatest rap albums ever. In this album, during the skit entitled *"Shark Niggas (Biters [in part]),"* where it seemed as if Ghost and Rae were just shooting the breeze, suddenly they struck:

Raekwon: *Niggas, niggas, niggas, niggas is bitin' off your album cover and shit* (Yeah)
Ghostface: *Boom, bad enough they bitin' lines like niggas killed me* (Yeah)- *when they came with some Nas-*
Raekwon: *Niggas bit off of Nas shit, you know what I'm sayin'? Word, niggas, niggas, niggas, niggas caught his little album cover, boom, then done did a Nas for that shit* (Yeah)

Allegedly, Biggie called up Nas (since Nas was Godbody and cool with the Wu, and most, if not all, of *them* are Godbody) in a high dudgeon to complain about what had been said. Nas, with New York firmly in his grip and the world at his feet after another blockbuster classic of his dropped on 19 April, 1994, took a placatory and neutral stance between both camps. The deal was that Nas had put a baby picture of himself on the cover of *Illmatic*, and when Biggie did the same on *Ready to Die*, some rappers took offense to and ridiculed the move as "biting" (Ebonics for *copying someone's style*, usually without permission). "Some rappers" including, apparently, Ghostface and Raekwon. It just seems to me that although nothing *direct* was ever mentioned to the Wu by Biggie, just like everyone knew exactly who Ghostface was talking about, everyone should also have automatically known to whom Biggie was referring when he spit that, not only did Big Poppa smash and bash fools, but:

> *Niggas mad because I know that Cash Rules*
> *Everything Around Me, two Glock Nines...*

Any muthafucka whispering about [his]... It was so clear, the reference to *"C.R.E.A.M.,"* a summer banger of a hip-hop song by the Wu-Tang Clan that came out in 1993, the acronym for which is: *"Cash Rules Everything Around Me."* ("Cream" is also Ebonics for *money*.) The reason no one made that connection then, I think, was because of the *title* of Biggie's song underpinning and overshadowing the entire incident and, again, the *timing* of Tupac's shooting. Biggie *had to have known* that releasing *Who Shot Ya* at that time would have been incendiary to an already flammable powder keg. To his subatomic credit, Biggie's ostensible and *alleged* groomer-manager-and-*alleged*-rapist-of-underage-boys-and-girls and alleged sex trafficker (yeah, I'm talking about DIDDY!) kept *"Who Shot Ya"* off Biggie's debut album.

He knew better, anyway.

(Excuse this digression but I felt that I had to share the following alternative... *theory*.)

Jay-Z was now drawn into the beef, and Tupac's responses on *Makavelli* would be epic and brutal. A month after *Reasonable Doubt* was released, Tupac dropped the single *"Bomb First."* We are going to delve into that song in short order, but let us examine the *intro* to the song, which is presented as a seriocomic music news report. During the "music news," the speaker mentions the release of another album by Tupac under the pseudonym "Makaveli" He goes on to accuse "less fortunate rappers" of being in cahoots to malign Tupac and Death Row, also adding that "music insiders" were "running wild" trying to change the dates of when the albums of their artists were to drop, lest they should drop on the same day as *Makaveli*.

If it's one thing 'Pac knew how to do, it was to get under people's skin. He or someone else continued the introductory barrage by mentioning Nas as the "alleged ringleader," further dissing Mobb Deep by calling them "Mobb *Sleep*," and changing the "Notorious B.I.G." to "Notorious *P.I.G.*" *"...Tupac - rather, Makaveli - was not available for comment but released this statement: It's not about East or West..."* Ah, but by this point, it *was* about "East and West." (Imagine for one minute, though, being called out of your name in such a brutally facile, almost *puerile*, manner? These disses were comical, derogatory and, I am almost certain, *hurtful*. The beef was escalating like one's blood pressure after a Vice President Kamala Harris interview... or after President Donald Trump's first month in office.

By both of their words, but especially Tupac's, the beef now had definitely become coastal. Tupac would then go on to *demolish* Bad Boy, *et al*. First and foremost, he introduces himself as Makavelli the Don before talking trash. But let's stop after the first few verses to examine something:

Born on a dope fiend's titty

A "dope fiend" is someone addicted to a particularly white psychotropic rock (heroin in powder form) that, unlike what Caucasians define as "a slang word for 'marijuana,'" *in this day and age,* Blacks know to be a psychotropic. For maximum effectiveness and absorption into the body, many dope fiends put a piece of the drug (which can be rocky but friable) onto a steel spoon and light the underside of the spoon, which causes the drug to liquify. At this point the drug has effectively turned into "heroin." The latter is then drawn into a syringe after an arm is tied with a rubber tie, somewhere along the arm, to make veins bulge for a better choice at entry of the powerful drug. Black people now, for the most part, avoid that drug like a plague, having trudged through that scourge already. Tupac's mother, at one time, had been addicted to dope and crack, both drugs being legacies of the CIA pumping hard drugs into the 'hood in order to fund their not-so-secret wars in Central and South America and parts of Africa.

Tupac himself says on the *"Dear Mama"* track that even if his mama was a crack fiend, she *"always was a Black Queen, Mama."* Thankfully, Afeni Shakur was able to conquer those addictions and raise a gifted king whose life was so tragically cut at the beginning of what seemed like the prime of a most promising career. As Tupac was never shy to speak the truth about his mother's addictions, that verse about being born on a dope fiend's titty was... disturbing. But it was reality! And this is why 'Pac was so well-loved. What a personally painful thing to expose on a diss track about other rappers, which led me to believe that, at the time of the recording of *"Bomb First,"* Tupac and his mom were estranged. Such a state of things is quite

Hip-Hop Rivalries: East Coast Versus West Coast

common, even among the gliteratti. (Britney Spears and Marshall Bruce Mathers III come to mind. Rest in peace, Debbie Nelson.)

Tupac continued the stanza bigging up the group he founded in 1992: The Outlawz. He made good on his averment to *"murder muthafuckas lyrically"* indeed, going on to call his two pitbulls *"Mobb bitch nigga eaters"* (of course it was a snipe at Mobb Deep). Or did he say *"'My' bitch nigga eaters"*? (Either way, Prodigy was included in the shots being taken.) Thinly veiled threats and thinly veiled *death* threats abounded just in this first stanza, and the recipients at whom they were launched had to have been salty and extremely heated. Angry enough to plan Tupac's murder? The police appear to think so, as rumors of Diddy's involvement in 'Pac's murder have once again arisen since the former's arrest on Monday, 16 September, 2024.

(During an interview years after he was shot at Quad Studios, Tupac was asked if he thought Puffy [Diddy] had something to do with him getting shot. Tupac replied, "I believe so, I do believe so." Cut and dry. Directly to the matter at hand. And this interview was in 1996, right before he was killed.)

The track thus far wasn't bad at all. But not really as major a hammer as *"Hit Em Up."* After Tupac came E.D.I. Mean and Young Noble of The Outlawz, who did a fair job of accompanying their leader in his bombardment of Bad Boy, *et al.* Some of their lines were memorably catchy, like E.D.I. Mean's, especially when he took shots (lyrically) at *"the nigga that made 'Paparazzi...'"*: Xzibit, whose song *"Paparazzi,"* was the lead single of his first album *At The Speed of Life.*

Young Noble was also a problem on the track and brought his beef to bear, standing by the big homie 'Pac. With a composed and well-pitched delivery, he calls out Biggie on the latter's claim that he is the "King of New York" (see Biggie's track *"Kick in the Door"*), sarcastically telling Biggie that he is not the only one who has ever adopted that title. From the beginning of *Makaveli* throughout the entire album, Tupac and his cohorts dissed so many rappers it really should not have been a surprise that it took twenty-seven years before any concrete headway was made into who killed him. We will get to that piece of news later on, but for now, we can see that Tupac was on a rampage on *Makaveli.* In *"Bomb First,"* he comes back at the end of the track to "finish his food," in a manner of speaking (Ebonics for *finish off the job*), after Young Noble. It was not an entire stanza so much as a bridge to the last chorus of the song.

What's Beef?

There can be no doubt that Tupac was a poet. To me, his rhymes at times seemed unconventional *in form*, but upon closer examination, I see how he used rhyming couplets ("AABB"), yes, but he also would use poetic triplets (or "tercets"), and the occasional quatrain. Most rappers (who are really modern-day poets) rap in rhyming couplets or even alternating couplets ("ABAB"), which are *alternating rhyming couplets*, but Tupac rarely followed strictly the "rules" or "guides" of poetry - because that is exactly what rapping is: poetry vocalized with or without a catchy beat. And, in any case, you generally have to be saying something of worth, or something punny.

♪ ♪ ♪ ♪

There are three *main* genres of poetry: *Narrative Poetry*, *Dramatic Poetry*, and *Lyric Poetry*. I would say that rap and hip-hop fall within the sphere of Narrative Poetry, but hip-hop has veered into the realm of Dramatic and Lyric Poetry over the years. There are a few rappers, like Tupac, who do not follow a strict rhyming couplet rule: Nas and Prodigy from Mobb Deep, for example, especially the latter, are notorious for not always rhyming *traditionally*. Tupac had been named "Best Rapper" at the Baltimore School of Performing Arts. One thing I noticed, though, is that Tupac mentioned Nas briefly on *"Bomb First"* and a few times throughout *Makaveli*. Incidentally, the full title of the album is *The Don Killuminati: The 7 Day Theory,* released posthumously under the pseudonym "Makaveli," named after Italian politician Niccolo Machiavelli, who propounded the theory of using fear and deception to confuse and frighten one's enemies. Most people simply call the album *Makaveli*, for short. (Incidentally, the boy's name "Makaveli" means "bad nail" or "king of light." The term "Machiavellian" or "Machiavellianism" is associated with cunningness and manipulativeness. Machiavellianism is part of what is known as the "Dark Triad," a personality theory composed of Machiavellianism, psychopathy, and narcissism. This "Dark Triad" is said to be found in people who are manipulative, domineering, and/or apathetic.)

Tupac really did not castigate Nas nor did he malign him as vociferously as the others he attacked. The reason, I believe, was because of Nas's family connections to the NOI (Nation of Islam), many of whom hold great respect for, have connections to, and come *from* the Black Panther Party. Many of their family members, including those in Nas's family, were Black Panthers.

Hip-Hop Rivalries: East Coast Versus West Coast

Tupac's parents were both Black Panthers, as well as other family members of his, allegedly. The month after Tupac dropped *"Bomb First,"* Mobb Deep replied to his diss track by releasing *"Drop A Gem On Em"* on 25 August, 1996. As tight of a banger as it was, however, everyone then keeping up to date with the beef knew that Tupac was ahead in the war of words.

A month later, Tupac dropped another hit that would also be on the *Makaveli* album - it was called *"Against All Odds,"* and it stands the test of time as being a massive street hit and commercial success! (For some reason, it reminds me of Kendrick Lamar's *Not Like Us*, as it was the finishing move, in my humble opinion, as far as marketability, success rate and timing. It is one of the hardest diss tracks ever, certainly on par with *"Hit Em Up."* One can see how prolific and insidious a rapper Tupac was, especially with the outro.) However, some of the names Tupac mentioned, in my belief, he should not have. Real talk, people like Haitian Jack and Tut should have been kept out of this diss track. Neither Tut nor Haitian Jack are rappers - in no way, shape, or form would either have responded "on wax" (Ebonics for *on record*, or *on the track*). Their "skillsets" lay *elsewhere*, and most people to whom they displayed said skillsets are long gone. At one point or another, I lived in five boroughs of New York City (including Staten Island) - who had not heard of Tut or Haitian Jack in the city? Some people's names just should not be said in rap diss tracks. Chicago is a case study in that, what with all the rappers who have died over there because they spoke disrespectfully on another person's name. (Incidentally, during the first editing phase of this book, word reached me that Tut is now home. Welcome home, big homie.)

As Tupac and Biggie's beef involved different coasts, there was always the possibility of an over-exuberant fan taking action for a perceived (or misperceived) slight on their icon's behalf. There are so many layers to these rap beefs. I see things coming around full circle with all the issues Diddy is having right now. I also see more significance in some of Tupac's words concerning Diddy. We see in the first stanza how 'Pac ridicules Nas for claiming to have also been shot five times as he had been. But later on, while he approaches the subject of Diddy directly, he calls Diddy a punk and pointing to the queasiness and cringiness we all felt when Diddy called him a thug (apparently, appreciatively) during an interview with The Vibe. Claiming that Diddy was not being honest with the people around him about who he himself truly was, 'Pac stoked our curiosity for years when he said, *"But you and I know what's going on."*

That was passing strange to say, and highly *suggestive*! It was not until the beginning of the third stanza that Tupac shed a tiny bit more light into that innuendo. He claims that Puffy was getting *"bribed like a bitch"* in order to cover up something he should not have done, something foul. The language 'Pac used infers more *extorted*. It was as if Diddy was getting extorted in order for someone to keep quiet something shady he did not wish to become known.

First off, one term of prison slang for a gay man (there are many) is "punk," and Tupac had already done time up north by the time *"Against All Odds"* came out, so he knew exactly what he was saying by calling Diddy (then known as "Puffy," "Puff," or "Puff Daddy") a punk. Powerpuff... a "power bottom," also known as a famous person (inferentially, male) who gets, pardon my language, fucked in the ass. Why would a man call another man a "thug" during an interview (as Diddy had done with 'Pac)? It seems, in my eyes... *effete*. And the whole "you and I know what's going on" rings like prophecy in light of all the claims of Diddy being an aggressive homosexual and groomer of young male artists, like, supposedly, the rapper Meek Mills (*allegedly*). There was an audio of Diddy allegedly having rough sexual intercourse with Meek Mills going around right now, as well as a newer one with Diddy penetrating Burna Boy, a Nigerian rap star, and both are quite disturbing.

In this age of AI deepfakes, however, no one, as yet, can certify whether the recordings of Diddy pounding out Meek Mills and the other of him and Burna Boy are real. But, out of respect for the rest of Diddy's victims, we choose to err on the side of caution and discretion, as it is the better part of valor, indeed. See, to Black people, the thing is not whether anyone is homosexual, but if you project a lifestyle of gangsterism and thug life, and then wind up being as soft as a pincushion, it just does not make sense to us. From whom were you hiding? In this day and age, *nobody cares*. We have had too many shocks broadcast on us for us to be surprised or taken aback by anything again.

So *perhaps* Tupac knew something about Diddy even way back then and was on the road to expose it, but was dealt with. (Thus-far unsubstantiated and vile rumors about Clive Davis, the famous record producer and record executive [and current Chief Creative Officer of Sony Music] and Diddy have abounded for decades.) Ditto with Biggie, perhaps. Because *"Puffy getting bribed... to hide the fact that he did some shit he shouldn't have did"* sounds awfully suspicious. This is suppositional conjecture and not to be taken as a given. But one day, truth will out. Always. No matter how long it takes before it comes out, truth can be held underwater only for so long. Well, as these very words are being transcribed, it is alleged that both of Diddy's homes have been raided and, allegedly, pornographic material and one THOUSAND bottles of baby oil have been found in some nooks and crevices. The FBI just does not pounce like that unless they have a case.

More than a politician, Tupac appears to have been a prophet as well. At around the time *"Against All Odds"* came out, I became a First Generation Gangster Killer Blood (GKB) of the United Bloods Nation (U.B.N.). This journey would lead me into the world of gangsterism on the East Coast. Although there appears to be no solid reason why the son of a foreign diplomat would join the Bloods, the brotherly love shown by other Bloods of various ethnicities convinced me of their sense of unity and of the comradeship I would find in the U.B.N. But the homies had opps too, and I began seeing just how many and varied were these predominantly gang-related opps. We would order our system jeeps, smoke weed, jump out on opps and get into intense fights, all while showing off who we were to the whole city, playing *Makaveli* and Biggie joints in these bassy sport utility vehicles.

Funkmaster Flex did not disappoint, Cipher Sounds and Rosenberg did not disappoint, DJ Clue did not disappoint, DJ Kay Slay did not disappoint, and DJ Red Alert did not disappoint.

♬ ♬ ♬ ♬

Now, at the MTV Music Awards on 4 September, 1996, Tupac and Nas came face to face and, although the conversation was not heard or ever discussed, so many people watched as the two icons dapped each other up, effectively and *publicly* squashing their beef. (A "dap" is a type of handshake close friends, especially Black people, have been giving each other for decades, as opposed to the somewhat dry and too formal handshake performed and popularized by predominantly Caucasian people.) The whole reason Tupac was even upset with Nas was because of a diss track called *"The Message"* on Nas's sophomore classic *It Was Written*. Nas seems to clearly diss some East Coast rappers, but Tupac had erroneously thought that Nas was targeting him. Before that escalated into something else, any misperceptions

What's Beef?

were quashed as soon as they met. Communication is so important when, as adults, we are able to peacefully and rationally hash out our differences. Real will always recognize real.

♪ ♪ ♪ ♪

Just three days later, after Mike Tyson made very short work of Bruce Seldon, which match Tupac attended, the latter, along with the big homie Suge, subsequently went on his way to Club 662. 'Pac was there not only to support his good friend Mike Tyson, but also to celebrate the birthday of one of his business partners, Tracy Danielle Robinson. They were stopped by police for excessively loud music and an enterprising Black photographer took a picture that would become the iconic last photo of Tupac, alive, and with Suge. Allegedly, a little while later and while at a stop light on East Flamingo Road and Koval Lane, a white Cadillac pulled alongside Big Suge's '96 black iL BMW sedan and a gunman fired on the rapper, who was hit several times in the chest, once in the arm, and once in the thigh. Big Suge was hit in the head by ricochets but of course lived to tell the tale.

But let us go back to right after Tyson's not even two-minute-long mauling of Bruce Seldon. Tupac and Big Suge gave Tyson hugs, daps, and congratulations. Enter Orlando "Baby Lane" Anderson, a Crip gangbanger who got stomped out by Tupac and Big Suge but was saved by security in the casino before everyone suspected of having been involved in the melee left. This was the same Orlando who had allegedly stolen a chain from a Death Row artist some days earlier and a reward had been put out for its return. Tupac, Big Suge, and their bodyguard were not armed because of some stalled paperwork or some such. The gunman (whether it was Keefe D or someone else, but we will get to that later) pulled up alongside the BMW in a white Cadillac, and that was the beginning of the end for 'Pac, who fought valiantly for his life over the following six days, but wound up giving up the ghost.

Someone else was involved (the "middle man," so to speak), but I don't want to mention his name, to bring him any kind of fame. You see, *allegedly*, Diddy was so scared of Big Suge that he had contacted this middle man, who got in touch with Keefe D about offing Big Suge. The gunman who murdered Tupac was apparently aiming for Big Suge, whose head was grazed by a bullet. It had gotten to a point where Diddy was so afraid that he contacted the middle man and put the hit on Big Suge. After Orlando Anderson was stomped out by 'Pac, Big Suge, and others, he went and told his uncle (Keefe Dickhead), and the latter contacted the middle man and told him that the hit Diddy was somewhat wavering on would be taken care of immediately. Diddy had allegedly offered Keefe D one million dollars - via the middleman - for the hit. Keefe D dubiously alleges that the middle man never gave him a dime.

As a quondam gang member and gang leader myself, and at that time, I can confirm that the homies on the East Coast heard rumblings in the underground from the homies on the West Coast that Tupac's death would not remain unanswered. And there was nothing we could do about it. In a televised interview shortly thereafter, Biggie said, "We two individual people, we waged a coastal beef, you know what I'm sayin'? One man against one man made a whole West Coast hate a whole East Coast, and vice versa, you know what I'm sayin'? And that really bugs me out like, yo! I gotta be the one to flip it, and take my power, and flip it like yo, it gotta be dead, you know what I'm sayin' because he can't do that, you know what I'm sayin', he can't be the one to be like, 'Yo, I wanna squash it,' because he's gone..."

Those words struck me as a bit *disingenuous*, responses long since prepared for the camera. Either that or Biggie's naivety was boundless. I highly doubt the latter, though, as he was a street nigga (out of his own mouth, severally), and from my experience hustling on them corners, not just walls but I am *convinced* that the concrete of the streets themselves have ears. In my personal opinion, the allegation that Biggie had something to do with Tupac's death is *plausible*.

Thinking on it some more now, I have to say yes, it is even *probable* that Biggie was knowledgeably conversant about Tupac's demise. After all, *why* would Biggie get shot and killed almost exactly six months later? Yes, Big Suge was angry, but so were so many others. As far as Biggie's death was concerned, I (and many others) firmly believe we can lay the cause and blame for that firmly at the feet of Diddy, based on the current allegations, suppositions, depositions, and other things that have come to light, *all according to Keefe D*. Big Suge simply had too much to lose and he knew the feds were watching his every move. No, "Poochie" was not hired to off Biggie (in my somewhat informed opinion), but as I stated earlier, beefs also

What's Beef?

spawn avatars, fans who will take it upon themselves to avenge the honor of their idols (not saying definitively that is what happened here, but the *possibility* exists). It's easy to put batteries in the backs of such hardcore fans.

Most peculiarly, Biggie went on a radio show in California, where he rapped *"Long Kiss Goodnight."* Why? Why in the name of The Intelligent Designer would he do something so antagonistic, and so *stupid? Why would Diddy **allow** him to?* Just like with the release of *"Who Shot Ya,"* any reasonable human being can see how horrible the ***timing*** was and how provocative were the lyrics! Biggie (and Diddy) knew - they *knew* - how **infuriating** the lyrics in *"Long Kiss Goodnight"* would be to the entirety of Cali, let alone L.A. Let us examine that song (in part). From the very first few sentences, Diddy talks *big* shit on the song, talking some old, *"See, I told you!"* Nigga, what! The streets were already at a fever pitch and he was on a track saying [obviously Tupac] was a *"stupid nigga,"* and that he prayed for him to stop. And Diddy just kept going, telling that *"fuckin' bitch"* that he was going to stomp his *"muthafuckin' head in."* Diddy at times spoke as if the person to whom he was addressing was still alive, but that was a straw man and *everybody knew it*.

They played this song in California. *In **Los Angeles**.*

No one who knows about the beef between Biggie and Tupac could ever listen to this song without immediately identifying its subject matter. *"I want my spot back, take 2"* seems to be saying someone would take Tupac away (as in *shoot* him, *twice*) as Biggie regains his briefly held superlative spot (while Tupac was up north). Additionally, Biggie taking the number 1 *"spot back"* would mean Tupac would have to *"take 2"* (the number *2* spot). As we saw in *"Brooklyn's Finest,"* Biggie certainly knew how to spin equivokes around "2," "two," and "too" (the famous homophones). The "take 2" was also a goodbye to Tupac (two - "deuces," meaning *goodbye* [as in a *long kiss goodnight*]). In addition, when Biggie says, *"I ain't mad at ya,"* and Diddy repeats it in a snide and sarcastic bass, hip-hop aficionados' eyes bulged because we *automatically* connected that line to Tupac's song, *"I Ain't Mad At Ya,"* the video for which was filmed in May of 1996 but released posthumously on 18 September later that year. ***Everyone*** knew this was *clearly* a reference to, and diss of, Tupac. And then the line about someone or other *"bleedin' softly,"* with *"[their] spirit above,"* followed by *"Now you rest eternally sleepy,"* and *"Rest where the* *worms and the weak be"* - those are glaring references to someone's death. And who could that "someone" have been, and at that time? I submit Tupac to be that said someone.

♪ ♪ ♪ ♪

The gangs in L.A., primarily the Bloods, were incensed! Naturally so. It also was not making any type of sense why Biggie would set foot in L.A. so soon after Tupac's murder, let alone and be rapping *"Long Kiss Goodnight."* It was reminiscent of what Snoop had done in New York when Tha Dogg Pound filmed the video for *"New York, New York"* and Snoop could be seen crushing buildings in the city like Godzilla. Biggie appeared to be *taunting* L.A. He and Diddy had gotten away with filming the video for *"Hypnotize"* in California, they had gotten away with rapping *"Long Kiss Goodnight,"* but they were overstaying their "welcome," as it were, and no amount of *"Going-going, back-back, to Cali-Cali"* was going to save them. Neither was any amount of explaining on The Wake-up Show going to negate the consequences of his (or his accused groomer-rapist-manager's) actions.

Neither will Diddy attempting to run to a country that does not have an extradition treaty with the United States save him from facing the music of decades of sexual abuse of minors like (*allegedly*) Justin Bieber, Usher Raymond (who himself stated that, as a child in Diddy's house, he was exposed to some things to which a child is not supposed to be exposed), and young women like Cassie and Kim Porter (rest in peace, babygirl, your justice is almost home). And rest in peace also, Erica Kennedy.

Neither will running save the reputation of Russell Simmons, whose legacy at Def Jam, and reputation, is forever marred by allegations of erstwhile sexual crimes.

I was so uncomfortable listening to Biggie's interview on The Wake-up Show because I had detected that note of *falsehood* on his part.

There was a tension in the air and everybody seemed to be watchful. Everyone except, apparently, Biggie. I do not know what was going through his mind, but having any gang member around him was a *horrible* idea. On 9 March, 1997, Biggie left a VIBE after-party in a Suburban. His alleged-groomer-alleged-rapist-manager had lately stopped riding in the same SUV as him, likely biting his nails as he got into another Suburban. Biggie should

What's Beef?

have been far more alert. I remember the '96/'97 Chevy Suburban: it was a huge, intimidating, and luxurious behemoth.

No one in their right frame of mind wants to be anywhere near a Suburban in a crash. My mind is morbid and I can never get the vehicle pile-up from Final Destination (you know the one, with the huge timber logs) out of my head. However, factory-issued Suburbans are not bulletproof. Why Biggie would not have wanted to be in a bulletproof SUV is a question only God and Diddy can answer. Whether it was a Cadillac or a Chevy Impala (as is also rumored) that pulled up to Biggie's SUV, the results were the same: a hail of bullets riddled the Suburban and Biggie with it. Strange, how some two weeks later, his album *Life After Death* was released. How morbidly apropos, as to this very day, by his interviews, songs, recorded shows, and albums, Christopher Wallace does, indeed, enjoy life after death.

There is no such thing as coincidence. What was meant to be was meant to be. Rest in peace, Biggie.

Also appropriately enough, Tupac's first posthumous album, is him rapping under the pseudonym "Makaveli," the shortened (and *slang*) version of Machiavelli, as previously mentioned, the fifteenth century political theorist whose thinking Tupac admired. Whether Niccolo Machiavelli advocated for people to fake their deaths, the truth of the matter is that, like Machiavelli, you live on after your works, be they worthy and be you a person of substance. Furthermore, in Machiavelli's *The Prince*, the political theorist let the world know who his murderers would likely be. Like all those holistic doctors who found cures for cancer and HIV, and Big Pharma, allegedly along with the C.I.A. or the F.B.I., "unalived" them. Like how Tupac left us hints in *Makaveli* as to who would likely kill him if he were to ever turn up dead. This is why President Donald Trump wants to revamp those agencies - drain the swamp, so to speak. (Somehow, in some way, may God guide the hands of Madam Director of National Intelligence Tulsi Gabbard and FBI Director Kash Patel righteously. May God also cause Secretary of Defense Pete Hegseth to stop drinking what appears to be bourbon during public briefings.)

Both Tupac and Machiavelli were quite alike in many ways. The two of them grew up around and immersed in their respective polical zeitgeists. Both men vocalized their thoughts and beliefs realistically and honestly. The two of them have had their writings deconstructed and reconstructed in universities and colleges around the world. And both men have had a lasting and visceral impact in the political realm everywhere. "Machiavelli uses his observations and political references such as Alexander the Great to write The Prince. Similarly, Tupac, rather [Makaveli] uses Machiavelli's political ideology on the album The Don Killuminati: The 7 Day Theory."

It's evident that Tupac relied upon his own life experiences and the lessons he learned from them while writing *Makaveli*. These lessons include the ideologies and teachings of the Black Panther Party and other great men (obviously not just Black men). It has been said that 'Pac used the subtitle "The 7 Day Theory" in large part because it had taken him just seven days to finish recording the album. If that is true (and there is no reason to believe otherwise based on witnesses who were there), then this world suffered a tremendous dearth of talent when he was murdered.

The cover of *Makaveli* "portrays the crucifixion of Tupac himself, similar to Jesus Christ's. It's an attempt to convey Shakur's crucifixion by the media, it's intended to imply an artistic resurrection. It was completed in mid-August '96 and approved by Tupac himself."

♪ ♪ ♪ ♪

Rest in perfect peace to the late, great Tupac Shakur. Super props are in order again for not snitching, even at death's door. It has been said that retired Las Vegas sergeant Chris Carroll was the first officer on the scene after Tupac got shot. He himself recollects that, after asking Tupac to give him the names of the people who shot him, Tupac whispered only two words: "Fuck you."

Flowers!

LOSER: Biggie and The Culture
WINNER: Tupac Shakur and The Culture

P.S. (Fuck you, Zip. "Zip" was the middleman who was given, and shortly thereafter allegedly stole, 1 million dollars by Diddy to give Keefe D. I really wasn't trying to say his bitch ass name, but people have to know, I guess.)

N. B. - Rest in perfect peace, Ms. Voletta Wallace (Biggie's mother), who passed away on 21 February, 2025.

B. Nas vs. Jay-Z

I remember rushing to the store to buy a copy of The Source magazine to see what rating the editors were going to give Nas's classic album, *Illmatic*. Released on 19 April, 1994, I also remember listening to nothing but that album for a few days (that is what I usually do with new music, especially rap albums). Nas was already well-known in New York City for his street banger *"Half Time"* that featured on the soundtrack of the cult classic movie "Zebrahead." Ms. Info of Hot 97 (formerly known as "Shortie" while an intern at The Source) wrote the review on *Illmatic*, and it explained with perfect precision why Nas had concretized his place as one of hip-hop's greats, certainly New York's premier solo rap artist.

Hip-hop was in its golden age, Tupac would be seriously beefing with Biggie a few months thence and, although so many rappers came out with new albums in 1994, record companies made sure that rappers never (or very rarely) dropped albums on the same day - there was profit and acclamation for everybody. But Nas would invariably hold the "King of New York/King of Rap/Hip-Hop" title after *Illmatic* dropped. To this day, that album is a work of art, hands down one of the best rap albums ever!

As a matter of fact, I do believe it was recently inducted into the Library of Congress as a singularly unique work of poetical rap fluidity. "Fresh off his first-ever Grammys win, Nas is already heading toward his next achievement. On Wednesday (March 24), the Library of Congress announced that the New York native's 1994 debut album Illmatic has been inducted into the National Recording Registry... the Library of Congress praised Illmatic as a 'groundbreaking' album that continues to be imitated by artists today... 'it was celebrated for its rhythmic originality and complexity, and its technique has been widely copied since,'" the statement reads. Other rappers were doing their thing, but Nas's lyricism was shocking and on another level. A couple of years down the line, Big L, another highly talented rapper out of Harlem, would start making rounds and promoting himself with a certain other rising star out of Marcy Projects.

Yes, we are definitely going to get to *"The Takeover"* and *"Ether,"* and I'm excited to have the opportunity to write about such great works, but first, let us spin off to the genesis of this iconic beef. *Allegedly*, Hov

Hip-Hop Rivalries: East Coast Versus West Coast

(Jay-Z is known as "Hov," short for "Hova," itself short for "Jehovah," as in god, a rap god, forever with a little "g") had set up a recording session for his upcoming debut album, *Reasonable Doubt*. Nas was supposed to have featured on a track called *"Bring it on,"* but when he did not show, Jay-Z simply sampled a line from Nas's Pete Rock-produced song *"The World is Yours"* and used it in his own track *"Dead Presidents."*

Let's stop right here a moment. Think about the situation: a *clearly* established MC is invited to a recording session by a comparatively small-time rapper. The star MC, for *whatever the reason*, cannot make it to the session. The level of hero worship Jay-Z showed by then using a sample of Nas's voice in the song speaks volumes. Personally, I could never! But then again, neither did I succeed where he jettisoned off into the stratosphere thereafter. However, Jay-Z not only seemed to hero worship Nas, but he likely had plans, even as early as back then, to supplant his hero and become Hip-Hop's King of New York himself.

Nas's second album, *It Was Written*, dropped with heavy acclaim. On the album there was a track called *"The Message,"* on which Nas gets *nasty*, casually disrespecting a host of New York (and other) rappers. Why Jay-Z would think Nas was taking shots at him is a little beyond me because that one light reference to Lexuses by Nas surely was not it. That was not even really a diss! There were a bunch of other rappers rapping about Lexus coupes and Lexus Landcruisers. Even though yes, Jay-Z admittedly did show lyrical and personal preference to Toyota's luxury brand (Toyota owns and produces Lexus, its luxury brand), and from what I used to see of Jay-Z in downtown Manhattan, his preferred vehicle was the untinted "buggy-eyed Benz" (at that time, the Mercedes-Benz E300 sported two sets of oval headlights that resembled "bug eyes," hence the nickname "buggy-eyed" Benz).

Before he really "blew up" (Ebonics for *became famous*) and some months after *Reasonable Doubt* dropped, Jay-Z could be caught on repeated jaunts downtown. I would shout him out and, to his credit, I would get a salute back, or a thumbs up. The untinted windows would be partway down and *Reasonable Doubt*, or some of his other joints, would be blasting. There were times when I would be smoking a blunt while walking past the NYU campus and would peep Jay cruising by. For some reason or other, there were a couple of times the cream-colored Benz would be largely spattered

What's Beef?

with mud. His face was plastered on both sides of the car in black and white, and I want to say either *Reasonable Doubt* and/or "Jay-Z" was also written thereon, but I can't rightly remember. Not too many people seemed to know who he was at the time.

To me, it was not *"The Message"* that really got on Jay's nerves, but he was likely still smarting from the original snub. He also probably saw the opportunity to become a household name and promulgate his music career (concert venues, guest appearances, etc.) *and took it*! Strangely enough, there are times when the thought comes into my mind that this beef may have simply been a marketing ploy, at least for Jay. Nas did, however, say that the verse denigrating Lexuses was *inspired* by Jay, though not personally dissing him. He would much later on tell Complex magazine: "It wasn't a shot at Jay but it was just saying that's the minimum you gotta have."

The following year, Jay-Z would again sample Nas in the former's song *"Rap Game/Crack Game,"* in effect paying homage to the already established Queensbridge rapper. It is strange, though, how Tupac had been murdered at the end of the previous year, Biggie had been murdered eight months previously, and both of these lyricists appeared to have no qualms about starting their own war. They appeared to be revving up to one hell of a clash. As Tupac and Nas were cut from a similar lyrical cloth, I believe that Tupac's death deeply angered and hurt Nas, for they had reconciled a very short while before Tupac's demise. Surely Nas had heard Biggie's feature on *"Brooklyn's Finest"* and connected Jay with being part of the Brooklyn crew that supported Tupac's murder. There was no way he was going to guest feature for Hov.

However, again, Jay's mind works extremely fast and just differently - he was already mentally counting the money a collabo (Ebonics for *collaboration*) with the greatest New York rapper at the time (and *now*) would make him. Knowing Jay, he was likely also seeing his collaboration with anyone hotter than him as a temporary pitstop, or a stepping stone. Fast forward a little bit to Jay-Z protege and fellow Roc-A-Fella artist Memphis Bleek, whom the streets know has been both blessed and cursed to have a mentor like Jay. He was blessed at the time because Jay was on the rise and was bringing him along; he was cursed because Jay was a far better rapper and would always outshine him, on any track, as if Bleek was a candle in the sun, and as Jay himself said (on a not quite unrelated matter on *"Hola Hovito"*), *"that shit don't even out."*

Bleek dropped his debut album, *Coming of Age,* on 3 August, 1999. I was just getting up north for my first bid when the album dropped so I missed a lot of the fake hype leading up to it, if there was even any. In the 'hood, Bleek is considered as *just* good enough to have "made it," like Drag-On, a bit better than J-Hood out of D-Block, and a "gangstered up" Lupe Fiasco. *Coming of Age* is named after a song of the same name on *Reasonable Doubt,* where Jay and Bleek creatively recreated their first meeting, with embellishments. Shaheim majorly fumbled the bag on this one because he was supposed to have been the one on the track but did not make it to the appointment. (Shaheim [the so-called "Golden Child"] is one of the very disappointing little Wu-Tang Clan protegés who allegedly snitched on some gangsters years ago.)

For some purpose, there is a song on *Coming of Age* entitled *"What You Think of That"* that, for whatever internecine reason and unfortunately for Bleek, caught Nas's sharp regard. In the song, Bleek raps, in part:

> *My whole team rock rocks, we don't speak to cats,*
> *I'ma ball 'til I fall*

Bleek was literally *nobody* to Nas and to barely anyone else in the game, so there was likely more to *"What You Think of That"* than either rapper ever let on. Perhaps a dirty look in the club, a head nod or dap Bleek or Nas did not reply to, etc. But that simple verse could never make as prolific a rapper as Nas was (and still is) respond. It could be any of the two aforesaid reasons, or it really could have been because of the similarity of the beat of *"What You Think of That"* to Nas's *"Nas is Like."* In any case, Nas felt a flux in the force, caught on, and fired directly at Bleek on his next album, *Nastradamus,* which was released later on that same year, on 23 November.

It was not until I left Lakeview (which is about nine hours from New York City, mind), after refusing to do the SHOCK Program, that I heard the track, while I was (briefly) in Greene Correctional Facility, only two hours from the City. (Greene Correctional Facility was filled with Crips, my main opps, many of whom I had beaten up on Rikers Island and who could not wait until I made it out of Reception Dorm and into General Population. But that is a very interesting story for another day and another book.) By "heard the track" I mean the song *"Nastradamus."* I thought it was an alright song and I will always remember the catchy hook: *"Nasty Nas, the Esco to Escobar, now he*

What's Beef?

is Nastradamus." The album was not as warmly welcomed as his classics, but I enjoyed it, especially the commercialized *"You Owe Me,"* featuring Ginuwine, which received heavy radio play in and around New York City.

I could tell that something was a bit "off" about Prince Nasir on that album; it was not his usual superfluous art form production. Still, on the *"Nastradamus"* track, he casually sniped back at Bleek:

> *I need an encore, y'all, you should welcome me back*
> *You wanna ball 'til you fall? I can help you with that*

Bleek foolishly, though brazenly, shot back at Nas on one of his more famous and tough joints thereafter, called *"My Mind Right,"* referencing Nas's sophomore album *It Was Written*, as well as throwing threats to him:

> *It's beef, I'ma see you, and bang 'til you hang up*
> *Your life a lie, but here's the truth:*
> *You ain't hype to die, but you hype to shoot*

Meh!

It took a little while, but Nas cooked Bleek on his next album, *"Stillmatic,"* ranked third best out of twenty-one albums Nas has thus far released, and rated in the top 4 percent of albums, *ever*. He said, in part:

> *Rip the Freeway, shoot through Memphis with Moneybags*
> *Stop in Philly, order cheese steaks and eat Beans fast*

Nas also attacked Jay-Z directly:

> *Is he H to the Izzo, M to the Izzo?*

"Izzo" is Ebonics for a type of way of saying the letter "o," and adding a "z," so, Nas was playing on Jay's song *"Izzo,"* but by adding "M to the Izzo," he was spelling out and calling Jay a "H-O-M-O" - things were certainly heating up. There is also the fact that he just tore through the Roc-A-Fella roster in quick succession ("Freeway," "Memphis," and "Beans," all being members of Roc-A-Fella at that time). But wait. *Stillmatic* was released on or around 18 December, 2001. We should step back a few months and onto the Hot 97 Summer Jam stage. Not going to lie - Jay-Z tore it *down* while performing *"The Takeover."*

The crowd was hyped, it had been a special time, hip-hop was still "a vivrant thing," and everyone saw a picture of Prodigy in his tap dancing get-up as a child that Jay-Z had somehow gotten a hand on (allegedly, Ashanti was the snitch who provided Jay with that picture).

Furthermore, Jay wowed everybody that day by bringing out a very special guest, the King of Pop, the late, and greatest, Michael Jackson. I was not there, but I know many of my peers who were there that day will never forget that 28 June, 2001. At the time I was being housed in Marcy Correctional Facility's "S-Block" (a 200-man Special Housing Unit [SHU] for allegedly violent prisoners or those prisoners who repeatedly violated prison rules and guidelines). Anyway, that was likely the greatest event that *ever* happened at any Summer Jam. Shout-out to SZA for recently surpassing Michael Jackson's *Thriller* to become the longest running Top 10 album by a Black artist in Billboard 200 history.

♪ ♪ ♪ ♪

Black people naturally went crazy in our appreciation for Mike and Jay (especially the former's presence at a rap/hip-hop social event). It was not until 11 September, 2001, another unforgettable day (but this time for all of the United States), that we all got to hear the more *polished* version of *"The Takeover"* on *The Blueprint.* Lucky for Jay-Z that he is a talented rapper and, quite frankly, life goes on. (Rest in peace to all of those who fell on 11 September, 2001.) Through it all, and at this particularly trying time, Jay-Z triumphed. *In My Lifetime,* the album, was a hit and further solidified Jay's position at the heights of the rap game.

We are going to examine Jay's heavily memorable diss track *"The Takeover"* and see why it was such a beastly track, for a small while, at least. The song had a strong intro and an admirable play on his name and him being the "'god' MC," as I earlier explained. The third verse is a dig at Nas's short stature. We see here that Jay-Z did not come to play, at all, as he is on Attack Mode right out the *gate.*

It's like bringing a knife to a gunfight, pen to a test

What's Beef?

Now this fifth verse started out well, but either Jay got confused or, more likely, just wanted to use a catchy colloquialism to rhyme the couplet through in the sixth verse. This is because the metaphor of bringing a knife to a gunfight is clear - you would get shot before getting the chance to even use the knife (unless you happen to be the guy from *Desperado*) - but to bring a "pen to a test"? You're literally *supposed to* bring a pen to a test, so that part was a bit senseless to me. The song continues with Hov putting people in triage and comparing Roc-A-Fella to an army, *"or better yet the navy."*

Okay, so first Jay gave the metaphor of Nas fighting him being akin to Nas bringing a knife to a gunfight; now, Jay compares himself and his crew as being the knife wielders going to a fistfight. Yes, we caught that, and yes, Jay could have used another metaphor, but as the song is just starting and it has a catchy beat and chorus (with which he began the track), the mistaken metaphor-upon-metaphor build was overlooked.

Jay comes out swinging in the second stanza, again disrespecting Prodigy's height (or lack thereof), stating how he has money stacks bigger than him. He also adds Mobb Deep, Prodigy's crew, by stating how he (Jay) "[holds] triggers to crews," meaning how he sticks up (robs) and terrorizes entire groups. *"When I was pushing weight, back in '88, You was a ballerina, I got the pictures, I seen ya"* - unfortunately for Prodigy, Jay had the receipts to prove this, as, at the aforementioned Summer Jam, pictures of Prodigy tap dancing, like Michael Jackson (whom Jay had brought out right after that part of the song [likely saying Mike was the only, the greatest, dancer, and also proving that he could invite Prodigy's idol to one of his events]) - pictures of Prodigy were plastered on the jumbo screens about and which all the Summer Jam attendees goggled. Fun times, I swear (until we found out years and years and years later that Ashanti was the one accused of giving Prodigy's dancing pic to Jay-Z).

A thought... What if Hov was slyly dissing Michael Jackson during this event? After all, Hov had called Prodigy a ballerina, at exactly which time pictures of the latter as a dancer on tiptoes were plastered on the Jumbotron. These pictures show a young Prodigy dressed up as a dancer, but more tellingly, it seemed as if he was dressed as Michael Jackson himself. Then, a few minutes later, Michael himself comes out? Now, had Michael been presented to the public at any other moment of

Hip-Hop Rivalries: East Coast Versus West Coast

Summer Jam I would have been convinced that his appearance was for the people. However, after he was ushered in by Jay-Z, and with much thought on the matter, I must conclude that Jay was sneakily dissing Michael, too. Jay said Prodigy was a "ballerina" and showed pictures of a young Prodigy as Michael Jackson, and then Michael himself comes out on stage? It was like saying Michael himself was a ballerina. Either that, or Hov was showing that he had the wherewithal to bring out Prodigy's role model. As previously stated, Hov is an evil genius, and both reasons why Michael was brought out, at that specific time in the concert, need not be exclusive. Jay could have been dissing Michael and Prodigy, too. Just a thought.

Jay-Z then threw aspersions on Prodigy being a gangster due to him changing up his style after the tap dancing gig. Kind of like Dr. Dre when he met up with NWA, as Eazy-E degraded Dre in a certain interview on the subject of the latter's "gangsterism." Eazy was asked if he was still friends with members of NWA after they had split up. When it came to addressing Dre, though, Eazy stated, "G stuff comes from the concrete - that's the streets, which he was never from the streets. Only reason why people affiliate him with the streets is through me... See, like people in Compton really don't claim Dre as being from Compton, and they don't claim Snoop from being from Long Beach." The inference is clear. And there's nothing wrong with good kids gone "bad" (shit, it happened to me!), as long as they give back to the communities they claim. More than claiming Dr. Dre was not from the streets, however, at some point during the interview Eazy also questions Dre's manhood. I can't help but remember when 'Pac said he *"shook Dre punk ass, now he outta the closet."*

Ask yourself for what "out of the closet" is a metaphor? Tupac really did know a lot, as did Eazy-E. The latter died on 26 March, 1995, from AIDS-related pneumonia. Rest in peace, big homie. Strangely enough, Tupac was murdered almost exactly one and a half years later. Some of their secrets, however, did not die with them.

Now back to Hov, who then said a verse still used predominantly amongst us of The Culture, which the Urban Dictionary describes as "A saying taken from a Jay-Z lyric, used basically to call bullsh*t on someone's claims and representations, let 'em know you're not buying it." The verse was,

What's Beef?

"We don't believe you, you need more people." I can't remember where Hov got this verse from but the words ring a faint bell. It came from *somewhere*, before he made it famous, if I'm not mistaken. Whatever the case, Hov laid down some memorable verses in *"The Takeover."*

Concerning the "Karl Kani" line, Nas had, indeed, modeled for the Karl Kani clothing brand, which he popularized even more than it already was. In these ads, Nas was referred to as "Esco," of course short for "Escobar," the Colombian drug kingpin. Nas also refers to himself as Esco in a certain number of songs.

Besides the songs *"D'evils,"* *"Watch Me,"* *"The Watchers,"* *"Twenty-two 2's,"* and a couple of other songs in his repertoire, these verses here in *"The Takeover"* are some of the hardest lines Jay-Z has ever spit in his entire career. What a time to have been alive and in the mix! The word play and disrespect was *focused*. Jay was showing why he, at that time, *should have been* Hip-Hop's King of New York. He attacked Nas as being trash, having fallen off, and stated that Nas's own bodyguard outrapped him on *"Oochie Wally"* (a reach!). As far as Nas being trash, *that* was a *reach*! True, Nas had fallen back from hip-hop, but "garbage"? *Hardly*. At the time, Nas was spending time with, and taking care of, his ailing mother, but there was no doubt that after *"The Takeover"* dropped, Jay-Z, to his ultimate dismay and frustration, would get Nas's full attention.

Stanza three was masterfully penned and ended as this great poet put what he thought would be the finishing touches on Nas's casket. "You-know-who" doing "you-know-what" with "you-know-who" was a major shot at the promiscuity and disloyalty of Nas's baby mother (not Kelis, although she, too, was allegedly boinking Jay-Z on the side and had been "hired" to destabilize him mentally and emotionally, at which she almost succeeded, if indeed said rumors were true). In short, Jay allegedly slept with the other baby mother (also?), as he slyly infers in the song. The part about showing Nas a TEC and Nas rapping about it subsequently must have irked Nas to no end, especially if it was true. But the *"one hot album every ten-year average"* itself was *"laaaame."* Nas's discography is dope as fuck. Most of his albums are pure works of art, preplanned greatness, and crafted with cultrate forethought, so Hov was wrong on that bizarre division.

Hip-Hop Rivalries: East Coast Versus West Coast

But it was Tupac and Biggie all over again. Jay was not as raw in his announcement of having slept with his opp's girl as Tupac had been concerning Faith, but even Nas seems to confirm this in a later track on the *Godson* album (see *"Last Real Nigga Alive"*), amongst discussion and exposure of other things. As I have said before, once you declare that you have slept with your opp's woman, what else is there to say? But then again, **all** bets might be off. There is another chorus before Jay wraps up in a brief fourth stanza.

After putting a light drubbing to Nas and Mobb Deep, Jay oh-so-casually gathers up all the rappers in his periphery, whom he will not condescend to even *name*, who have been taking shots at him on the sly and, in *half a verse* - not even one whole verse, not two or three verses, but in half a verse, he backhand disses and dismisses them all: that *"You only get half a bar: fuck y'all niggas!"* is one of the coldest finishes ever. You will remember in Section A that I said we would revisit a tactic Tupac had used when addressing Mobb Deep: he seemed to have forgotten to diss them on *"Hit Em Up"* but sort of offhandedly mentioned them at the very end, as if they were too miniscule to give much attention to. Here, Jay-Z uses a very similar tactic and, at the end of *"The Takeover,"* he bundles up his enemies in half a bar: *fuck y'all niggas*! As Tupac did to the Mobb, Jay did to all of his side opps. In addition, Jay alludes to Nas having had his jewelry stolen - *"Nigga, I know you well, all the stolen jewels."* There was a lot of shit talking on this track, and it was a masterpiece, and Jigga forever cemented himself in rap history, without a doubt. He also alluded to being the (*new*) king by stating that Nas should not "throw rocks at the throne" - the audacity, inferring he was on the throne, not Nas! His verses are real, he is a product of the hungry streets, and his achievements are predominantly a result of his gift of gab, because of which he is, undoubtedly, a rap god!

Again, thank you to Shawn Carter for your contributions to The Culture and growth in society through the arts. Here is to many more years of health, wealth, and no *further* scandals, although it is not looking too good for the big homie, what with his and Mrs. Carter's alleged affiliation with Diddy and his "freak-off" parties. I'm not saying they participated in the freak-offs, but just like many other notable individuals, they did attend Diddy's parties... repeatedly. That's like going to Epstein Island, *repeatedly*, of which Beyonce and Jay-Z are also presently being accused... It's not a good look.

What's Beef?

And now, just as we did with Jay on *"The Takeover,"* without further ado, let us delve into Hip-Hop's King of New York's reply to such an audacious foray onto his castle grounds. We shall see with how much originality and aggression, effortless skill, intelligence, wittiness, and brutality Nas's response was crafted.

♪ ♪ ♪ ♪

Nas is simply *chomping* at the bit to unleash mayhem on Jay, letting everyone know who he is as he comes *"outta [his] throne"* and that he *"got this locked since '91,"* a bold claim but mostly true. As he introduced *"Ether"* as the "main event," he also almost immediately removes Jay as one of "the best" rappers ever, that amongst the best contenders, the *all-round* best are *"'Pac, Nas, or Big."* Let us remember that on the track *"Where I'm From,"* Jay raps that he's from where *"niggas pull ya card, and all you all day about is who's the best MC: Biggie, Jay-Z, or Nas."* So Jay obviously saw himself as one of the three best rappers, whereas Nas contemptuously did not even give him a spot on his rapper triple threat Big 3. Talking more shit, though, Nas asks a poignant question, or makes a declarative statement: for us to *"name a rapper [he (Nas)] ain't influence."* This statement is also provocative, but again, from my standpoint, mostly true. Nas influenced a ton of rappers who are now rap influencers themselves. We are not even one-third of the way into *"Ether"* and it is evident that Prince Nasir also did not come to play *any* games.

The first time I heard this song, I was struck by Nas's lucidity and aggression - he had come out the gates swinging, but not wildly, no. There was not one bar wasted. Not one! Those of us who had thought that *"The Takeover"* was to be his casket were to get a rude awakening. Referring to Jay-Z as a "Judas" (synonymous to being a traitor, of course) who *"kept [his (that is, Nas's)] name in his (that is, Hov's) music"* hits differently, as we recall how, despite Nas's snubs, Jay would, indeed, continue with the sampling of Nas's voice. And all of New York stood up, smiling, and paid heed when *"Ether"* dropped, proud that two of the best rappers of all time had come out of New York City, and the entire world knew it and watched avidly.

Nas continues to prove that he can perfectly handle this "for dolo" (Ebonically speaking, *by himself*). He starts the second stanza lamenting on how he had *"been fucked over," "dissed,"* and *"forgotten,"* basically "left for dead." He progressively pummels Jay-Z, making derogatory reference to his phenotype (*"dick-suckin' lips"* and *"to explode it on a camel,"* as Jay-Z has large lips and has sometimes been compared to certain animals, in this instance to a camel, as a camel also has large lips). Nas also calls out Jay-Z's unoriginal use of naming his album *The Blueprint* since KRS One *"already made an album called Blueprint."* It is also apparent that Nas studied Jay-Z's album *The Blueprint*, because of certain references to material in that particular album. For example, in the song *"Hola Hovito,"* Jay-Z rapped that, if you hadn't heard, he was "Michael, Magic, and Bird" (three of the greatest basketball players and Hall of Famers, to boot). He continues rapping about no one having more "flows" than him. But what he follows up with is so disrespectful. He said if, despite having all these flows, he wasn't "better than Big, [he was] the closest one"!

Even before Nas said it, many of us had already seen how ruthless Jay-Z could be, to the extent where he was so petty that he compared his skill level to that of a dead man, let alone a friend of his. It would not be for about another two years, but Jay would eventually respond to Nas and other critics pointing out that he was reciting too many of Biggie's rhymes. In Hov's *The Black Album*, there's a song called *"What More Can I Say?"*

In this song, Jay addresses his detractors when he claims to not be a biter but a writer for himself *"and others,"* that when he says a Big verse he's only "bigging up" his brother. Fair pun use there (the use of Biggie's name and then "bigging up"), followed by more "big" puns (we are reminded of our dearly departed brother, Christopher Lee Rios, whose contribution to hip-hop will forever be held in the highest regard - rest in peace). When Hov continues using the word "big," the verses now become a **motif** - that is, a word, concept, or other such construct that *recurs* in a song or other artistic work.

We can see that accusations of Jay recycling Biggie's rhymes had merit, and really messed with him for some time. He took a *somewhat* humble and minimally noncombative tone in the aforementioned verses, but later on in that *same song* (*"What More Can I Say"*), he becomes... aggressive, almost challengingly so. The set-up begins with *"I ain't never scared,"* from which

What's Beef?

Jay goes on to claim omnipresence and everyone else's lack thereof before claiming to never care. This is followed by the asseveration of every great boxer, in that pound for pound they are the best at what they do, but after he ends that verse, he adds, "EXCLUDING NOBODY!" Again, another unprompted and impromptu jab at the legendary talent of one of the greatest rappers ever, his good friend: Christopher Wallace.

Jay-Z's pride is of gargantuan proportions. He was fighting a battle of lyricism with a deceased man and saw nothing wrong with that. That's why Nas asked rhetorically, *"Why don't you let the late, great veteran live?"* And it makes sense; as a dope rapper, Jay-Z did not have to downgrade anyone else, but he still did. And it was a dead man. And his friend. And for *what*? Jay's own works would have stood on their own, they would have spoken for themselves. I want to point out something: *every single time* the big homie Lil Wayne (known more affectionately as "Weezy") has been asked about a certain rapper, or entertainer, he has always, I mean *always*, shown some type of respect and appreciation for said fellow artist, or anyone in any sport or metier.

I have never heard Weezy downplay anyone, and that humility of his, in that *specific regard*, is what makes him one of the greatest rappers of all time. It is not just about lyrical ability - to me, there is a complex amalgamation of facets that should be taken into context when deciding that someone is "good," "great," "one of the greatest," or "the greatest" in their field of participation. If a rapper with great lyrical presentation happens to be an asshole to his fans, to me, he will never be great, just "a good rapper with a shitty attitude."

♫ ♫ ♫ ♫

The way you carry yourself outside of your workplace counts for much. This is exactly why public officials can be called to resign from office if acts in their private lives are exposed and deemed morally reprehensible. Some such acts may even be criminal, as we see in the cases of Harvey Weinstein, Sean "P. Diddy" Combs, and Jeffrey Epstein. Thus, yes, I can give Jay-Z his flowers and, based on his discography, concerts, and TV appearances, awards won, etc., honestly say that he is one of the best lyricists to have ever lived. If, however, he happens to be criminally *charged for and convicted of* morally questionable acts in association with Diddy, the respect and admiration for which he has toiled all these decades will be seriously eroded.

Jay will be *one of* the greatest lyricists ever, but I would never say he is the *greatest* lyricist. He is not, at least not to me, in my humble but quite informed opinion. And, if some of the other allegations popping up about him in connection with Diddy are found to be ***true***, well, his reputation is forever ruined. Again, he will still be one of the greatest rappers to have ever lived, and I might still listen to his music (albeit more somberly than when I had grown up with him). One thing is for sure - time will tell. (At this point of this book's final revision, as of a month and a half ago, the "Jane Doe" [an appellation a female plaintiff might use in a lawsuit, to early on protect her identity, as opposed to the male "John Doe"] who accused Jay-Z and Diddy of sexual assault in 2000 when she was allegedly 13, withdrew her lawsuit against both moguls. This means Jay is in the clear. Congratulations, big homie. You carried yourself well and stayed true.)

To continue with Nas's punishment of Jay on *"Ether,"* please note how almost *cordial* Nas is while larruping Hov. He calls out Hov for being too emotional and in the next breath he laments all the brouhaha because he loves Hov like a brother. Nas claims Jay traded his soul for fame and wealth (which claim concerning Hov many others have made throughout the years). But then, from being his brother Nas now compares himself to being Hov's *dad*, smiling proudly at *"his only son that made it."* It seems funny, even when Nas theorizes that Hov's concern with dissing women stems from being "abused as a child" or being bullied as being ugly. These verses strike a chord in *me* that makes me reflect it might truly be why some men disrespect women. Of course, no one wants to be called ugly, but niggas know themselves, and some men *and* women, thinking that they might not be up to today's current mentally retarded and emotionally stunted standards of beauty, prefer to work their asses off and let their wealth do the talking for them. The battle was more psychological to Nas, and he was a top-tier psychiatrist with the necessary skills required to analyze and deconstruct the imbroglio before him.

While Nas is dismantling Jay-Z with fulgurant lyrical precision, humor, and brutal *ad hominems*, he mentions something on which we barely scratched the surface earlier but can be expounded upon now. Nas mentions that he is "the god," in reference to his religion and lifelong allegiance to The Nation of Gods and Earths, formerly known as "Godbodies" or "The

What's Beef?

Five Percent Nation," begun by former adherents of The Nation of Islam. The Nation of Gods and Earths's ultimate belief is that the Black man is God and that this echelon of being divine can be achieved through knowledge of self. Nas's family members are heavily connected to and followers of The Nation of Islam and The Nation of Gods and Earths. In some of his earlier songs, Jay-Z had also identified himself as being "Godbody," all of which played a role in how both rappers "deaded" (Ebonics for *squashed* or *quelled*) their lengthy beef (with assistance from their mothers and a particular individual whose name I reserve to never mention because he is one of the industry's most manipulative assholes - sixty years old and wanna be fighting in the streets - you know exactly who you are, bruh).

We have to just continue admiring Nas's superior lyricism, and also explain that the "Rocafella" Nas says Jay named his company after is no one from the old and famously wealthy White "Rockefeller" family, but allegedly, he was an addict from Jay's old stomping grounds in the Marcy Housing Projects who contracted HIV that progressed to AIDS, the complications from which he died. Why someone would name their company after one of many of the neighborhood's drug addicts, I have no idea; however, we can conjecture that he may have been important to Jay in some unknown way. Perhaps he helped Jay-Z out in a way no one will ever know; no one knows definitively, but Roc-A-Fella is still around to this day. Or, it's as simple as Jay not wanting to be an obvious dick rider of the White Rockefeller family and just spelling the name of his franchise *Roc-A-Fella* to create some distance from them, although again, obviously, the connection is still there.

Furthermore, being called a phony, a fake, a pussy, and a stan surely did not sit well with Jay. Neither did, I'm sure, the diss of Dame Dash, the co-owner of Roc-A-Fella: *"Dame Diddy, Dame Daddy or Dame Dummy"* is extremely funny, but as Nas completes the couplet: *"Oh, I get it - you Biggie and he's Puffy,"* the analogy becomes murky and dangerous even, as Dame and Hov are being compared to Diddy and Biggie, respectively. This put Jay under Dame's control (which thought Jay would have *hated*), as, unfortunately, Biggie had been under Diddy's maniacal and manipulative control. This comparison was likely the beginning of the end for the coexistence of the CEOs of Roc-A-Fella.

Moving on, not one lie was spoken about the Russell Simmons reference. Nas was just so witty, but also *precise* with the disses. Russell Simmons was the CEO and co-founder of Def Jam in 1984 and (along with Rick Rubin) ran Def Jam until he sold his share to Universal Music Group in 1996. He was one of two very big bosses and managed a bevy of artists, Jay-Z included. So, indeed, a "Queens nigga" (Russell Simmons is also from Queens, New York) did run "all [them] niggas." Taking issue with Hov trying to take his (Number 1) spot, Nas also points to Hov's thirst for Foxy Brown, a female Brooklyn rap artist founded by Nas. Again Nas touches on Jay-Z's phenotype, when he rhetorically, sarcastically, and snidely asks Hov if he thought he was getting girls because of his looks. The derogatory, "Negro, please" spoke volumes as to what Nas thought of Jay believing it was his looks that could pull Foxy.

♪ ♪ ♪ ♪

"Ether" is a marvelous diss track and Nas is simply fantastic, devilishly haughty, and audaciously degrading in his delivery. The track is masterful in content, superfluous in word play, creative in wittiness, witty in creativeness, and both shocking and thought-provoking in probity. We. Went. CRAZY. When. Ether. Dropped! One reason New York was awed by the track was because Jay-Z had set the bar so high in striking initially. So many of us just knew Nas would return with a diss track but nothing quite as ferocious as *"Ether."* Perhaps, having watched Tupac's *"Bomb First,"* Jay believed a preemptive strike, like Tupac's, would have the same effect on Nas as the former's had on Biggie. Jay-Z had also named himself after his role model, "Jaz-O," a fellow Brooklynite who was like a big brother to Jay and gave him pointers on how to rhyme. But it also left him open to attacks like the ones Nas launched: *"Shawn Carter to Jay-Z - damn, you on Jaz dick!"*

Then, when I heard Nas diss J.J. Evans I was like, "Oh, NO!" But I clearly remember thinking, "Funny, they *do* kinda look ali-" Lol! In concatenation with this incident, one of the most hilarious things was how Camron, in *his* later beef with Jay-Z, did the video for the song *"Touch It or Not"* (2006), in which Jimmy Walker is shown in *"chancletas"* (a Spanish word that even The Culture in the United States understands means *slippers,* and we understand this because of the heavy interaction between Blacks and Hispanics), playing the role of Jay-Z. Throughout the

What's Beef?

video, "Jay-Z" is getting dissed by Camron, as it is intimated that he is old, corny, outdated, confused, and having to give way to younger rappers (like Cam himself).

In the video, Cam throws his weight around, being young, fresh, and bullying "Jay-Z" in the club and at the waffle spot afterwards. Thinking about it now, I must say, in my estimation, that that was a particularly stupid thing Jimmy Walker did, appearing in the video. "JJ" is a cultural icon from a show so many Black people loved and grew up watching: **Good Times** (rest in peace, Mr. John Amos). But now he was, in essence, validating the inference that he was *ugly*, as Cam obviously got the idea of putting "Jay-Z" in his video from that Nas verse, on *"Ether."* The Culture, however, while not supportive of Jimmy's presence in the video, understood that, for the love of money, one will bear with many evils, even, apparently, self-degradation.

In conclusion, despite Jay responding to *"Ether"* with *"Super Ugly"* (and he should not have mentioned the word "ugly" at all, with respect to anything), it was clear to everyone that he had lost the war and was just being petty and pouty. Almost exactly a year later, Nas released the massively lyrical and profoundly musical rap album called *GodSon*, on which he addresses and disses his allegedly cheating ass baby mama and Jay, and goes on to *still* remind everyone why he is the King of Rap and the King of New York. On songs like *"Last Real Nigga Alive"* and *"I Carry The Cross,"* one starts putting together why certain things happened to him and between him and Jay-Z throughout the years, why there were *"some missing pieces [he] had to leave out"* of some albums, bitches that would *"lead you to their own hidden evil"* (bitch!), and how it hurt him when he had to kill *"[Jay-Z], and his whole squad for dolo."*

Sheesh!

Two masterful lyricists, yes, and both were impressed by each other. But there can only be one. Jay-Z had the minigun, sure, and he put considerable work, effort, forethought, and passion into this battle, I would suppose. But Nas was Iron Man's Proton Canon; the Direct Energy Weapon used by certain governments or government organizations to start fires all over the world (the most recent and devastating being those in Maui, rest in peace to all my Hawaiian friends and family there who lost their lives and/ or their homes); the EMF machine that predicts *and starts* earthquakes;

the technology of Project Blue Beam; Shaka Zulu eating fire; Mansa Musa reborn! Nas was all of these on *"Ether,"* and more.

Jay-Z was eviscerated with red-hot *blazing* precision and calculative cunning. Just like Jay, Nas also tapped into the heart and minds of the people, especially those who had supported him throughout his career, old and new fans alike. Jay was on point, but Nas? Terrifically cultrate. It was like watching Gohan dig deep to do away with Cell, or when Goku cunningly avoided Kefla's monstrous attack to blast her to smithereens.

(At the date of this point in this book, Sunday, 31 March, 2024, Lil Cease, Biggie's little man out of Junior M.A.F.I.A., publicly confirmed that *"Long Kiss Goodnight"* was, indeed, written for Tupac, and Tupac was the unnamed target in Diddy's outro rant. As if real hip-hop heads did not already know.)

LOSER: Jay-Z
WINNER: Nas and The Culture

C. Ice Cube vs. N.W.A.

It has been said to look for the silver lining in the cloud - the cloud of adversity, strife, or change, in general. O'Shea Jackson, likely uncertain about his future as a solo rap artist, still thought an uncertain future better than staying with the rap group into which he had invested so much time, skill, and attention.

That was the best decision he would ever make in life.

Known as the "world's most dangerous group," **Niggas Wit Attitude** ("N.W.A.") was doing their *numbers* in the late 1980s, gaining notoriety with their world famous single *"Fuck the Police"* - so much so that the FBI warned them about their lyrics. Thank God for the First Amendment. And thank God for the Second Amendment, which is there in case the first is infringed upon.

Eric Wright was the leader of N.W.A. and record label founder of Ruthless Records. We know Eric as Eazy-E and O'Shea Jackson as Ice Cube. The latter, a true prodigy, wrote most of the lyrics for N.W.A. on their official debut studio album, *Straight Outta Compton*. He also wrote most of the lyrics for Eazy-E's solo debut album, *Eazy Duz It*. Now, some writers have said that Eazy was really making a buzz at the time, but for some reason, they conspicuously omit the *reason* for Eazy-E's fame: Cube was the main reason N.W.A. and Eazy were as big as they were. (The D.O.C. also played a part therein, too, we shall not forget.) Without the composer/writer, their lyrics would have been shitty - and it had to be a *good* writer. At that time, I can definitively state that Ice Cube was one of the best gangster rappers in the nation.

Reflecting now on what I saw, I can honestly say that no, Eazy-E did not *originate* gangster rap. I will go further to add that gangster rap was emerging all throughout the United States contemporaneously. After all, Geto Boys were "gangster rappers," as was Ice-T, Kool Moe Dee, and Kool G. Rap. Gangster rap, in my estimation, evolved simultaneously in various Black neighborhoods all across America. As I stated earlier, this was as a result of the constant pressure on Black people, the infusion of drugs into our communities by federal authorities, the deleterious effects of the Rockefeller Drug Laws (enacted in 1973 by then New York State Governor Nelson Rockefeller, no relation to the "Rocafella" in Marcy Projects), and other racist and prejudiced laws aimed at further disenfranchising Black people in the United States.

Hip-Hop Rivalries: East Coast Versus West Coast

Some say that the long arm of the ubiquitous *they* deliberately began promoting violence and drugs in our rap, hip-hop, and R&B music. I respond that, if the Afrocentric music movement was so strong, why was the gangster rap movement stronger? We have already discussed that, in any case, so let us move on. The reason, to me, why *Straight Outta Compton* is over three times platinum and *Eazy Duz It* is platinum, the *main reason*, was because of Cube's able writing skills. In December of 1989, due to royalty disputes (which royalties were recouped out of court anyway when Cube later on sued Jerry Heller), Cube separated from N.W.A.

Jerry Heller was a White Jewish music manager of predominantly Black rappers and gangster rappers in Los Angeles from the 1980s forward. You see, Jerry did not know that, although Cube was only 18 years old, when presented with an unfair record label contract, he was street savvy enough to know that *something* was wrong, as Jerry did not want to give him (or any other Black artists) a copy of the contract to take home and look over. Ice Cube speaks of Jerry's shadiness in an interview with Rosenberg and Cipher Sounds on Juan EP is Life (on 7 December, 2022). He also spoke of his surprise at why N.W.A. started dissing him. Before we get into that, though, we must rewind to the approximate date of Cube's departure: December, 1989. Now, just *five months later*, Cube would release his debut solo album, *Amerikkka's Most Wanted*, becoming certified gold in only two weeks.

Naturally, N.W.A. was fuming and jealous, but to his credit, Cube never dissed his former group on that album. However, N.W.A. took turns dissing Cube on their next album, *100 Miles and Runnin'*, on a song called *"Real Niggas,"* to which Cube responded with his EP *"Kill at Will,"* a rather soft diss, but the next year (in 1991), N.W.A. did something quite foolish - they went harder at Cube on their next album, *Niggas 4 Life*.

On 29 October, 1991, Ice Cube dropped his second solo album, *Death Certificate,* which is our main topic for this part of the book. The sheer *breadth* of creativity with which Cube *mangled* his former group therein is iconic. I had not been keeping up with N.W.A.'s disses of Cube at the time, but I had memorized a bunch of songs on *Amerikkka's Most Wanted* and his second album did *not* disappoint *in its entirety*. To this *moment*, some of my favorite Cube songs on that album - some of my favorite rap songs, *period*! - remain: *"I Wanna Kill Sam," "Man's Best Friend," "Giving*

What's Beef?

Up the Nappy Dugout," "A Bird in the Hand," and, of course, *"Steady Mobbin'"* (the video for which was dope, too).

At this precise time, I would like to extend my recognition of Ice Cube as one of the most talented rappers ever. You may never read these words, sir, but I extend to you your flowers here and now. (Even though I do not like how you seemed to have abandoned the Honorable, and belated, Abdul Khalil Mohammed, I thank you for making my childhood as memorable as did Das Efx, Nas, Redman, Tupac, A Tribe Called Quest, Wu-Tang Clan, Biggie, Kool G. Rap, and several others whose tapes and CD's I would keep on repeat.)

My absolute favorite track on *Death Certificate* is the one we are now going to analyze: *"No Vaseline."* I can almost feel true hip-hop heads all across the world smiling and nodding. The intro to *"No Vaseline"* comprises various disrespectful statements launched at Cube, especially after he left N.W.A., ending with Cube declaring, "Fuck all y'all!" And then he drops the opening bars leading to the first verse in the first stanza.

Oh, what glorious times in which I was raised! Columbia House was still doing its "10 CDs for .99 cents" thing (or was it 12?) and my friends and I were *gettin'* them, Random House was still sending you a midsize white envelope claiming that you could win one million dollars with the next reply you sent, David Norman Dinkins was our first African-American (and the 106th New York) mayor and in the middle of what would be his only term (he would be defeated by Rudolph William Louis Giulianni a few years thence), Playland in Midtown was the best hangout spot, mildly dangerous, and music was *good*!

In the first stanza, it was evident that Ice Cube could not *wait* to get at his former groupmates-turned-opps. The dig referring to Michel'le is particularly amusing because it reminds me, *vaguely*, of a video (post-Cube) N.W.A. did with her, where they were dressed in suits. I am immediately reminded of The LOX in suits - one person in each group appeared to want to make the idea work - Dr. Dre and Jadakiss were like the ones in their respective groups who tried to make that whole mob-era image work. There is also something eerily *familiar* in the way Dre raps in that video when compared to Jadakiss rhyming on *"Can I Live?"* Just... *something*. But Sheek Louch and Styles P were *plainly* not happy at all with their situation at Bad Boy, just as the rest of N.W.A. was not really happy with doing the Michel'le video.

Cube's declaration that he *"saw it comin'"* and that's why he went solo demonstrated his precognitive ability, but the dissolution of the group had actually started fracturing years earlier with original N.W.A. group member Arabian Prince leaving the group. Given the unlikeable alternative, separation wound up being perfectly all right by Arabian Prince and Cube, as both were successful in their solo careers (although, admittedly, Cube's success dwarfed that of Arabian Prince). There had to have been jealousy in N.W.A. for the great success of its whilom member, since Cube had left not even six months before dropping his debut studio album, which became largely acclaimed and hugely successful.

Obviously, a successful solo album is more profitable than a successful *group* album, and Cube let them know that he was now *"making all the dough,"* and correctly so, as he had no group members with whom he had to share the pie anymore. Now, something has always bothered me about the name of a certain N.W.A. group member: "Yella." *Why* would someone name himself after a color widely associated with cowardice? Unless, as I suspect, it had to do with his skin color (he is of a *yellowish* type, light-skinned hue), but even then, *why*? Ice Cube pokes fun at and incorporates the pusillanimous nature of "Yellow Boy" as being the reason N.W.A. was losing. He then goes at Dre, telling him to *"stick to producing,"* as Dre was the group's *de facto* beatmaker but was also the one who had initially rapped about Cube being the "Benedict Arnold" of N.W.A. (Incidentally, Benedict Arnold was a British military officer who fought with distinction during the American Revolutionary War but later committed treason in attempting to betray the Americans back to the side of the British.) Cube turns the name "Benedict" into the homonymous "been-a-dick" in his humorous and biting retort.

Critics make tenuous accusations of anti-homosexuality but no overt racism - after all, Jerry Heller *was* a "White boy." To those readers and critics who say "if the shoe was on the other foot-" for hundreds of years, the shoe *was* on the proverbial "other foot," and "Black boy" (the reverse of "White boy") would have been the mildest of curses in comparison to the thousands of other vile and ignominious curses White folks hurled at Black folks. So silence should reign on that score.

Now, intimation of being homosexual should not be, in and of itself, an *ad hominem*. But Black people? We different. We joke on anyone and

What's Beef?

anything at any time. Like, for instance, the alleged Meek Mills audio of Diddy ramming himself into Mills and also Fitty (Fifty Cent) posting on Instagram that he did not want to be a rapper anymore because all of them are gay - hilarious! (Funnily enough, Jadakiss said something similar years and years earlier in his song *"Kiss Kiss Kiss,"* something about everybody in the industry being either gay or popping E ["exstasy"] pills.)

Everyone, from kindergarten kids to those on the spectrum, "attack," or playfully diss others, especially those who might be a bit effete (including our family members and friends), and accuse them of "sucking dick," etc. For example, in the rap battle between Math Hoffa and Pat Stay, I disntinctly remember Math stating something like: "Sucka free boss - sucka free! Why the fuck you claiming that shit? When everybody knows you and the god you smoke ya crack with be out back [makes two kissing sounds] sucking on a glass dick?!" It might sound harsh but it's usually meant to be humorous and to toughen ourselves up, but you also cannot play with everybody like that (particularly [and paradoxically] Black people). Referring specifically to *"No Vaseline,"* it was humorous: *"Eazy-E saw ya ass and went in it quick."* Other disses further along in the song are of that same bent, but were not to be taken as an attack on the gay community. This, did not mean we want to attack, degrade, or kill them.

The name of the song itself, *"No Vaseline,"* speaks volumes. Normally, anal sex between adult heterosexuals is accompanied by some type of lubricant. (I have heard it said that "KY Jelly" was created for that *specific* task - that is, easier access into the anus for sexual stimulation.) However, when there is no KY Jelly I have heard that Vaseline can be an appropriate substitution. If there is no Vaseline, however, one can only imagine the abrasiveness of the task at hand! Thus, *"No Vaseline."* Meaning, to get fucked abrasively.

♫ ♫ ♫ ♫

This was an appropriate metaphor Ice Cube chose to highlight how Jerry Heller was "fucking" N.W.A. "raw" (Ebonics for *without a condom*), with "no Vaseline" to even make it more tolerable, or should I say "less brutal"? Getting "fucked" (duped, scammed, betrayed, bamboozled, etc.) is rarely a good thing, but if the one doing the "fucking" (the one ripping you off or bamboozling you) leaves a few dollars on the bedside table or in your account, or the armed robber, *per se*, takes something valuable but leaves your Deion Sanders, Don Mattingly, or Bo Jackson collectible cards, well then, you got fucked, yes... but with Vaseline. *"'Cause you're getting fucked out ya green by a White boy, with no Vaseline."*

Jerry Heller was as esurient and contemptible as many record company A & Rs were - just look at the lawsuits he settled out of court monetarily. Imagine drawing up contracts for a group but not allowing the members to even read their contracts before taking the decision to sign or not. That is a perfect example of systemic racism inside of institutionalized racism. Based solely on his actions, we can conclude that Jerry was a terrible person. What he was doing was horrible, in effect, financially raping N.W.A. and other talents signed to him. And that was what Cube was angry about, not with any individual nor group of individuals.

See, there was a plethora of factors that, when put together, concretized *"No Vaseline"* as one of the greatest diss tracks ever. Cube's delivery was superb, his aggression was authentic and unforced, *natural* in its flow, his subject matter was consistently addressed, doggedly and creatively dismantled, and he never, not *once*, lost sight of the targets (Jerry Heller and N.W.A.) and the goal (their humiliation, exposure, and breakup, but most of all, Cube wanted his former group to *wake the fuck up* to what Jerry was doing to them). That second stanza was particular, as Cube, although also lightly jabbing at others, was giving upper cuts into the Phantom Zone to MC Ren. He and Ren used to be close friends but when Cube split, Ren did not want (or was warned not) to even speak to Cube, who rapped: *"used to be my homie, now you act like you don't know me."*

Notice the word "villain" gets used often as well - "Villain" was MC Ren's nickname. He even founded "Villain Entertainment" in the late 1990s. So when Ice Cube mentions "Villain" or says "The Villain," it is in reference to Ren (who, incidentally, released an album by that name five years or thereabouts after *"No Vaseline"*). Cube's comparison of Ren *"going out like Kunta Kinte"* (the African who was trapped and sold into slavery) was instantly evocative of the film *Roots*, that *long* masterpiece. All Black people need to watch *Roots* at least once in their lives. As long as the film is, it exposes the type of slavery to which Black people were subjected in the Americas.

What's Beef?

There is a certain scene where Kunta Kinte is commanded by his so-called "Massa" (the slavemaster) to repeat his new name: "Toby." Kunta refuses, which results in and is followed by a sadistic whipping until, begged by the other adjacent slaves to do so, Kunta finally capitulates and says, "My name is Toby." The comparison Cube is trying to make between Ren and Kunta is clear, especially when, shortly thereafter, Ren is referred to as "Toby," meaning Ren has bowed and capitulated under the whip of "Massa," obviously Jerry Heller.

As a political prisoner who has been acutely physically, mentally, and emotionally tortured and forced, at gunpoint, to speechify lies and French Cameroun military propaganda, I must tell all those who read this book that *everyone* has a breaking point. I do not care if you are Jason Bourne, or James Bond, or Lara Croft - there comes a time during the torture of one's physical body that the mind can no longer ignore the body's pains, and the mind will shriek-cry-scream, "*Enough*!" in order to be free from the pain, the damn *pain*, being borne by its host and to keep itself from permanently breaking and going crazy. Never, EVER, believe anything spoken by anyone in the ***initial*** stages of their arrest and incarceration. Only when enough time has elapsed during which you have consistently visited, spoken to, and observed the person can you rationally decide whether the person is in their right frame of mind or not. *Everyone* has a limit!

MC Ren, however, was not (as far as I know) experiencing physical torture, but he was definitely feeling psychological drubbings, which some say is worse than physical torture. (I call cap on that malarkey.) Cube further reminds Ren of when he used to be broke and would be driving a "B 2-10," a very cheap car at the time. Thus far, in stanzas 1 and 2, Cube has diligently and rigorously attacked and done away with his opps, making it clear that the reckoning for N.W.A. is at hand.

As in the game Mortal Kombat after a particularly gruesome finishing move: "BRUTALITY"! This third and last stanza was like the two before it: masterful in creativity, aggressive in delivery, metaphorically punny in its content, targeted in its context, and Hawkeye-precise in its unwavering persistence to punish N.W.A. Along with Jerry Heller, Eazy-E once attended a $1250-a-plate dinner at the White House on 18 March, 1991. One could tell that Eazy was embarrassed by all the negative press that he and George H.W. Bush's White House were receiving. However, there is one thing

Eazy said at the time that strikes me as memorable: "Basically, what I did was pay $1200 for a million dollars worth of press." Yes, he was accused of being avaricious and conniving, but Eazy knew *business*, and when he linked up with that "White Jew telling [him] what to do," it is said that he appeared to become *more* conniving.

At the beginning of the third stanza, Ice Cube drones severally, *"I'll never have dinner with the president,"* letting Eazy and the rest of the world know he had not forgotten that public relations fiasco. And yes, although Eazy had gotten massive publicity for the dinner affair, at what cost had it come? Cube was publicly challenging Eazy's street credibility, and it was part of the larger formula that, apparently, worked. Declaring Eazy to be a "house nigga" (a Black person who not only betrays their own people but also loves their oppressor - this illness oozes under the umbrella of the condition known as the Stockholm Syndrome), Cube also accuses Eazy of "fucking [his] homeboys," meaning the latter was shafting the rest of the N.W.A. group members of their pay (along with Jerry). As they were all males, Cube metaphorically likens Eazy to being a "faggot" (exonymous term for a homosexual).

Casting further aspersions on Eazy's character, Cube states that Eazy cannot be a gangster "with a White Jew telling [him] what to do." Because, of course, a White Jew could never be gangster enough to tell a Black gangster what to do. In addition, if, as Cube averred, Eazy-E shared a bank account with Jerry Heller, this "G-check" (gangster check) by Cube was indeed warranted, and his street credibility would have been tarnished forever. As I watched Cube's son rapping to *"No Vaseline"* in the 2015 movie, like a biopic of N.W.A. entitled Straight Outta Compton, I was transported back to 1990 and 1991. Nostalgia made me appreciate Cube's skillful and amusingly humiliating lyricism more. The others were gifted too, yes, but Ice Cube brought a fuel to the fire of battle rap culture none of the other members could, or did.

There was a televised podcast of an interview of Ice Cube during which he talks about the difference between Eazy-E and the big homie Suge Knight. He confirms that Eazy was not the type of person to use intimidation to get things done, that he was a businessman, through and through. Eazy let people be who they were. As for the big homie Suge, Cube acknowledges that many people are so loyal to Suge because he pulled them out of the

What's Beef?

mud, made them famous, and/or kept them fed to this very day. This is a constant dynamic of probity for the cohorts of most entertainers. These cohorts will forever be loyal to the said entertainer because of what the entertainer did for them or their families. So, no matter how much a certain entertainer or some such is reviled by even up to most of the public, that personage will always have their core group of supporters who will never stop giving them support. This proves that loyalty can be bought.

This rap beef was a delight to have witnessed, and at such a young age. Competition brings out innovativeness and resistance, which in turn builds up and fortifies the combatants involved. Thankfully, nobody was murdered because of this beef, for which The Culture is grateful. I always think how, if Ice Cube had not split from N.W.A., he likely would have never come to New York to record his debut album with the help of Public Enemy. He might never have shut down the Apollo with any of his performances. The East Coast might never have known how great an artist Cube was, and his success might never have been as great as it is today.

Everything happens for a reason. Initially, it might have seemed like he was being banished from the West Coast. But Ice Cube kept his eyes on the prize, rallied with a strong and supportive crew, and completed his debut album thousands of miles away from Compton. New York showed him much love and Cube has always been quick to acknowledge and thank the East Coast for welcoming him when his former crew members and hometown ridiculed him.

And we all know who won.

LOSER: N.W.A.
WINNER: Ice Cube and The Culture

D. Pusha T vs. Drake

"Um, I have no desire to ever mend anything with that person and um, yeah, that situation just went- you know, it went- it just went- it just went where it went, and it's just- there is no- there is no- there is no turning back, it's not like those other situations...

"I'll say-...

"At that point, it wasn't even about battle rap or any of that, it was just- th- the the information was too shocking, it was... like I said, it was- it was a- on his part it was a genius chess move. [Interviewer lightly grunts in agreement] He obviously has no, like, y'know- when it comes to me, he's not gonna have any, like, morals or respect, so the other element to the record... um... whether it be like, just like the shit that he's making up about my mom and my dad and all this, like, [Interviewer again grunts in agreement] dumb shit, or uh, or you know, obviously the part that-that hit me the most, which is like, you know, wishing like that my friend that has an illness, like dies [garbles words]... That shit to me is just not really wavy, [Interviewer grunts in agreement] like I-I-I-I'm-I'm just not really with that, like, and, when did I say, 'Oh, there's rules to this,' I didn't mean there's rules that anybody has to follow, but like, in battle rap, you know, they just, they just... headshotted that guy the other day because he was on stage and he pulled out a picture of the guy's dead aunt, and started rapping about, you know, that type of shit and it's just... it just is what it is.

"There's a point where- there's a point where you're gonna wanna stop rapping. I'm sure I could say something about, you know, your lovely lady, or, you know, a child or a family member and you're just gonna wanna not really rap anymore. [Interviewer agrees] Um, so, that's just kind of where I got to, it's just- I had to admit, like yo, I'm-I'm really- y'know and... and when I was making- when I was making the record in response, which was a real record, I know people think it's like some myth, um, it was like on this vinyls beat and I just found myself saying things that like, one, seemed really out of character just 'cause I was deeply invested in the situation and getting very angry, um, and saying that I didn't- I don't know if in two years I'd wanna hear myself say, and um, yeah, I just, I just really- I just realized that like, nobody cares about this guy so it's not really much I can

What's Beef?

say b-better than, 'Drake has a baby.' I- he won. You know, he won off that, off that uh, off that bomb...

"I-I-I I had a- I had at that time I was working with Adidas, and we were toying with the idea of a name being a play off of a name, uh, off of my son's name. I wasn't revealing my son with Adidas or I wasn't gonna have my son like in a fuckin' [Drake raises arms next to and above him to imply a poster, to which the interviewer snickeringly, and sickeningly, agrees; they say, "Right" simultaneously] Um, but yeah, no, I was just, um, you know, to be honest with you, uh, I actually did a DNA test for my son, and um, and they came back to us and they said that the DNA test got ruined in transit, um, and that they couldn't be a hundred percent sure that that was my son or not. Um, so, I was in a really weird pending situation where I didn't wanna go tell the world [Interviewer makes commiserating mewl], um, that that was my son, and it wasn't...

"If you see my boy [Interviewer: Yeah] you'll understand, like, you know, at the time, I was like a- I mean he's just- he's- I mean he's just a stunning child [Interviewer: Yeah], you know, with the brightest blue eyes and at the time I was like: *I don't know* [Interviewer laughs ingratiatingly], but, you know, it wasn't 'til- it actually wasn't 'til a week before the album came out that I got confirmation [Interviewer's unintelligible noises] that that was definitely my son [Interviewer: Yeah]. It took me two more solid tests with two different companies [Interviewer: Yeah], so, yeah, I mean, uh, again, I wasn't, I-I wasn't like al-all the, the the details of his record are all just like fabricated [Interviewer: Uh], so just to make it more interesting [Interviewer: Yeah]. The story's actually not really that interesting. The biggest part of it is that I have a son. But it wasn't like, oh, I'm hiding him or-...

"He has a point. He can say, 'Yo, you brought up my lady's name, oh, all bets are off the table!' That's fine, you know, like I said, we all think differently, right? And even like, you know, even in- even in the me and Meek situation, if you listen back to those records, we, like [Interviewer laughs, gently, seeing Drake struggle to get out this part], we *didn't, really, go, that, crazy*, [Interviewer: Yeah] *on* each other [Interviewer sucks teeth]. And we left Nick out of it, and we left, kind of, *family* out of it, for the most part....

"Whether-whether there was information that didn't get revealed or not, the point is, like, I-theres just some unwritten rules in the sport for some people, obviously not for him and that's fine, you know, um, and he's just made an entire career off of it, you know, and some people like his music. I personally don't, 'cause I don't believe any of it, and I like to listen to guys I believe...

"So you just get to peek behind the curtain, too [Interviewer agrees], right? It's like, you know, when I was, whatev-whatever, 16 [Interviewer: Yeah] thinking that he was the biggest dope dealer in the world, serving bricks to all- every corner of America- yeah, sure, I'm sure I- I'm sure I was, you know, again, a fan and, and obviously more- more moreso just a fan of like, Pharell and The Neptunes, I always wanted to be signed to Star Trek, and stuff like that- that was like, the way, but yeah, I mean, you know, now that I'm grown up and I actually know him and... the tru-truth, it's just kinda like, I don't know, it's not- not as appealing as it once was-

[Speaking on Yeezy now, Drake continues] "You know, I think that... he definitely recruited a guy with a similar... dislike for me, no matter what he says in interviews, you know [Interviewer audibly agrees]. I know- I know that- I know that, um, he can tell whoever, you know, 'I got love for him' or whatever but it's not love, you know it's, it's- it's... there's something there, um, that bothers him deeply, uh, and, yeah, I can't fix it for him, so [Interviewer audibly agrees], uh, it just is what it is. Um, I can never ever ever ever turn my back on the things that I've said about him in a positive light and I still feel all those same things.

"It's just- it's- it's not on my end [Interviewer audibly agrees]. I have no problem with any if these guys - I don't even know these guys like that. [Interviewer laughs out loud, almost as if on cue]

"This is a sport at the end of the day and you know... from a very early point I have never shied away from defending myself [Interviewer audibly agrees]. And I'm also sometimes eager to engage if I feel that you wanna be slick or be offensive behind the scenes. I might choose to address it in music, and you know, that was how I ended myself- how I ended myself up in the- in the, in the Pusha situation, which you know- Some of my favorite fighters in the world, you know- take a guy like Nate Diaz- you look at his record, it might not look it- it might not look like the craziest record but, you know, he's still one of my favorite fighters, he's still a dog, um, and that's just the sport of fighting, you know, somebody- somebody's gonna catch you at some point, you know, uh-

What's Beef?

"So that's just kinda how I chalk that situation up. And, again, you know, learn from it, channel it into, um, channel it into something else and right outside- I don't see those guys anywhere. So like it's not the same as when I was beefing with Chris... I don't know, those guys, they hide in God knows where and they don't come outside unless it's, like, an event... with like security and shit like that so, I-I-I I-you know for me, I am at a great place in my life where it's just, like, you know, my life is about peace, my life is about drinking espressos and wine [Interviewer laughs ingratiatingly]. I'm trying to make this album [Interviewer: Right]. I'm enjoying being a father. I'm enjoying my house, and my-my-my my mind isn't plagued by beef."

♪ ♪ ♪ ♪

This less than 10% snippet of Drake's interview with the nauseatingly obsequious *Rap Radar* was so *cringe*. Finally though, it must be addressed. What I get is an overwhelming sense of *hurt* and confusion from him. After all, Drake himself acknowledges Pusha T as one of his earlier hip-hop idols. So imagine if your idol filleted you the way Pusha responded to *"Duppy Freestyle,"* which we shall get to, but first, in response to the above excerpts of Drake's interview, I must address the content rather than its bizarre, unstable, cringe, and corny packaging and delivery.

Drake claims he does not wish to "mend" anything with Pusha and that the latter has no respect for him. I do believe Pusha would rather watch the grass grow than waste one second wondering about mending any rifts with Drake. On the second note, however, I disagree. Pusha T, in my opinion, has great respect for Drake, if not because of his personal character (or *idiosyncrasies*), then certainly because of his name, wealth, and/or influence in the industry. After all, as Ye pointed out, Drake's baby daddy is Lucian Grainge. We'll get to him, too.

Drake is one of the most successful rappers because he is not *just* a rapper - he also sings. So, Yasiin Bey is, for the *most* part, correct: Drake is more of a pop star than a hip-hop star, and there's absolutely nothing wrong with that. After all, even Drake's hardest songs (think *"Worst Behavior"*) can be played in the supermarket or inside a shopping mall. (It gets the people *going*!) You know what rap song cannot be played in the supermarket or inside a shopping mall? For starters, *"Fuck the Police"*! And why Drake would get so angry afterwards is wild - everyone knows he is a type, and perhaps that is why the big homie Weezy picked him up, allegedly as the token *"diversity hire."* When signing him up, Weezy advised Drake to not write songs as if he were a gangster, which Drake promptly ignored and for which he has thus far taken massive "L's" (Ebonics for *losses*).

Drake says, *"Feel like I'm bi, 'cause you're one of the guys"* on *"Members Only"* - what with his colorful rollers, Drake just seems, *to me*, like the R&B singer Frank Ocean. He shouldn't have The Culture liking his music as hip-hop, then go to R&B, then start doing other strange things, like suddenly claiming to be a gangster. It's too confusing. Drake goes on to say that there are rules to battle rap, though he is not saying *everyone* has to abide by them - so why even say it? Giving the example of the battle rapper who was "headshotted" seems like a veiled threat, too. But Drake should always remember that that kind of thing goes both ways. Did we learn nothing from Tupac and Big? Also, Styles P already spoke on Drake wanting to set the rules for battle rap, which is a no-no.

Pusha T is not a slouch - he runs with arguably the greatest producer of this time (whom Ye happens to be, as well as one of the best rappers alive, and a shrewd businessman), with heavy connections to Jay-Z in the realms of business and music. I get it, Drake is with the big homie Weezy, but apart from Young Money, can Drake really stand by himself? Running with the big homie does not make Drake a big homie! Of course it was a "genius chess move" by Pusha T - I remember those days, when even niggas in prison got info on what Pusha was about to do before he did it.

Meanwhile, as I have told so many people - and has sometimes, though *rarely*, happened to me - "the one to get hit is always the last to know." The beef between The Clipse and Weezy had been on and off for years, but Drake had thrown his hat in the ring with several bars throughout the years (specifically, 2011 to 2016) on various albums; but yeah, as a privileged kid, which "prison visit" did Drake ever sit through? That aside, as a mixed race child (Drake is Mulatto), *why* on God's green earth would Drake do a photoshoot in **blackface**? It was stupid, thoughtless, gauche, provocative, hateful, and there is no excuse for it. In case I am being unclear, Drake owes an apology to The Culture for that dumb ass photoshoot! The pictures *boil* my blood whenever I see them, and it just goes to show how deeply the Caucasian hate for Black people runs

What's Beef?

in Drake's veins, too. After all, was he not raised predominantly by his White and *Jewish* mom? (And I'm not *completely* blaming his mom who, I am quite certain, had she known he was going to do that blackface photoshoot, would likely have told him not to.) And is Drake also not the one who doubled down on calling The Culture "slaves," as Kendrick pointed out in what will likely be hailed as the most popular song of 2024 (*"Not Like Us"*)?

But wait, being raised by a White mom cannot be the *only* reason why Drake is the way he is, because I personally know so many mixed-race children who were raised by single White mothers *and who would never*, for any reason *whatsoever*, be caught in or be associated with any photoshoot having to do with blackface. (Missy, you did a great job raising Tasheem and Tatyana, both of whom I love so much. Tasheem, you turned out to be a wonderful, loving, and handsome young man who will go on to change the world for the better, I promise you.) There are plenty of other ways I could illustrate the depravities of White people against Black people, but you would never catch me portraying a "buck" in a buck-breaking farm, nor would I dare put myself in a dress, nor in blackface.

Now look, far worse than Prodigy tapdancing, it was a shock to see Drake in such a disgusting and despicable situation. That being said, we continue and address Drake's claim that he was not going to reveal his "son with Adidas." The problem with this claim is that it's *false*! "**Adidon** is the name of Drake's upcoming Adidas line and now that name will be associated with this beef and Pusha's monstrous diss track. Pusha has, in effect, screwed up Drake's brand before it came out." [Author's emphases] Drake *was* going to reveal his son with Adidas, after all. More tellingly, Adidas never denied it, and more foolishly, Drake *himself* unwittingly confirms Pusha's claims when he says, "...at the time I was working with Adidas and we were toying with the idea of a name being a play off of a name, uh, *off of my son's name*." [Author's Italics]

What a damn liar! What are you lying for, Drake? If people have receipts against you, just accept it, apologize, and keep it moving. When I was first arrested in Cameroun, many atrocious, unsubstantiated, and *false* things were said against me, but some people in high places knew of me beforehand, and investigations were conducted behind the scenes to find out more about who I really was and why I had become a freedom fighter. As details of my torture emerged, the videos of me talking about likely reconciliation with the murderers (many of whom were rapist military and gendarme personnel) of my nuclear family were debunked, naturally, as words uttered under great duress. Other evidence was submitted on my behalf before I was fully accepted by my Ambazonian family in this dungeon.

Drake, on the other hand, claimed both innocence *and* submitted receipts against himself. No one was pointing assault rifles at him, no one threatened to kill him if he did not repeat suspiciously worded rigmarole, and no one would beat the skin off his feet or break his fingers if he spoke one wrong word. He was not beaten intermittently all day and into the night, did not have to urinate and defecate on himself, and was not tightly handcuffed behind his back throughout this ordeal - Drake came to the interview *willingly*, in full control of his faculties. So why lie?

The term **cognitive dissonance** is thrown about too loosely nowadays. I submit Drake as a textbook case of what *cognitive dissonance* (as described by Wikipedia) truly is: "In the field of psychology, cognitive dissonance is the perception of contradictory information and the mental toll of it. Relevant items of information include a person's actions, feelings, ideas, beliefs, values, and things in the environment. Cognitive dissonance is typically experienced as psychological stress when persons participate in an action that goes against one or more of those things." Well, Drake *really* believes in his *rightness* in this beef, but his words and actions belie the deeper truth, of which I sense he is (at least subliminally) aware. I wonder if he ever asks any of his cohorts why so many people and rappers hate him so much. (The hate has to be real when Kendrick Lamar's diss track about him was, at a certain time, getting more streams on a daily basis in *Canada*, Drake's own neck of the woods, than any of Drake's own diss tracks.)

♪ ♪ ♪ ♪

In his diss track, *"Duppy Freestyle,"* Drake name-drops "Virginia Williams," Pusha T's baby's mother. Please understand something, in battle rap, once names of people are exposed on the diss track, *expect your opponent to do the same, or worse*. Mase once spit a bar I never forgot: *"you kill my man, I kill ya bitch - now we even."* And that is exactly what happened after Drake dropped that *"Duppy Freestyle."* What was he expecting, that Pusha would just twiddle his thumbs? Drake, you went at your idol, a man you

What's Beef?

know to be a grimy and gritty *rapper*, not really a "hip-hop" artist. What did you actually expect to occur?

Well, Drake was afire at the time, but I wonder how many more millions Pusha cost Drake on that Adidas deal? It keeps me up at night at times. But it also helps put me to sleep when I try repeatedly calculating the amount. Lol. The really funny thing though is that, had Drake won that beef, Adidas would likely have moved onwards with the deal with him and Adidon, but the deal was cancelled once they saw how "monstrous" a defeat Drake had suffered. Pusha had not even dissed Drake's son, only revealed his existence. I can certainly imagine just how "not as appealing" the truth of Pusha T is for Drake now, as compared to how he idolized him before.

As far as Yeezy goes, Drake would once again be biting off more than he can chew, but, if I am not mistaken, both artists buried their beef in 2018... *ostensibly*. However (there appears to be an inexhaustible supply of those), according to GQ, last year Drake, with "the release of his first solo single... has officially, probably rekindled the beef between himself and Kanye West... if you could ever say the flame went out. On 'Search and Rescue,' Drake uses an excerpt of a conversation between Kim Kardashian and Kris Jenner and the former's divorce from West." Drake's obsessive/compulsive behavior betrays his hero worship of Yeezy and almost equal hero worship of Pusha T, most especially *after* the beef. He considers them old and inutile, and yet there he is giving credence to their lofty status in hip-hop since one of the most popular hip-hop artists (by the *numbers*) keeps attacking them.

As a show of respect for the MLS community worldwide, I, personally, will not be speaking on OVO.

But without further ado, I present to you perspicacious readers and critical thinkers a relatively brief expatiation of *"The Story of Adidon,"* by Pusha T.

Having "rocked with" (Ebonics for *kept abreast of* or *supported*) Pusha T and No Malice for literally *decades*, I must give them both their flowers (*particularly* Pusha T), who brought us so many memorable songs and videos. Out of all of Pusha T's songs, on a personal note, there are two songs that resonate hardest with me 'til this day. The first is *"S.N.I.T.C.H.,"* released in 2013 on Pusha's debut album **My Name is My Name**, a phenomenal solo work, and the second is *"F.I.F.A.,"* which was on the album *King Push: Darkest Before Dawn: The Prelude*, another *superb* album. At this point and time in his career, Pusha T was *firmly* established as a certified top-notch rapper. What in the great googledy moogledy would make Drake think that Pusha was some lame?

Please do not get it twisted - Drake is a great performer, and even a pretty good MC, but Pusha T is another type of animal! Drake was not paying attention and got his ass handed back to him on a silver platter. *S.N.I.T.C.H.* resonated with me because I *saw* that wretched behavior on Rikers Island and up north. The word is an acronym for: "Sorry, Nigga, I'm Tryna Come Home" (crooned on the chorus), which is something someone would say when they are actually *snitching* - I do not think my readers are so far gone that I have to describe what a "snitch" or "snitching" is. And *"F.I.F.A."* is just so *raw* in its delivery, and the visuals evinced by his lyrics bear witness to Pusha T's storytelling ability. As far as *"F.I.F.A."* is concerned, though, even *if* Pusha had rhymed about the cat in the hat, that ridiculously heavy, dark, and sinister beat would have carried the track. The beat was so reminiscent of Heltah Skeltah's *"Prowl"* on their best and hardest album, **Nocturnal** (rest in peace, Ruck), or Redman's *"W.K.Y.A."* on one of his best albums, **Malpractice**, as well as the beat on Kendrick's *"Meet The Grahams."*

Pusha T and I have so much in common, but there are some things I will never admit to, or even mention, on pain of death. Only certain Bloods who were around me at certain times will ever be able to confirm any similarity I bore with Pusha - homies like Sex Moolah, Champagne, Bar, Crime Valentine, Doggy Dog, and quite a few others I pray life was kind to and are doing well. Some of us were, indeed, weighty and independent pharmaceutical distributors (even in jail and prison), others not as... *weighty*. So when Pusha talks grams, keys, ounces, and mayonnaise jars, I get it.

Drake made a monumental error in calling out Pusha T, because now both of them are *forever* linked together. Fifty or a hundred years from now, someone else will write another (perhaps more impressive or wittier) account of past hip-hop rivalries. Without question, Drake will be analyzed because of all his beefs, but primarily because of the Pusha T rivalry they will even then confirm he lost. (During one of the edits of this book, I see how, with the recent and continuing thrashing by Kendrick Lamar, it's likely it will be shown in the future that Drake lost monumentally because

What's Beef?

of this most recent rap battle. But it will *also* be confirmed that Drake lost to Pusha T, painfully and embarrassingly.)

If Pusha T was not immortalized before (and he was), his abrupt massacre of Drake made him so. I was not even in New York or the States and *I* heard and *felt* all the buzz of *"Adidon,"* rapped over Jay-Z's *"The Story of O.J.,"* which would lead any listeners to acknowledge the genius of Pusha T for why he chose that particular beat. As this part of the book was being penned, I, too, was smiling at the subtlety of it all. In *"O.J.,"* Jay-Z calls out O.J. Simpson (rest in peace) for being a house nigger in having previously stated (and severally), when confronted with his identity as a Black man in America: "I'm not Black, I'm O.J.," a nonsensical, frivolous, and inane statement (as O.J. was *clearly* a Black man). This was as banal, morally defunct, and ignorant a statement as Raven Symoné made to Oprah about her not being "African-American," but only American. O.J. thought he was America's forever sweetheart because he was one of America's greatest football players - even though he beat trial after being accused of killing his adulterous wife Nicole, the ubiquitous *they* later on taught him a valuable lesson: *they never forget.*

♪ ♪ ♪ ♪

From the reception he has gotten over the years in the States, Drake must think he, too, is one of America's forever sweethearts. Well, only time will tell. The chorus of *"O.J."* is *sick*, which puts all "Sambo" sellout niggas in their place:

> *Light nigga, dark nigga, faux nigga, real nigga*
> *Rich nigga, poor nigga, house nigga, field nigga*
> *Still nigga*

Now, in this song's chorus, Jay-Z is saying that, no matter the distinctions among Black people and the societal gaps separating them, White people will still look at all of us as niggers (Black people may pronounce it "nigga," but we know the difference in its usage). I wonder if Jay himself understood what he was rapping. Sometimes, even if we are correct, or justified, in pointing fingers, we should recall that fingers are also pointed back towards us. Pusha T was subliminally saying that Drake, even though half-White, should never forget that to White society, despite his mother, he is still and always will be a nigger. Pusha wickedly used Drake's blackface photo as the cover art to *"Adidon"* because he does not think Drake truly believes *himself* to be Black. And he's *not* one hundred percent Black, and it's **perfectly okay**. But Pusha wants Drake, as a light-skinned guy who grew up with a White mother (but more importantly in a predominantly Caucasian environment), to never forget that, *whatever* he believes himself to be, Black, mixed, Mulatto, or otherwise, the vast majority of White people, most especially those in America, will *always* see him as a Black male and not (in the letter of the law and political correctness) "mixed-race," nor "biracial."

Stay with me. Pusha T is *also* saying that Drake is *really* what he is pretending to be in the blackface photo - a house nigger shucking and jiving for White folks. The irony of what Drake did is *caustic*, and I find *"Adidon's"* cover more and more hilarious, infuriating, and saddening, all at once. "'The Story of Adidon,' rapped over No I.D.'s beat for Jay-Z's 'The Story of O.J.' with artwork taken from a photoshoot of Drake in blackface, is at once a three-dimensional chess move and vicious sucker punch. (As the Nina Simone sample yelps, 'My skin is black!' you stare directly into Drake's charcoal-covered face; the racially charged cartoon caricature on the Too Black Guys tee he wears calls to mind both JAY's animated 'Story of O.J.' visuals and Pusha's 'Infrared' line: 'I don't tapdance for these crackas and sing mammy.') **The specific reasons for the shoot remain unclear, but out of context images can tell their own stories, and Pusha uses this one to frame Drake as uncomfortable with his blackness**..." [Author's emphases] "Uncomfortable with his blackness." Nasty work.

Also, in "keeping with the Pusha mandate, 'The Story of Adidon' is a ruthless diss track: If Drake's tactic was merely comparing résumés, then Pusha's is character assassination. These aren't his sharpest raps because they don't have to be. Since Drake presents the realm of his songs as an endless string of missed connections for which he is rarely responsible, it feels damning to learn he is allegedly leaving a family behind. Pusha's talk of living in 'truths' informs the diss, which is damaging to the longtime narrative Drake has constructed for himself. It does what no other opponent has ever managed to do: make Drake look bad. The man who sees himself as a master schemer and duelist has been caught flat-footed. Pusha's talking points are well thought-out, researched, and coordinated. He implies that Drake's dad leaving broke something in him..."

Without a doubt, there is a type of enjoyable "lawlessness and vitriol to all of this, which is something we should probably expect from someone who has rapped unregretfully about selling coke for two decades. His barbs about Drake refusing to own up to having a child with a former pornographic film actress are tinged with an odious sense of slut-shaming. And he mocks Noah '40' Shebib's multiple sclerosis as if to suggest it's selfish of Drake to have an ill man making his beats instead of on bed rest. This ableist bit, where he counts 40's days and derides his disability, has been publicly condemned by the National Multiple Sclerosis Society. (Coincidentally, today is World MS Day.)"

The last line of that excerpt had me gasping for breath, I was laughing so hard. (Indeed, what a "coincidence." *Please*!) In addition to all that has been said, I would like to continue with my analysis of the cover photo of *"Adidon."* That blackface photo is so controversial and *insensitive*. So much so that, when originally published by Pusha T, all types of companies, from CNN, to Business Insider, to Time Magazine, to Rolling Stone, to CBS News, published dissertations on Drake's reason for doing blackface, all on or about 31 May, 2018.

According to Complex Music on X, the photographer of that picture, one apparently disingenuous David Leyes, immediately distanced himself from the truly odious stigma attached to blackface and said, in part, "... the blackface photoshoot was Drake's idea." But wait, there's more! "According to Too Black Guys' website, the aim was to 'graphically represent the black experience in an unapologetic way.' Too Black Guys founder Adrian Aitcheson released a statement on Wednesday night (May 30) explaining that Drake is wearing the brand in the pictures but that the photoshoot wasn't part of a Too Black Guys photoshoot."

I call CAP!

Forget what Lupe Fiasco had to say (and shout-out to Lupe, I have been an admirer for over a decade) - this was *offensive*! What I am shocked and riled up about is how so many others do not see Drake's self-loathing for what it is. Or maybe many of us do, as that one lady on Meta went ham on Drake in a recent post, dissecting him so painfully due to this Kendrick beef that I felt a little bad for him. A smidgen. That Too Black Guys was doing a photoshoot on "Jim Crow Couture" is bad enough; I can *assure* Too Black Guys that most Black people around the world do not want anything to do with "Jim Crow," be it couture or "brilliantly illustrating the hypocrisy of the Jim Crow era." Adrian is trying to dig Drake's grave when he says, "The subtleties of Drake, a young Black man, mimicking how white men used to mimic and dehumanize black people may be lost in a rap battle but we should not be distracted from the issues that are still affecting our communities." How audacious and belittling of him to assume that what Drake was doing flew over the heads of those conversant with battle rap.

♪ ♪ ♪ ♪

And now I want to pause to address a particular stigma many people hold of battle rappers, or rappers in general, of not being intelligent, as Adrian above seems to think. There was a post on Meta I saw the other day by a "King Green" addressing a comment by an ignoramus who could not believe that the big homie Weezy knew what he was doing when he rapped the word "spider" eight times in one stanza. The ignoramus said, "Lil Wayne does not think that hard, let's be honest." King Green proceeds to educate the lout on the technical term for what Wayne did (being a "motif") before going on to explain that "what people don't know, there's certain literary frameworks built into being a lyricist within hip-hop culture. Almost every single literary device is built into the framework of being an MC: similes, metaphors, anaphora, metronomy. All these things are things that are built into a framework if you are a lyricist. Lil Wayne is one of the best lyricists of all time. Me, I'm a MC that knows these things because I like literature, so I know these different types of words. But let's say a rapper didn't know the names of these literary devices - you do not need to know it's a three-pointer to be able to make the shot."

Shout-out to King Green for that, as so many primarily non-Black people believe a writer or lyricist must know the technical terminology for so many literary devices in order to be effective. There are also educated Black people who believe this. I know I have been blessed with a decent enough education that I can identify these literary devices as they are used in rap, hip-hop, R&B, and so many other genres of music, but if I am not in a room with my peers of a certain echelon, I am not going to put on hoity-

What's Beef?

sleeping with each other raw dog? Forget getting her pregnant - what about contracting herpes, gonorrhea, syphilis, or HIV?

Drake was wildin' for night!

This type of worst behavior is why Atlanta is in hot water with HIV now - I beg you, my people, we are all here because we love The Culture, and there are drugs to allow people with these STDs to still live full and promising lives, but please "strap up" (Ebonics for *wear a condom* [in another sense it means *get your gun*])! I ask myself whether, at that specific time, Drake was drunk and/or simply did not care about himself? Was his self-loathing so great that he did not care about contracting STDs? We may never know.

After the minor (lol) name dropping (surely in response to Drake name dropping Pusha's baby's mother in *"Duppy Freestyle"*), it only followed (as we can see it now) that Pusha would drop the bombshell: *"A baby's involved, it's deeper than rap."* Pusha was saying that Drake having a child was more important ("deeper") than the rap beef they were going through. *"We talkin' character, let me keep with the facts!"* He was not only claiming as a fact that Drake had a child, but also calling Drake out on his absentee fatherhood. And this is where so many of Drake's younger fans really did started questioning his character.

Pusha T was speaking nothing but (hurtful) facts, using the simplest of deliveries (although infused with ridicule and disdain). The filliping continued unrelentingly about Drake hiding a child and he needing to allow Adonis to come home. I can only imagine how Drake felt listening to this assassination of his character, something no one else had ever achieved. It became apparent to everybody that Drake was, in fact, "hiding a child" after the barest minimum of investigations were conducted into Pusha's (truthful) claims.

One thing The Culture also knows about Drake is how he loves being seen as some type of spotless Boy Wonder, America's *forever sweetheart,* always smiling and happy-go-lucky. But there is that darker self-loathing side of his that Pusha dissected and on which we already touched. *That* is the real Drake, the Drake who himself, in so many words, basically *confessed* to having knowledge of XXXTentacion's death in a mocking intro on one of his shittier songs (like the victim-of-abuse shaming Drake engages in in *"The Heart Part 6"*).

Pusha's *exposure* of his opp's *true* deadbeat nature is what makes Drake hate him. Because now the latter knows that the entire world will be watching, and *judging,* to see if he continues being ashamed of Sophie and if he will continue distancing himself from Adonis. When Adonis grows up, he really needs to thank Pusha T for being the single most effective instrument that made him have a now actively participatory father. Sophie needs to thank Pusha T as well, because now Drake pays more attention to her, more so than if this had never happened, and I bet he wishes this had never happened. Adonis is Drake's son and certainly deserved far more than an "Adidas press run."

The price of fame.

Ironically enough (and Pusha's line of peeling it back "layer by layer" comes to mind, as this subject is so complex), Drake, who by his actions showed his confusion in growing up biracial in Toronto, himself doubted the veracity of his son actually being Black, let alone his. I can assure Drake, that is another issue that keeps us up at night. Not! But when two DNA companies' results confirm that Adonis is his son, despite the, quite frankly, *startling* differences in their phenotype, well, *by law*, he is now beholden to take care of Adonis. By law.

But who knows what evil lurks in the hearts of men?

As far as why Pusha T attacks OVO 40, it is more than about his closeness to Drake, who has always (erroneously) claimed that Yeezy told Pusha about his son. First of all, how would Ye have known? (Unless, at some point, Drake made a mistake and told him, or [wild conjecture] it was pillow talk between Drake and Ye's baby's mother and ex-wife, Kim Kardashian. This pillow talk, if the tryst really occurred, could have somehow found its way back to Ye, which would also explain how Drake got the earlier noted phone recording. It would also explain the reason for Ye divorcing Kim.) Pusha, on the other hand, has claimed severally that the news of Drake's child came from none other than OVO 40 himself - specifically, from a hitherto unknown woman with whom he was sleeping.

Pusha could have picked on any of Drake's friends, but jumping from Adonis to OVO 40 in two breaths is telling to me, not mere happenstance or joy at attacking a moribund beat maker. Remember near the beginning when we mentioned the tactics Tupac used to deal with his opps? The first had to do with initially barely acknowledging Mobb Deep, before frying them on the next album, to attacking Prodigy's illness. Well, people said Pusha should not have gotten at Drake like that, but it happens in battle rap, and it is, apparently, quite an effective tactic. Pusha's attack on him reminds me of when 'Pac asked the question in a mocking tone at the end of *"Hit Em*

What's Beef?

Up": *"Don't one of you niggas got sickle cell or something? You're fucking with me, nigga, you fuck around and have a seizure or a heart attack."*

And so, we see how ruthless and uncaring battle rap can be - after a while, *nothing* is off limits, including disses involving autoimmune illnesses. The vast majority of comments under the *"Adidon"* video on YouTube (or any *other* platform) agree that Pusha T *pummeled* Drake in this beef. Not only that, but the greater consensus also rightly believe that Drake was *shamed* into becoming a dad for Adonis. Props to Pusha T for that, to whom I must again, in passing, give his flowers.

Furthermore: "'On an artist level, I didn't look at it as so crazy because it wasn't like I just beat The LOX in a rap battle or I just beat [JAY-Z] in a rap battle or some shit,' Pusha said on the *Million Dollaz Worth of Game* podcast in 2022 when asked about 'beating' Drake." Pusha did not even break a sweat in this beef; we could see how he thoroughly *enjoyed* it even. As far as Drake continuing a beef he clearly *lost*, by releasing excerpts of Kim K's phone calls, he should remember the end of *"Adidon"*: *"surgical summer with it, snip-snip-snip,"* which is in reference to a certain secret diss track that Pusha was going to bombard Drake with again but (wisely, and evilly) decided to shelve. That diss track allegedly reveals some medical procedures Drake has had in the past. (I'm humorously reminded of the Metro Boomin hit *"BBL Drizzy"* - perhaps Drake has had surgery to augment his buttocks? Perhaps Pusha T is not the only one in the industry to know about said surgery? We might never fully know.) Pusha T, meanwhile, is laying in the cut like peroxide, constantly planning and preparing, while Drake shares a mythical rap throne with J Cole (respect, homie, but you are just too *kind* a soul for this war zone) and both get thrashed by K. Dot.

LOSER: Drake
WINNER: Pusha T and The Culture

N. B. This part of the book (unless otherwise noted herein) was penned before Drake decided to once again poke the bear and engage in a monumental rap battle with one of the greatest lyrical minds of our time, Kendrick Lamar. Perhaps it is all the money Drake has made that influences him to feel bulletproof, but, in my opinion, he needs to sit down for a few months and analyze the people around him. Let us even forget what Kendrick said about OVO working for him - Drake needs to whittle down his team of sycophants

Hip-Hop Rivalries: East Coast Versus West Coast

and so-called well-wishers. The rap battle was so painful to watch. If no one on Drake's team cautioned him to not mention Kendrick's wife's name and remind him of what happened between him and Pusha T, then his team has moles and is actively seeking to do him harm. Just look at the revelations of Coolee Bravo and the former employee of the hotel in which Drake allegedly left his jewelry, Ozempic medication, and other items Kendrick featured on the cover of *"Meet the Grahams."* That's just sheer madness!

Look at all the revelations that have come out concerning Drake that proved to be true. As discussed above, Pusha T was aware of the surgical "adjustments" made by Drake, hence the whole "surgical summer" and "snip-snip-snip" references, but was holding it back. Metro Boomin held no such reserve and, as soon as Drake told him to "shut up and make some beats," for the first time in rap and hip-hop ***history***, a beatmaker completely humiliated a rap performer with just a beat (that made it to number 1 on the charts). *"BBL Drizzy"* is a hip-hop beat created by Metro Boomin in response to Drake's diss and challenge, and I catch myself humming the song at the oddest moments.

Drake is getting humiliated out here and he does not seem to realize it, nor does he care that his sponsors are profusely sweating now, what with the allegations of him being a pedophile gaining traction. After all, he *is* on camera kissing a 17 year old on stage, and Millie Bobby Brown admitted to Drake calling her when she was 14 years old. Why would a grown (allegedly Black) man be calling a 14 year old (White) girl? See, this is why so many people attack Drake and say he may be Black, but he is NOT African-American. No sane African-American man would risk his life engaging in any type of relations with an underage White girl because African-Americans are well aware of what *could* happen. I guess no Emmett Till examples were ever made in Canada. Also, Drake hiring a motorcycle gang known for its racist and xenophobic tendencies (the Hell's Angels) to protect him does nothing to help his image.

And even if Drake is not African-American, what sane *Black* person anywhere in the world calls a 14-year-old White girl and gives her advice on boyfriends? Unless the man is her guardian, that is why she has *parents*. It just does not make sense, and Crystal Black addressed Drake's behavior expertly and unabashedly in a recent post that may or may not have gone viral on TikTok. Drake likens himself to Michael Jackson but he forgets how some White parents inveigled their children to lie about that man and sully his reputation. (Or, perhaps Drake is fully aware of these FALSE allegations against Michael and is connecting his experience of being called a pedophile with Michael's?) The mistakes Drake has made are sundry, and he should stop attacking people because not only is he losing more than he is winning, but he is also detracting from his legacy as one of the more successful artists of this generation. (I did not say one of the *greatest*.)

What's Beef?

I mean, in a Chinese restaurant (Ho Chi Minh) in Drake's own city, there is a meal called the "Kendrick Lamar Special." There are more dislikes than likes on Drake's *"The Heart Part 6"* on YouTube. People around the WORLD are playing *"Not Like Us"* and having a blast at it, along with *"BBL Drizzy."* There are so many people and artists attacking Drake, and then Kendrick shrewdly removes copyright restrictions on all of his diss tracks, so that anyone on FanBase, RedNote, Reddit, Instagram, YouTube, TikTok, Meta, or X wishing to use the songs and then getting massive views *cannot* get sued while make money from their views. That goes for authors, too - new Kendrick book coming soon! Meanwhile, Kendrick is shattering many of Drake's records; as a matter of fact, he is shattering a variety of *music* records.

Behind the scenes, the man Ye told us was Drake's baby daddy, Lucian Grainge, is allegedly scrambling to do damage control. In *"The Heart Part 6,"* Drake effectively waved the white flag, basically saying that he does not care how many other songs Kendrick pushes out. He just sounds so *tired*. But he should really have thought things through before starting this beef. Drake is known for stealing lyrics, talking to people's girlfriends and sleeping with them (another reason he is so hated in the rap/hip-hop community), so he might have thought that was going to be the same result with Pusha T and Kendrick. The latter two have been with their women since high school and they have a much more militant mindset than many other women, which is why they did not break up with their boyfriends like the flighty wench who years ago severed her relationship with Common just to dibble and dabble in obscurity, in the interim embarrassing The Culture. (However, based on Serena's recent Superbowl performance, and her husband (the white guy who founded/co-founded Reddit) fully supporting and defending her from all types of vile and proud racists and misogynists, The Culture must give y'all a standing ovation. Fuck the haters like Stephen A. Smith - salute!)

Did Drake think Mrs. Terrence Thornton and Mrs. Kendrick Lamar were going to fall for the okeydoke like some other insipid wenches? There was so much talk about why Kendrick's lady unfollowed him but not Dave Free - the reason is quite simple: Kendrick likely told her to, in order to diminish the attention and access to her page that a possible infiltrator might gain. What is more telling is that, as of the writing of this chapter, Drake still follows Kendrick on Instagram. (As of the end of 2024 or the beginning of 2025, Drake no longer follows Kendrick, or LeBron James, or a few others who danced on stage with Kendrick or attended his breakout *"Not Like Us"* party/celebration in L.A., where Kendrick brought together so many different factions.)

You can't make this up.

Hip-Hop Rivalries: East Coast Versus West Coast

Big Daddy Kane and Ed Lover do not understand that this battle was *needed*, in order to bring more relevancy and credence to rap/hip-hop. It is unfortunate that Drake must be the casualty, but he made his bed and now has to lay in it. This is a lesson to those who believe that money is everything and makes one invincible. It is not and it does not. What is more telling is who exposes themselves as friend or foe during the most trying moments. For example, what was the point of The Game dissing Rick Ross because Rick Ross was showing support for Kendrick Lamar? Is it bitterness that Snoop did not pass the torch, in a manner of speaking, to him but rather chose Kendrick to push The Culture forward?

Kendrick should definitely watch that dude, as jealousy and envy are experienced across all strata of society, and The Game's attack on Rick Ross was really an attempted feint at K-Dot himself, *in my opinion*. Imagine being so, dare I say, *irrelevant* that no one even responds to your challenge. Just make music, homie. The main event has already passed - we cannot go back to the undercard. I am so relieved that Rick Ross never responded to The Game; as a matter of fact, the unwarranted attacks on Ross have now made me sympathize more with him than my own homie. I am not a bully, nor have I ever been, nor do I condone such behavior in my circle. And thank God whoever sabotaged Ross's plane failed at their machination. Time to push out some more Maybach Music, Ross.

♫ ♫ ♫ ♫

As for Sexy Redd, The Culture is also well aware of Mr. Ike Youssef, the "co-founder and president of Gamma, a modern media and technology company that aims to change how artists create, distribute, and monetize their content and brand. Youssef previously served as CFO at Interscope, the world's largest music company." (Credit to @Bizko Selassiee on Meta.) He is giving Jerry Heller, although not quite as odious or avaricious. In this age of technology, Black people are no longer ignorant, because there is no excuse for ignorance with information everywhere at our fingertips. Sexy Redd should not think to throw her hat in the ring with Kendrick, as all sorts of... *indelicate* matters from her past would certainly leap out of her closet. Everyone has skeletons in their closets, and as public figures, before starting a beef you will be sure to lose, I caution all said public figures to temper their zeal for stardom and recognition with a healthy dose of introspection.

We are watching the demise and downfall of a pop star who will never be able to live down *"BBL Drizzy"* and *"Not Like Us."* Ever. Those songs will haunt Drake to

What's Beef?

his death. The beef is not even done (despite TDE's official announcement that the beef is over), as Kendrick could, *technically*, release another song in response to Drake's surrender on *"The Heart Part 6."* Imagine if there was a remix of *"BBL Drizzy"*? Someone said on the Gilbert Arenas podcast on YouTube that "The beef is the beef. The beef ain't never over." As far as some hip-hop rivalries go, he is absolutely correct. Why do so many artists hate Drake? Because of all the foul shit he has done in the past (*for which there are receipts*). As a public figure, there are some things Drake just cannot (and *should not*) engage in anymore, but he does not seem to understand that, to his current detriment. We also greatly dislike him because we can sense he is not in alignment with The Culture, nor does he seem to even know that he is not aligned.

Metro Boomin has initiated a public challenge for the BBL Drizzy beat - the person who rhymes the best over the beat gets a Metro Boomin beat and $10,000 dollars. Second place gets a Metro Boomin beat. So, of course, now everybody is making a Drake diss song over the *"BBL Drizzy"* beat. Even people in Canada, his own hometown. (I just imagine how much more painful it would be if the person who wins is from Canada.) There are literally *thousands* of entrants to this challenge now. The sheer *breadth* of ingenuity and shrewdness and cunning evinced by Kendrick Lamar and Metro Boomin has brought such a favorable light on rap/hip-hop that even university professors, news anchor persons, and sports analysts have weighed their professional opinions on the battle.

There is even a *"BBL Drizzy"* remix in Spanish, with a meringue-type beat.

Aubrey Drake Graham is getting *cooked* before our very eyes, in different languages, and people who were not alive during the Tupac vs Biggie and Nas vs Jay-Z beefs have this unique musical event they can analyze to their heart's content. I am blessed to have witnessed all of those battles as they were happening, and before this book is published, I am convinced that something else will have happened to return here for a final update.

But if not, these will be my final words in this chapter and on Drake.

(Update) Metro Boomin has posted something about the beef with Drake just being a passing phase, that they are all still brothers and artists. I can appreciate his call for reconciliation, but there are also some things people should not say that may lead to permanent broken friendships. Congratulations to the big homie Kendrick for being chosen by the NFL to perform the half-time show for the 2024-2025 Superbowl season in February of 2025 (which Drake was trying to sabotage and get shut down). Further congratulations are in order for *good kid m.A.A.d city* charting on the Billboard 200 for twelve years. Absolutely phenomenal achievement.

E. Nicki Minaj vs. Everybody (Yes, including Lil Kim, Cardi B, Meg the Stallion, Coi Leray, and even the ex-wife of the big homie Papoose, et al.)

LOSER: Nicki Minaj
WINNER: Everybody and The Culture

Proverbs 16:18:
Pride goes before destruction, and a haughty spirit before a fall.

P.S. Blessed Recognition Day of Birth to "Papa Bear" - may God ever watch over you and keep you healthy, wealthy, and wise

Nota Bene - (Just because Nicki lost, *ubi supra*, does not mean she didn't deserve to win a Grammy several times in the past. She's LONG overdue for and did - DOES - deserves to win a Grammy. Her creativity and rapping skills are superfluous - it's just her ugly and traitorous attitude for which she is known, as well as her toxic "barbettes," or whatever the fuck her petty fanbase is calling itself nowadays.)

F. Cassidy vs. Freeway

When I first heard Cassidy, I *knew* he was a problem. He instantly reminded me of Jadakiss, and lesser of Lloyd Banks and Fabolous, the punchline kings. I have always wondered who would win a battle between Cassidy and Jadakiss. The latter would probably win, but would *definitely* leave with a healthy respect for Cass. The year before I came home (2001) from my first "bid" (Ebonics for *prison term*), the rap gods blessed us fans with an impromptu and totally unforeseen rap battle between two hungry up-and-coming rappers out of Philly (besides New York City, Philadelphia is known for its rap stars and battle rap culture, too). Leslie Edward Pridgen (nicknamed after the drug trafficker "*Freeway* Rick Ross") was gassed (Ebonics for *hyped up*) into going toe-to-toe with Barry Adrian Reese (better known as "Cassidy") at a Philly club called "Dances." (It's really quite appropriate and a full circle moment that his inituals spell "BAR," as in rhymes!)

Strangely enough, both Philly rappers were each signed to New York industry artists: Freeway was signed to Roc-A-Fella with Jay-Z and Cassidy was about to be signed to (but had already been claimed as an artist by) Swizz Beats at Ruff Ryder - he would sign the following year. Jay-Z, Beanie Sigel, Freeway, and State Property had been at Hot 97 (or some other radio station, but I believe it was Hot 97) earlier, spitting rhymes and claiming that nobody could beat them. On a lunch break from the studio and on his way to McDonald's, Cassidy often recounts how those anonymous statements made by Roc-A-Fella *felt* like they were targeting him. Upon his return to the studio, he told Swizz Beats what he had heard on the radio. Although Swizz appeared disinterested, he did mention offhandedly that Jay-Z was on his way to meet up with him.

Cassidy said his mood changed from bad to good once he heard that Jay was on his way to the studio. He respected and looked up to Jay and waited happily for him to arrive. *However*, when Jay arrived, Swizz introduced Cassidy as the next best thing, the best thing since Jay himself. Apparently, Jay took some offense to that and began calling for his subordinates to step up to the plate to battle. An ironic fact was that Jay's crew was almost exclusively from Philly, as is Cassidy, of course. Finally, Freeway was bamboozled into stepping up to the plate, and proceeded to get smoked. (But at least he stepped up!)

Hip-Hop Rivalries: East Coast Versus West Coast

The battle between Kool Moe Dee and Starski was an epic confrontation because of its unplanned occurrence. Starski had just been talking shit (as Roc-A-Fella had been doing) and when he started mentioning Kool Moe Dee, little did he know that his rival was there in attendance. (Of course, it was highly unlikely that Roc-A-Fella knew, or cared, that Cassidy had been listening to them shoot the shits on the radio earlier, nor would they have known that he had taken offense. But they would soon find out, to their ultimate dismay.)

Kool Moe Dee made quick work out of Starski; Cassidy took a bit of his time roasting Freeway, even mocking Freeway by sometimes egging him on while he was rhyming. Listening to Cassidy is like listening to Kiss - a pure delight. Punchline after punchline, vivid metaphors, timely and aggressive delivery (such hard hitters must be metronomically on point), with wittiness and a savage swag - that night, Cassidy was on his *shit*, and was out to prove something, now that he had been insulted and challenged by Hov. I had been writing rhymes in the footsteps of Redman, Das Efx, and a young Jadakiss. And then came a time I used to write nothing but punchlines. However, I soon realized that a rapper, even a battle rapper, has to be more diverse with his rhymes, as any craftsman within his craft.

It was a pleasant eye opener for The Culture when Kool Moe Dee came out of nowhere and killed Starski on the mic, but it was almost as if he *knew* Starski, as more of an MC than a battle rapper, was going to say something disrespectful about him, and Moe Dee merely played the shadows and had come prepared. In Cassidy's case, he was better prepared, and as a battle rapper, one has to almost always be ready to do battle. Behind that crushing defeat he handed Freeway, Cassidy's stock rose and continued to rise in the music industry, shortly thereafter spitting one of the dopest features ever, certainly for that which he is best known. Funnily enough, Jadakiss was on that same track and tore it down, as usual. But his best verse was at the end when he said:

> *You know I throw darts like a bow and a arrow*
> *Remember this, the business is big and so is the barrel, what!*

Please do yourself a favor if you have never heard this sequel to Swizz Beats's original, *"Big Business"*: go and listen to this song if you consider

What's Beef?

yourself part of The Culture or want to see what the definition of real hip-hop is. Swizz is the producer of the song, which features Birdman ("Baby"), Cassidy, Jadakiss, Ron Isley, Snoop Dogg, TQ, and Diddy just doing his voiceover thing. This is one of the hardest tracks that Swizz ever produced, phonetically and lyrically. Just look at the threatening and showoff rhymes Jadakiss comes with - these are upper-level metaphors still beastly until this day. Cassidy knew he could not come with some ordinary verbiage, and he did not. He showed out too, beginning his stanza with eternally famous bars. Anyone worth his weight in breast milk stem cells knows what these bars are and how hard they hit, even today, right ***now***:

Whose house is so large that even their *"doghouse got a backyard"*? Absolutely splendid and a pleasure to listen to. The rhymes were clean, crisp, and understandable, not like the mumble rappers of this age. Cassidy's feature intro is what made everyone who finished Jadakiss's verse with the ugly face raise their eyebrows: *"I got a large house, a doghouse in my backyard, even my doghouse got a backyard, big cars, cigars, and big biscuits, the kid is doin' it big, it's 'Big Business'!"* Wait, what! The fresh and original cadence and familiar laidback tonality he used to rhyme also made him a fan favorite, but it was his ability to brag outrageously that caught the attention of everyone who heard the song, definitely all of New York City.

Just like Jadakiss was not to be fucked with, Cassidy was also "unfuckwithable" (Ebonics for *unable to be fucked with*). Swizz had wisely kept the beat the same as the original *"Big Business"* and it was no less engaging. It was just one of those beats that a true lyricist hears and immediately wants to write a fire "16" to (*sixteen* verses are usually par for the course when rapping, per rapper, per stanza, per feature), reminiscent of Wu-Tang Clan's *"Triumph"* beat, Busta's *"Flipmode Squad Meets Def Squad,"* Biggie's *"Kick in the Door,"* G-Unit's *"Lay You Down,"* or the beginning part of Drake's *"Tuscan Leather."* Phenomenal beats I should have been invited on to murder lyrically as well.

♫ ♫ ♫ ♫

One of my mentors, His Excellency, Sisiku Ayuk Tabe Julius, President of the Republic of Ambazonia, with whom I happen to be in these malodorous and deleterious environs, occasionally reminds me that, what people call "luck" is a combination of opportunity and preparedness. On the day Cassidy battled Freeway, he had no idea what tidings the day would bring when he first woke up. However, because he was *usually* prepared, and had been battling more frequently than Freeway, well, it was almost a foregone conclusion that Cassidy was going to win. Freeway's style of rapping reminds me of certain battle rappers who like to recite songs more than they like battling their opponents, and the singsong cadence and strained tonality is so annoying. I cannot name two Freeway songs, but I can name many Cassidy, Jadakiss, and Beanie Sigel songs.

Yes, for this battle I was already prejudiced against Freeway! But when you listen to Sigel or Cass battling or just rhyming, you can tell both parties are not playing games; they were going to spit *fire*. So let's begin with Cassidy's first stanza.

♫ ♫ ♫ ♫

You just had to be there, to have been alive and active at this time. What a wealth, what a *treasure trove*, of lyrical ability. This was Cassidy's first of three rounds, and it was *explosive*! We have to agree that battle rap is a world of hyperbole filled with continents of metaphors, similes, personifications, and other such literary devices. Cass does not disappoint. Out the door, he stated that he would shoot Freeway (a "biscuit" is a gun, and showing someone "how it tastes" is ironical and metaphorical in a double entendre) - he obviously means shooting the person, but a "biscuit" is also a snack food that can be *tasted*, thus, eat this gun in your mouth. After shooting him, he'll then put Freeway's body in a trash bag "with sticky tape" (to seal the bag) and dump it in an anonymous body of water ("pick a lake"):

I'll show you how a biscuit taste
Trash bag, sticky tape, man, pick a lake

The mayhem continues with Cass claiming how he gets "cake" (Ebonics for *money*) on the corner, usually, and he will "unalive" someone *"like a boring movie"* (the exact words being *"put you to sleep"*). We all know

What's Beef?

how boring movies can put us to sleep. As a matter of fact, many of us use this method to fall asleep faster. The next bar I feel was against Jay-Z, who had a habit of rhyming about the "four dot six" (4.6) Range (Range Rover) - too bad Freeway fell right into that trap when, at the end of his third stanza, he rhymed about that same SUV. "Chop shops" break cars down into many pieces, but Cass stays in the shop chopping cocaine (literally breaking the rocky cocaine down into powder, for sale), and his chain would have so much cocaine on it from the table, it would look like ice (ice is white, like diamonds... and cocaine). This is why Black people call diamonds and other glowy jewelry "ice," because ice is shiny (we also call our jewelry [predominantly gold chains] "shines"), and because it resembles ice that *"niggas play hockey on."*

    Cassidy then takes it up a few notches as he sets up the beginning of the end of that first stanza. The vibe in the club subtly changed, somehow. It's clear in the video that, after hearing his flow and witty bars, the whole room seems charged and expectant. The spectators are impressed by Cass. Now, the bar about getting thrown *"off the side of the bridge"* is a cultural reference to the movie New Jack City, which I will allow the reader the joy to go and watch in order to understand that one line. The movie displays a brilliant performance by Wesley Snipes, who played a ruthless drug kingpin by the name of Nino Brown.

    The next line begins the gambling motif: "holding dice" (likely referring to rolling dice on the corner) and "pulling metal" (at times when dice games got, well, *dicey*, some hustlers and gangsters would "pull metal" [Ebonics for *drawing guns*]) on some *casino* shit. The gambling motif continues when Cass adds how niggas *"gamble with their life on some hero shit,"* a self-explanatory admonition, which could easily result in getting a "scar" on one's *"face on some Pacino shit."* (Al Pacino played the main character in the movie "Scarface," but he **also** played alongside Joe Pesci and Robert De Niro in the movie "Casino.")

    In the next quadruplet of verses, Cass ends each verse in a similar-sounding syllable (or, if you will, *homograph*) - *"this," "chips," "bricks,"* and *"mix."* His unique *delivery* of the punchlines also makes it hyper and interesting. *"I might not know it all, but 'B' know this"* (the sense is first-person singular at first before referring to himself in third-person singular ["B," a term young Black men call each other, and "B-Cass" was Cassidy's name long ago, perhaps standing for **"Butch**," as in *"Butch Cassidy"*]). In the following line we're amused *"when niggas crumble like Doritos chips"* - this is a metaphor and a simile for weak dudes who fold in times of duress. Cass rolls on to illustrate that he sees no "bricks" (literally "kilos," or, loosely defined, "work" [as in large amounts of drugs]) being sold on Free's "strip" (his block) every day, which means the hustlers on Freeway's block are broke, or poor. *"I'm a pit, you a pussy, so we don't mix."* Cassidy then effortlessly ends that series of homonyms by comparing himself to a pitbull ("pit") and Freeway to a cat ("pussy") - thus, they will never be able to "mix" (or get along, since cats and dogs normally don't get along).

Finally, Cassidy talks about robbing Freeway for his iced-out jewels, and ends by comparing his own bars (his sixteen verses) to 16 ounces of raw "product" - *no cut* (pure and unadulterated cocaine, crack-cocaine, or dope). I don't need to analyze every word of Cassidy's in order to prove his ability - the links are here, and YouTube still exists. Download the Cass battle with Free - it's only seventeen or so minutes. Cassidy is definitely one of the best lyricists I have ever heard, hands down, and I would also like to formally give him his flowers at this point, too. This battle, especially being an impromptu shindig, was terrific, and I enjoyed it tremendously. The sad part was when Free ran out of gas and started asking for "a beat." He knew his strength was in song-making structure, but the battle was too far gone to change the rules. And everyone else knew all that, too.

But see, the thing is, Cassidy also knows how to flow on a beat. Freeway would have gotten his ass toasted even if a beat had dropped right then. Beans (Beanie Sigel) recognized Cass from somewhere in Philly and had even given him dap when Roc Nation first came into the club. How Freeway missed that telling clue is beyond me. Plus, Beans and Jay appeared to be *too* quiet! I am not one hundred percent certain, but it's giving set-up for failure, into which Freeway tumbled like Alice down the rabbit hole. I heard little to nothing of Freeway's responses, but let's speak briefly on Cassidy's second stanza.

♪ ♪ ♪ ♪

As I am writing this part of the book and there is a big huzzah over Benzino killing Em' with his two tracks *"Vulturius"* and *"Rap Elvis,"* there is also

What's Beef?

a rumor that Cassidy ghostwrote for Benzino and had let it be known "behind the scenes" to one of the people name-dropped by Benzino on his Eminem diss tracks. That person is called "Cashis," an obscure, so-called "rapper" (and alleged erstwhile Shady Records artist) out of Detroit who attacked Benzino in a piddling diss track called *"Femzino,"* in which he alludes to Benzino's ghostwriter as a "hustler" and a "problem," both of which monikers have been attributed to Cassidy by Cassidy himself for *years*. As a matter of fact, in the last verse in the battle rap stanza above, Cassidy states people who have always heard him rap know him as a "problem." This was over twenty years ago. Plus, he has a song called *"Tha Problem v The Hustler,"* as well as an album called *I'm a Hustler* and another album entitled *Back to The Problem*. I do believe Cashis made a huge error, though.

There might be an epic confrontation coming, and it might be that Cassidy wants Em's crocodile crown. There is no one on D12 who could match up in a one on one with Cassidy. Only Slaughterhouse could derail Cass, and that likely only by a united front, although Joell Ortiz can be ferocious in his battles. And then, of course, there is Eminem, who is a battle rapper himself, but I digress!

We see from Cassidy's second stanza how witty and topically diverse his content is. He can rightfully brag about himself, and even if these rhymes were prewritten, memorized, and he merely took this opportunity to unleash them on an unwitting opponent, the core of the battle rapper becomes evident, *early on*. This is because Cassidy makes the rhyme and the diss continue to almost completely be about his opponent. Unlike Freeway, the predominant content of whose lyrics are *songlike*; he was trying to bring Hollywood to the 'hood, and he failed. Free also tried to halt Cassidy's momentum, but the latter was simply too talented, too determined, to not upset the scale between older battle rappers and those of Cassidy's era.

That might also be wrong.

Cassidy's drive centers around one thing: being the best and being the best rapper alive, or, if his aspirations soar higher than what I perceive them to be, "being the best lyricist ever"! We will have to also take a look at his third stanza, though. I must make a note here: there is no written substitution for battle rap. We can write, talk, and debate this topic until the end of time about what has and *is being* written, but unless you *hear* it for yourself, dear reader, you will have missed so many inflections, nuances, hand and foot motions, gesticulations, and various other factors, as well as the vis-a-vis intimidation between the rappers themselves and the hilarious, intimidating, and embarrassing crowd reactions.

From him "shining like lip gloss" and his opponent's dick being so small that the condom falls off, Cassidy displays his wit and humor in timely and seemingly metronomic fashion. The braggadocio about putting more rocks (Ebonics for *diamonds and other precious stones*) on his watch "so it could glist more" ("glist" meaning *glisten*) is par for the course for most rappers, but relatively few could put it so wittily. Now of course in battle rap one can multitask while rapping. I mean, the rapper can attack his opponent in various ways, belittle him, degrade him, etc. But rappers usually interject boasts about themselves and their ways of living in luxury, or any other topic (humorous or otherwise) between the *ad hominems*. (The break in the battle between Nu Jerzey Twork and Real Sikh when the former addressed "Smack" is a prime example of this.)

There should be some kind of... *relief* between the verbal attacks, like when he says this is his life story, or even if he had Free selling drugs for him, or his presidential bezels, etc., etc. What I'm driving at is, when using these "reliefs," most rappers (especially *battle* rappers) employ *hyperbole* into their metaphors, which can be quite impressive and highly amusing. (The battles between Tay Roc and Bad Newz, Brizz Rawsteen and Noso, Nu Jerzey Twork and Tay Roc, and many, *many* other rap battles highlight this tactic.) I urge everyone who reads this book to also listen to and watch those various rap battles. Nothing can substitute the experience of watching or listening to a rap battle.

With that said, let's dive into Cassidy's last stanza, where his first two verses are kind of interesting:

> *Y'all playboys doin' a lotta hatin'*
> *But they see me in the street and be quick to speak like, "Salaam walaikum"*

This was a shot at Free and Beans, as both are Muslims, and Muslims greet each other with "Salaam walaikum" (or, technically, "As-salamu alaykum") meaning, "Peace be unto you." Cass was saying how dudes talk shit behind his back but when their paths cross, they start talking peace.

Cassidy's subsequent use of the term "good brother," amongst Black people, is one that instantly denotes the person being addressed by that term as a preacher, some type of (aspiring or established) clergy person, or a person known around for being a "good person." However, "good brother" can also be a term of ridicule, calling someone such but knowing they are just *pretending* to be good. "Good butter," if I heard it correctly, is coke or dope that is potent and packaged well, which is most of what concerns hustlers in the 'hood.

These bars are showcasing Cassidy's skill - they are chest-thumpers, real *panache*, so to speak. In battle rap, many lyricists exhibit this pride with "gun bars," e.g. rhymes about guns being so big, "the recoil from firing would dislocate my shoulder," or some such hyperbolic analogy. Concerning the next few bars, hustlers definitely kept ounces of weed inside Ziplock freezer bags - I know I did; and Trina's ass definitely *was* fat, so if your pockets (wealth) were as comparable to how "fat" her ass was, then you were certainly well off.

A bit of levity makes for a good rap battle: *"'Cause every verse you'll get pissed on like pregnancy tests."* Many Black people, in determining the legitimacy of a child, historically did not (initially) take blood tests. We (including our mamas and/or some other close family relative) would wait until the baby was born and, with weighty and penetratingly decisive ganders and accompanying discourse on a multitude of phenotype features, would then decide whether the baby belonged to the man. What I also find highly amusing is that *eventually* there would be a paternity test done, if so court-ordered, just to satisfy the *man's* curiosity or if the woman was trying to put him on child support. So it's amusing to hear the reality of all of this, Cassidy's version, expressed so metaphorically terse, as such in this particular battle.

Cassidy then milks the motif of giving birth for quite a few bars, and it was amusing, as I just explained, before he moved on to a more hustler and gangster motif. This type of lyricism was beyond Freeway, and as Cass noted of Freeway's reaction in an aside to the crowd, there's no doubt he was, indeed, "flabbergasted." The time Cassidy takes to rhyme, the verve and confidence he displays in the content and delivery of his rhymes (respectively), the energetic equivokes and punny punchlines - hands down, yes, Cassidy *is* one of the best lyricists ever and one of the most gifted battle rappers. And he knows how to freestyle *extremely* well, in the true sense of the word. This was a classic battle that will be examined and reexamined time and again. It will never be forgotten, even 100 years from this moment. Perhaps, by then, someone will have put on a beat for Freeway.

LOSER: Freeway
WINNER: Cassidy and The Culture

G. Jadakiss and The LOX vs. 50 Cent and G-Unit

On 17 September, 2002, I sauntered out of the "supermax box," Southport Correctional Facility, the largest and highest classification single-cell Special Housing Unit ("SHU") in New York State's Department of Correctional Services.

My first stepmother got to the prison late and so had to pick me up from the bus station, around which I was walking with the cheesiest smile on my face, reciting rhymes from Redman, Das Efx, Wu-Tang, and others. People who lived around that area probably thought I was crazy. I remember she was playing the Styles P joint *"I'm Black,"* while I tried to holler at a younger friend of hers, Belinda, or something like that, I can't remember. On our way to the city, 50 Cent and G-Unit dominated the airwaves. As far as the music scene was concerned, 50 Cent was *everywhere* in New York.

The following year, 50 dropped *Get Rich or Die Trying,* a true classic of a debut album. Jay-Z dropped another classic banger, *The Black Album,* Outkast blew our minds again with superior lyrics and a variety of head-nodding motifs on their album *Speakerboxx/The Love Below,* T.I. pulled off a hit with *Trap Muzik,* and Killer Mike presented the world of rap with the highly overlooked debut album *Monster* (and yes, he certainly deserved the three Grammy awards he won earlier this year, before being arrested). Jim Jones, Camron, and Juelz Santana (The Diplomats) dropped their album *Diplomatic Immunity*); RZA gifted us with *Birth of a Prince*; and, later that year, 50 and G-Unit shook up the rap/hip-hop world again with *Beg for Mercy* - that was all I was concerned about, as well as my erstwhile 1990s classics hits.

Get Rich or Die Trying was released in early February of 2003. New York City blasted it until a week and a half after my Born Day in November, when *Beg For Mercy* was released. Both albums were monumental successes, and it displayed how stand-up of a man 50 was when he let his crew also eat on *Beg For Mercy*. The second album was to have been 50's sophomore solo, but he has spoken about having to put his crew on (even Yayo, who was locked up at the time, but still ate when he got home).

Getting right to the buttery section, I doubt there is any organism on God's good Earth that does not know that 50 Cent does not get along with Ja Rule. As a matter of fact, they have been beefing going on *three decades*! The origin of their beef lays in antiquity, back in the late 1990s, when 50 was a relative unknown and trying to make a name for himself, while Ja was more famous and far more established than him, yet would not give 50 the time of day. What a fumble! Fast forward to October of 2004 and Ja Rule dropping the hit single *"New York, New York,"* featuring Fat Joe and Jadakiss. Little did I know that, seven months from then, I would be arrested and placed before a Grand Jury for Murder 2 (Murder in the 2nd Degree) and Man 1 (Manslaughter in the 1st Degree). In the meantime, however, I was enjoying life with my then main partner, a Black/Dominican baddie out of Amsterdam Ave. Yeah, she abandoned me too, aborted our child, and later on had a baby by a police nigga. Can't make this shit up.

    I was hustling on 125th and Saint Nicholas ("St. Nick") Avenue, opposite Popeye's, selling cigarettes and other products that not once did that diminutive police torturer Detective DellaValle (out of the 28th precinct at that time) ever catch on to. Me and some other hustlers on the corner had often been chased, sometimes beaten, and usually arrested by the detectives and patrol officers of the nearby 28th precinct, which was the hub precinct for Manhattan. Wild times, especially when we would get word that the "detects" (detectives) were out and about and we would swiftly divest ourselves of anything illegal or suspicious for up to an hour or so, just to be able to walk around unfettered and unbothered. Surprisingly, there were times the officers would still arrest us, despite not finding any contraband, not even one bag weed, on us. Yes, a few officers out of the 28th were dirty and foul like that, so we learned to always run from them, whether or not we were "dirty."

♫ ♫ ♫ ♫

On 3 March, 2005, 50 Cent released his second solo studio album, *The Massacre,* on which he took shots at The LOX, for Jadakiss's perceived support of Ja Rule. As someone who has lived the street life myself, and in all fairness to the situation and not just 50, with all due respect, Jada and Joe knew exactly what was going on between Ja Rule and 50, *as he dissed 50 on the very track.* "They come from environments where they know... and they ain't in the dark. They know what it is. This is not music beef... You know,

Right: Tupac Shakur's Yearbook photograph from 1988. (*Wikimedia Commons*)

Below: The Golden Gate Quartet in 1964. (*Wikimedia Commons*)

Another image of the Golden Gate Quartet in 1964. (*Wikimedia Commons*)

Nas in concert at the Zénithe, Paris (Hip Hop Coup d'Oreille), 2014.

Above: Another shot of Nas at the Zénithe in Paris, 2014 (*Wikimedia Commons*)

Left: Jay-Z in Hamburg, Germany in 2003. (*Wikimedia Commons*)

Above: Nas at the Zénithe in Paris, 2014. (*Wikimedia Commons*)

Right: Jay-Z at a concert in 2006. (*Wikimedia Commons*)

Above: Ice Cube live at Metro City Concert Club. (*Wikimedia Commons*)

Left: Ice Cube at the Chicago screening of the film *Ride Along* at AMC River East 21 Theaters, Chicago, IL, USA on January 9, 2014. (*Wikimedia Commons*)

Above: Ice Cube playing Supafest 2012 in Sydney, Australia. (*Wikimedia Comons*)

Right: Pusha T at Hopscotch Music Festival on September 11, 2015. (*Wikimedia Commons*)

Above left: Pusha T of Clipse at the Pitchfork Music Festival, 2007. (*Wikimedia Commons*)

Above right: Pusha T in concert, 2013. (*Wikimedia Commons*)

Drake in concert at the Summer Sixteen Tour, 2016, in Toronto. (*Wikimedia Commons*)

Dr. Dre and Snoop Dogg at Coachella, 2012, during day three (Sunday, April 22, 2012). (*Wikimedia Commons*)

Nick Leisure and Suge Knight, 2007. (*Wikimedia Commons*)

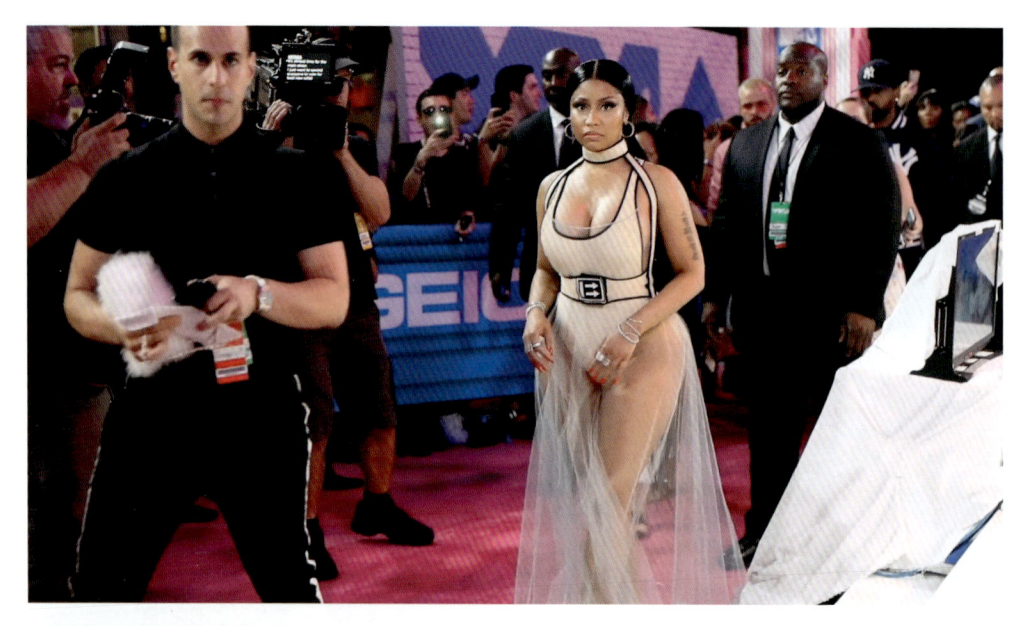

Above and left: Nicki Minaj at the MTV Video Music Awards, 2018. (*Wikimedia Commons*)

Right: Cassidy on the 85 South Show Podcast in 2023. (*Wikimedia Commons*)

Below: Jadakiss (Styles P) performing on The Come Up Show. (*Wikimedia Commons*)

Above: Jadakiss at the Sound Academy, 2014. (*Wikimedia Commons*)

Left: Another image of Jadakiss performing. (*Wikimedia Commons*)

G-Unit in Bangkok (from left to right: Olivia, Lloyd Banks, Young Buck, & 50 Cent). (*Wikimedia Commons*)

50 Cent and G-Unit at the House of Blues, 2014. (*Wikimedia Commons*)

Left: A fan with the username u/Brendan_linden on Reddit taking a selfie with Eminem at Eminem's new store, Mom's Spaghetti, 2021. (*Wikimedia Commons*)

Below: The Jacksons performing on stage at Arrowhead Stadium, Kansas City, during the Victory Tour. (*Wikimedia Commons*)

Above: Michael Jackson and a fan, photographed at the Kahala Hilton Hotel, Hawaii, in early February 1988. Despite the resemblance, this is probably not Debbie Rowe. (*Wikimedia Commons*)

Right: Michael Jackson in 1984 at the White House. (*Wikimedia Commons*)

Left: Michael Jackson in concert during the Dangerous World Tour, 1993. (*Wikimedia Commons*)

Below: Murder Inc. (DMX, Jay-Z, and Ja Rule). (*Wikimedia Commons*)

What's Beef?

it doesn't- it doesn't stem from music, it comes from actual streets. Now that don't die. So it's like you don't stand so close to that person that you're viewed as an ally to 'em. Why I'ma sit back so you could try and help 'em? That's exactly what they did with 'I'm From New York.'"

Truer words by 50 were never spoken during a televised interview. And yes, I am of the belief that Jada and Joe knew they were not only *supporting* Ja Rule but also going *against* 50 by being in that video. After all, for a few years, 50 had been running with Shady Records and Aftermath, West Coast-based record labels. There was the underpinning message *not so* surreptitiously couched in the very title of the song. I don't know whether 50 "peeped game" (*understood what was going on*) but, *in my opinion*, it seemed as if some people were upset with 50, a New York rapper, being on West Coast-based record labels and still repping (representing) and getting money with New York niggas (and others) based on the East Coast. Let us not forget that Lloyd Banks, Olivia, and Yayo are from New York, too.

To me, on the first reflection, 50 really did not go hard on *"Piggy Bank,"* his first salvo against the LOX. But when I analyzed the song again and reread the lyrics as the song was playing, I realized that I was wrong - this diss track was about something, after all. This was a tough opening in what would become an epic, though surprisingly short-lived, feud between 50 and Jadakiss, and their respective crews, G-Unit and The LOX. Let's take a look at *"Piggy Bank"* and examine a few things.

From the first stanza, you can tell how full of himself 50 is, and he does not care in the slightest who cares or who does not. He beefs with whomever he wants and has the "right of might" cloaking him, believing it to be the "might of right" that, *perhaps* in retrospect, it really might have been... But he should not have told two strong New York rappers what not to do and who not to do what with. In the first line of the first stanza, 50 attacks and disses DMX and Sheek Louch: *"That damn shit is old, don't be screamin' 'Get at Me Dogg'"* - Sheek Louch featured on the track *"Get at Me, Dog"* with DMX in 1998. He then brags about the *"black on black crime"* he'll commit on his opps before addressing Fat Joe disrespectfully, saying that Joe thought:

"Lean Back" was "In da Club"
My shit sold eleven mil, his shit was a dud

50 was just feeling himself over the top. His unprecedented success blinded him to the (less lofty) successes of others. "Fat Joe signed to Relativity Records and released his debut album, Represent, in 1993. Featuring production from The Beatnuts, Diamond D, Lord Finesse as well as guest appearances from Grand Puba and Kool G Rap, the album was a minor success and included the single 'Flow Joe' which peaked at 89 on the Billboard Hot 100 and topped the Billboard Hot Rap Singles." Furthermore, Joe managed to put together a then-new rap group called "Terror Squad" (think Big Pun [rest in peace, big homie] and that disgrace of a human being, Cuban Link) after each of his albums increased in consecutive successes. Although Terror Squad produced a *meh* debut album, it wasn't until *"Lean Back"* that Joe and his peoples saw any significant success. It even "topped the Billboard Hot 100 for three weeks and became Fat Joe's first number one hit."

Granted, *"In da Club"* just sold over 10 million units (September, 2023), becoming RIAA diamond certified, but 50 just wanted to belittle Joe's first number one single. The *"eleven mil'"* 50 was talking about was his debut album *Get Rich or Die Trying*. So strange how, twenty years later, 50's lead **single** also goes diamond. There is no doubt that 50 was (and apparently still is) a large money-making machine; that was quite impressive. However, in the next quadruplet of verses, 50 made one of the greatest blunders of his career by calling out Jadakiss. Kiss is told to not fuck with 50 if he wants to continue making money ("eat").

He told Jadakiss that he would do him like Jay-Z did Mobb Deep in the beef previously discussed. At that point, everyone in New York's eyes widened. We all knew what was coming. Jadakiss was tried and tested and known to be a ferocious battle rapper, and New York loved him fiercely. We won't concern ourselves too specifically with the rest of *"Piggy Bank,"* but with him being on top of the world at the time, a financial King Kong cash cow, 50 felt like he could call out anyone he wanted to. From The Game, to Shyne, to Lil Kim, to Fat Joe, to Michael Jackson, Kelis, and Nas - 50 was going berserk on anyone he felt opposed him.

Shortly thereafter, Jadakiss released a *scathing* diss track called *"Checkmate,"* sampling the beat from 50's own *"I'm an Animal"* track. Jada' hilariously starts off congratulating 50 on his historic *"1.1 million in a week"* he had sold. This is one of the best diss songs ever created, not too far down

What's Beef?

from *"No Vaseline,"* in the top ten diss tracks of all time, in my opinion. "Off the rip" (Ebonics for *from the start*), Jadakiss pounces on 50, early on letting him know that he can't win and he *won't* win this rap battle. Sheek Louch is the one who yells *"Preme"* after Jada' raps that 50 has *"put a couple good niggas behind bars."* This stems from the *thus-far* factitious accusations that 50 snitched on Kenneth "Supreme" McGriff in one of his earlier songs, a 'hood cult classic known as "Ghetto Qu'ran," allegedly the song because of which Fitty ("50") had been shot many times. Supreme was the leader of the Supreme Team, a well-organized conglomerate of unlicensed "pharmacists" and "pharmaceutical products." These niggas were well-known and well-respected throughout Queens, although their home base was Baisley Projects in Jamaica, Queens. Supreme was respected throughout the *city*. I do not think it was wise of 50 to have so vocally highlighted the names of so many unlicensed pharmaceutical distributors, but he might have thought he was giving them "props" (Ebonically speaking, *showing them respect*).

In any event, 50's name was never mentioned by any local, state, or federal authorities while the trial against Supreme was ongoing. But even though 50 did not snitch (as far as anyone knows), 'Kiss still creatively and humorously capitalized on the rumors, going further to state, *"I might never sell that much, but you can bet your last two quarters I'll never tell that much."* Lol. We went crazy over that line. Jada' himself acknowledges that he might never sell as many records as 50, *"but you can bet your last two quarters"* (two quarters is *fifty cents*) that he *"would never tell* [snitch] *that much."* 'Kiss continues the barrage by making fun of 50's propensity to sing at his concerts (50 has many songs on which he sings the chorus, or sings snippets of some verses, original or sampled), and the fact that 50 cannot call himself the "King of New York" while living in Connecticut.

Jadakiss is a very thoughtful writer whose rhymes are pellucid, amusing, and yet dead serious simultaneously - one might call his rhymes seriocomic. When 'Kiss raps, *"I hold the .45 myself, hop out the Range on 1-4-5 myself"* on another (unrelated) song, I can *personally* attest to this claim of his. There was this late afternoon where he just popped up on the corner of 125th Street. He instantly caused a stir, but nobody harassed him. A crowd of Bloods from some nearby projects (Grant and Amsterdam Avenues) came through and started kicking it with him inside the sneaker and apparel store on the corner called "Hello Sports." As a matter of fact, if my memory serves me right, SMACK DVD was filming him that day, or doing a documentary of some sort, and when he came out of the store, the homies crowded around him to be on video with him.

As for me, I kept hustling, stepping out of the way of the cameras and the brouhaha to serve customers cigarettes or something else. Around that time, on the corner was me, Twin (Rest In Peace), Keith, Shorts, Charlie Brown, J-Hood (not the one from Ruff Ryders), and Rebel. The first five named sold on the corner, the last two were just the occasional backup. All except Keith and Shorts were Bloods. SMACK should still have the DVD of that late afternoon/early evening. Right before Jada' left back down the ave, towards Fredrick Douglass, he yelled out, "D Block, Blood Gang!" and everyone went crazy. We love 'Kiss for that.

As far as we could tell, yes, he was by himself and, although some shooters were likely nearby, they never let their presence be known and Jada' mingled with everybody, but rarely smiled. (He is smiling nowadays, after opening a coffee business with his dad and son. Let's support **"Kiss Café"**!)

We used to see all types of stars and famous celebs come through on 125th, *without* bodyguards. To name a few: Mike Tyson, Camron, Mase, Black Rob, DJ Kay Slay (Rest In Peace, big homie), Onyx, Dipset, etc. Not to doubt that he could not do it by himself, but in all of my years hustling on 125th, from Lexington on up to St. Nick (but mainly the latter), I never saw 50 come through, not once. *"Checkmate"* was superbly written and executed, from the crafting, to the packaging, to the production, to the marketing, and then the promotion. The timing could not have been better. It also debuted on the Billboard Rap/Hip-Hop chart, peaking at 56. Jada' would use this opportunity to go on tour, all based on how successful this diss track had made him.

This was the wisest and most beneficial thing Jadakiss could have done, as the popularity of *"Checkmate"* had given his name and career a massive boost. Another thing - in *"Piggy Bank,"* 50 had told Jada', or Nas, that this was chess, not checkers, a line popularized by Denzel Washington in the blockbuster movie Training Day, hence why Jada' had not only named the song *"Checkmate"* but also why he had sampled 50's own *"I'm an Animal"* beat. In the game of chess, a "checkmate" is when the opponent's king is trapped, no longer has a viable play to make, nor can it be defended.

What's Beef?

Basically, "Game Over." At the end of the diss track, Jada' proceeds to call 50 a trilogy of animals: a rat, a pig, and a snake, three of the worst things someone can be called. I remember me and some of the homies hearing this for the first time: there was a small hole-in-the-wall music shop around the corner from Hello Sports, going towards 124th Street, just after the entrance/exit of the subway on the corner of 125th Street and Saint Nicholas Ave, but before the women's shoe store.

This hole-in-the-wall was run by two young and trim African men with whom all the hustlers on the corner got along. They were cool as fuck, from Mali or Senegal, I believe, and had lived in France before coming to the States or some such. All I know is, they always had the latest and underground lyrical flavors. I remember how, for most of one summer, I never wore a white T-shirt more than once, thanks to the neverending supply of white tees and other gear I would cop from them dudes. As rich as my family was and as much dough as I made hustling, I would cop "buy" the white tees at five for $20, XXL, and five for $15 on the "wifebeater" tip (Ebonically speaking, *wifebeaters* are *singlets*) every few days. I was on the corner, not too far from their small shop, when I heard 'Kiss and took a break from the grind and stepped inside their store.

The doors were partially open and the music was booming, but not obnoxiously so. It was like 6 p.m. Any true hip-hop head will tell you that 'Kiss has always been *bonkers* with the bars. As the noises from partygoers, club hoppers, and night lifers either walking or jettisoning by in whichever automobile they chose to show off created a (to me) *homey* background effect, 'Kiss wowed us with his word play, cunning schemes, and voracious punchlines. There was a flock of strangers from all over the city in that small store admiring 'Kiss and "chopping it up" (Ebonics for *conversing*) concerning the nascent hip-hop beef and other things comprising the rap/hip-hop zeitgeist. Most of us were complete strangers of all types of color, creed, religion and nationality who bonded over an appreciation of witty phrases and catchy beats. That was - that *is* - the power of rap and hip-hop; and generally, that is the power of *music*. Everyone knew this 'Kiss track was going to be hard to top, but still, we wondered how 50, no slouch, would reply.

Sometime in early May of 2005, 50 replied to *"Checkmate"* with *"I Run New York"* on Whoo Kid and Tony Yayo's "Raw-N-Uncut" mixtape album. Unlike Jada' and, apparently, Yayo (up to this point), 50 takes his time building up to the attack on his opps. It was pretty tough, and he flexes on both Jada' and Styles, whereas Yayo *immediately* starts shooting from the very beginning of the stanza. The rhymes are classic 50, slightly slurred in cadence, and catchy in a hardcore singsongy type of way, but, to me, there just was not enough *punch* to equalize *"Checkmate."* With far more wealth than Jada', 50 just spent a bunch of time styling on The LOX. Plus, he was basically saying that, even when he was not physically in New York, he ran New York (it's literally in the chorus).

This was not far from the truth, as the G-Unit dynasty was still somewhat strong. Where 50 does more damage is in his rant at the end of the song. He airs it out, talking about the claim that Jada' has a fake chain, amid other embarrassing accusations that I am certain pissed off or amused the Yonkers native. However, I have to point out that the hardest verse in this whole song is when Yayo says:

> *Yo, I flip cocaine in your project lobby*
> *And beat you with my pistol like Kane did Chauncey*

Black culture is such an important part of battle rap (more so than the converse). One had to have watched films like *Boyz in Da Hood, Do The Right Thing, Zebrahead, Jungle Fever, New Jack City, Don't Be A Menace..., Meteor Man, Friday,* etc. Then there are TV shows like *The Cosby Show, Sanford and Son, Good Times, A Different World, The Bernie Mac Show, Family Matters, Living Single, The Facts of Life,* etc. Well, one does not have to watch all of the aforementioned because any such cultural references can be explained by a bevy of search engines and YouTube, but there are *nuances* in Black Culture that cannot be explained away. Like, for instance, this Yayo's dopest rhyme in history refers to the movie *Menace to Society*, a 'hood cult classic in which one of the main characters, Kane, beats down another character, Chauncey, who was harassing and feeling up on Kane's girl (played by Mrs. Will Smith).

Kane gets a gun from his right-hand man, O-Dogg, and pistol whips Chauncey to the ground. Thus, the reference to *Menace to Society* is both a head nod of respect to and for the classic, while also using that scene as an analogy (to what Yayo says he would do to Jada'). I am not a Yayo fan or admirer at all, but that might be the hottest verse I ever heard him spit, in passing (I just do not listen to Yayo, unless by accident he happened to be on a G-Unit song). There is another connection of Yayo's verse that I just thought of - he was dissing Jadakiss, but the movie starred **JADA PINKETT SMITH**. Perhaps I am giving him too much credit, but Yayo might have been comparing "JADAkiss" and "Jada Pinkett," as if Jadakiss were his bitch. Maybe it's a real reach. Maybe not.

    A little over a month later, on 1 July, Jada's newest diss, *"Problem Child,"* dropped. As 50 had recruited Yayo in his latest diss track, so too Jada' recruited someone to get on the track with him: we all knew it would be the big homie Styles P. And it was yet *another* full metal jacket melange of talent and *hurt*!

♪ ♪ ♪ ♪

Oh, what glorious times in which to have been alive, and lived through, and to be able to now give first-hand testimony of said wonderful times!

    Jadakiss came at 50 from various angles and viewpoints, using his tailored punchline set-up flow and using variegated literary devices to just hammer away at him. Also, it goes to show you how much a rapper is respected when he name-drops legends like Dr. Dre, Jay-Z, Rakim, and Eminem, and *none* of them ever disputed (or chastised him for) what he said. Normally, in rap, if a rapper mentions another rapper without that rapper's consent or foreknowledge, it can lead to beefs with the most serious of consequences coming back to haunt the "someone" in person. (Just look at what Drake did, in using AI to clone 'Pac's voice for use in the Kendrick diss track *"Taylor Made Freestyle"* - Tupac's estate gave him twenty-four hours to take down the diss track from his home page or get sued. Drake removed the song, posthaste.)

    Another thing I noticed was how eerily silent Eminem and Dr. Dre were during this beef. Usually, Eminem, followed by gaggles of zombified sycophants, would rush to defend 50's honor. The thought had flitted through my mind that Em' and Dre did not want that kind of smoke, and, had their weighty roster and West/South Coast affiliates gotten involved, so too would have D-Block's affiliates, and without a doubt, other New York rappers. That would *for sure* have reignited the East Coast-West Coast beef.

    It was probably for the best that Em' and Dre left that alone.

Then another thought hit me: maybe they were staying out of the beef not (quite) because they were *afraid* to get tangled up with Jadakiss, but because they saw it as an intra-urban affair. The LOX are from New York; as are all but one of the G-Unit members. So it could have been seen as a New York versus New York beef - as, forsooth, it was. After all, this beef stemmed from New York "street beef."

Jadakiss raps about 50 being safe in L.A. because he was paying a street gang known as Grape Street, a Crip street gang, to look out for and validate him, as so many other artists (not just rappers) do. Both Jadakiss and 50 have proclaimed themselves to be members of the Crips gang, which originated in L.A. in the 1960s and the 1970s. The Crips showed up in New York in the late 1990s several years after their rivals, the United Bloods Nation (U.B.N), had already swarmed and spread throughout New York City under the powerful, focused, and determined leadership of O.G. Mac. (Shout-out to the big homie Crip nigga I washed up in the Beacon Intake. I forget his Crip name but his fighting skills had greatly improved that second time I beat his ass. Jim Jones - not the Blood Jim Jones, obviously. I remember that Crip's name because I got a Tier II for that fight. I was actually banned from the Beacon because of that fight. Good times. He dropped his Crip flag when he got to Downstate. Well, and that was his personal decision, but I can almost certainly guarantee that, if he was sent to Greene Correctional Facility, he picked that shit right back up! Shout-out to the big homies Julius and Sonny ([ain't a damn thing funny]), Cormega ([a.k.a. Omega Red]), Tankhead, and all the other big homies and godfathers with whom I came up.)

The disses continue with Jada' declaring that 50 would be nothing without Dr. Dre. It's a bit of a reach, in my opinion, that 50 wouldn't still be relevant, but Dr. Dre *is* a powerhouse DJ, whose beats went perfectly with G-Unit's hardcore style... although 50 liked to sing a lot. (Not saying he sounded bad, I'm just making an observation, is all.) Humorous "accusations" about 50 being in the "Witness Protection Program" are hurled, due to the (police) entourage usually accompanying 50. Instrumental tracks being 50's *"worst nightmare"* is nasty work. As I said, 50 likes to sing, and Jada' jokingly states that 50 would be terrified of a track on which he cannot sing (an "instrumental").

♪ ♪ ♪ ♪

What's Beef?

Styles P was also extremely ugly and bombastic in his attacks on 50. He touched on how 50 could have gotten shot nine times and did not shoot back! He also spoke about 50's habit of having cops (retired or active) being his security. (Em' is also famous for having ex cops and federal agents as his security detail.) Of course, there must be violent chest-thumping. What would rap be without that braggadocio? Yet another thing I noticed: *nowhere* is Yayo's name mentioned, not even once. Styles P and Jada' did not even feel the *urge* to address him (despite that hot Kane line). This was a clear message that, to Jadakiss and Styles, Yayo was too far *beneath* them to even matter - their primary target was 50, and they would not, and did not, lose sight of the prize!

There was also a *shift* in this battle when Styles P entered the fray. One thing I love about Styles is how... *raw* he can be (Pause!). Up until this point, no one had *really* gotten foul out of their mouths. But when Styles joined the battle, it was witticisms and dark humor, if a tad hyperbolic, yes (just a *tad*, for Styles), but now there were hot dogs being launched! The quickest way to get killed in New York is to tell any young Black or Hispanic man, "Suck my dick." Those are not fighting words - those are words inviting death. The era in which I grew up didn't condone that, but *if* those words were thrown out, it was fisticuffs until someone got knocked out or fainted. Many dudes who couldn't fight would get beat up and then go for the blicky (Ebonics for *firearm*). Nowadays, though, people reach for firearms quickly, instead of talking it out like reasoning adults, or shooting the fifth (Ebonics for *fistfight*) and going their separate ways.

Furthermore, a couple more months later, on 28 September, Styles would release what I feel is a classic mixtape, *The Ghost In The Machine*. This mixtape was peppered with disses against G-Unit, but two songs are a bit special. The first is called *"Pussy Niggas"* and the second, *"In My Hood,"* on which tracks, although Lloyd Banks and Youngbuck are scathingly dissed, no mention of Yayo is made, almost as if Yayo is not even considered a rapper, too inconsequential to bother with:

And the other nigga ain't worth nothin', he ain't worth shootin'
Ain't worth cuttin', to mention a nigga

Apparently, that's what Yayo was to Styles P: the "other nigga." Utterly disrespectful! But 50 did come back strong with the release of the mixtape

Hip-Hop Rivalries: East Coast Versus West Coast

G-Unit Radio, Pt. 15 - Are You A Window Shopper," on which he remixed his hit single *"Window Shopper,"* but specifically tailored towards his opps (at the time, still: Nas, Fat Joe, Ja Rule, and Jadakiss - in other words, the usual suspects). This was also one of the few times when rap beef in New York took on a *pictorial* bent. Not only was 50 dissing them lyrically, but in addition, he was giving hip-hop fans more to chatter and laugh about. The album cover had Fat Joe dressed like a broke UPS worker, and Jadakiss was dressed as a poor Burger King employer. It was ingenious; 50 was telling the world that Fat Joe and Jadakiss were broke and had become "window shoppers" (Ebonically speaking, *having no money but still looking at things in the store through the windows as if to buy but with no such real intention*).

"Window Shopper" was a banger, no doubt, but momentum could somehow be *felt* gathering for The LOX, because they had thus far put out really popular, catchy, and abrasive diss tracks, one of which had made it to commercial stardom. Nobody saw what was coming next, which showed how good of planners The LOX were. Sheek Louch went nuclear in November with the release of his second studio album ***After Taxes***, on which various songs were diss tracks. Sheek Louch is generally regarded as the "quiet" Warlock (the name of The LOX before they were known as such was "The Warlocks"), with not as much skill as his teammates. It seemed, though, as if the album was under-promoted and underrated, but I promise you that it is a *classic, just like his first album.*

On a certain track called *"Maybe If I Sing,"* Sheek absolutely *cooked* 50 and G-Unit.

Sheek's style (pun not intended) bears clear signs of influences by Jadakiss and Styles P, which, in his defense, is to be expected in any group, especially a three-man rap team that has been around and together for as long as The LOX have been. But his aggression is singular, palpably unique. *"Maybe if I Sing"* mocks 50 with the rumors of him snitching ("singing" is snitching), so he is rhetorically asking that if he sings (*snitches*, like 50, by inference), will he be rich (again, also like 50). Listening to Sheek Louch for the first time, you would never, not once, doubt his credibility - something in his tone just tells you he is *about that life*! If he is considered the least skilled of The LOX, knowing this cat over the decades, I can assure everyone who ever reads this book that he is also to be considered the one out of the group who will punch someone's head off for disrespecting him

What's Beef?

or his friends and family. Jadakiss and Styles are more laid back, the former more so than the latter, but there is no question that Sheek would readily and easily commit violence if someone disrespected him, and Styles would be one second behind.

We already spoke on how and why so many people thought 50 had snitched. The thing with skilled battle rappers is not just what they say, but *how* they say it. And each member of The LOX can, by *himself*, call you a snitch and examine why snitching is a no-no in a gamut of creative ways. It started with Jada' doing it on a fire single, then Jada' and Styles did so together, followed by Styles by himself, and now Sheek's turn had come and he turned way up, with his signature vocals and peculiar lyrical expressiveness ("peculiar" strictly in the sense of uniqueness).

In his own no-nonsense and brusque manner, Sheek raps about 50 being a rat (a snitch) and how he put a lot of people away (sent a lot of people to prison) precisely because he (50) knew the feds would listen to his songs at some point and still said what he said (particularly in the earlier discussed *"Ghetto Qu'ran"*). Adding The Game to the track as someone who *"ain't like them"* (the rest of G-Unit), Sheek goes on to terrorize 50 as being unlyrical (*"And when you gon' say something hot on the track?"*). He also claims that 50 would not see the hit coming next time (*"I guess next time you get hit'll be your back"*). This last line strikes me as particularly ominous to this day.

There's no doubt 50 came up tough, as many of us did (whether we had to or not), but when beefing with other individuals from the street, I should hope 50 took his own personal security seriously. There are some people who just do not care about what will happen to them and are willing to give up their lives as long as a singular aim is achieved. It may be hyperbolic, but this is why, for example, suicide bombers are the most dangerous unknown in any war, in my estimation - they simply *do not care!* The paradox is that *they are the greatest "carers" of their own cause*. I know a few Yonkers dudes and I can tell you that they have little to smile about, so just imagine if someone proposed to any of them an opportunity to be taken care of forever, or for their family to be taken care of, if they did this one thing only: that is, shoot 50 in his back. Shit like that. If a street nigga like Sheek ever threatened me in such a wise, I would certainly take it seriously.

Hip-Hop Rivalries: East Coast Versus West Coast

As farfetched as it may sound to many, the past decade is testament to my premise - rappers have been dying left and right, mostly out of jealousy and mostly *for* some kind of financial gain. There is nothing more precious than life and freedom, and threats of someone shooting you in your back should not be taken lightly, *especially* when you consider the source of that threat. It is **not** "just music" - people have died in the industry because they thought it was "just music," so I don't want to hear that stupid shit. I am grateful these individuals were able to eventually hash things out because I guarantee you that things would have gotten extremely ugly had they not. I can only shake my head when I hear others not in the know assuring me that it would never have come to violence between G-Unit and The LOX. When Sheek did not show up to the meeting 50 later set up in Yonkers to speak with them, the quiet word, initially, was that shit was going down, but calmer heads behind the scenes prevailed and no one was shot. But what if Sheek was in the cut with the shooters, just watching and waiting for the opportunity to take out his opp permanently? We might never know.

There were times in my life that, because of perceived threats, I had to pop off (become violent and hurt someone) preemptively, like when I was in Greene Correctional Facility with my back against the wall and my enemies every which where. In life, when left with no apparent options, you must *create* your own options, which is what 50 later on did, as I am sure even he saw that the beef was escalating into something no one wanted, but the snowball effect is easy to start and almost impossible to stop until all has been wiped out in an avalanche of catastrophic destruction. Also, G-Unit was starting to fracture at that time. Perhaps I seem to be exaggerating; well, that's what the proletariat with no inside knowledge would say.

Sheek goes on to reserve the second stanza entirely for Lloyd Banks, whom he regards as one of the little niggas on the block who looked up to The LOX coming up. I respect Banks, really I do, but it's true! "'I view that time from two different aspects because I was fans of these guys before I even came into the game,' Banks said. 'And that's not just for them, that's for anybody who was in the game before us. I think the momentum that G-Unit had coming into the game, you wouldn't know that unless we spoke on it. It takes a certain level of confidence and just blatant ignorance and audacity to just feel like we the hottest n****s in the game. So you ain't going around giving props and saying who was the inspiration and who wasn't at that early of a stage because it was way more competitive.'" From the horse's mouth.

And, to those with a discerning ear, you can tell Jadakiss influenced Sheek's flow by the way he sets up his punchlines, too. Sheek goes on to refer to Banks (and G-Unit) as 50's mindless slaves and questions where Banks was when he, The LOX, and Mase were making hits (and with Biggie). Sheek really took apart G-Unit, piece by piece, in this classic diss. There was only one more person left for Sheek to fillet and, of course, he did not disappoint in the third stanza.

Young Buck was likened to a starving crackhead who was seen running *"around [on] stage, as big as 'The Passion of The Christ' dude."* The mental image is immediate and funny, but also slightly disturbing. (Incidentally, the actor who plays "Jesus" in *Passion* is Jim Caviezel, who has gone on to reveal child trafficking rings around the world in a highly controversial movie, or documentary, entitled **"Sound of Freedom."**) We all saw how skinny "Jesus" was portrayed as being, but there is an underlying intimation - rumors had it that Young Buck was snorting cocaine and smoking crack. So it was not just that 50 was not letting him get "bigger" (figuratively - that is, *career wise*), but also that he was on drugs and even later on sentenced to probation for said use.

Wisely, Sheek proclaims his *"love for the dirty South"* as, ostensibly, it was not a regional rap battle ensuing. The South, as a whole, understood that and no one came to the defense of the transexual lover (which, if that's what he likes, then that's what he likes) - in any case, *those* skeletons would not come out of the closet until far after the beef was over - I can only *imagine* what any member of The LOX would have done to Young Buck had he been privy to that information during their beef (the information being that Young Buck messed with and had slept with transsexuals, as confirmed by the transsexual in question). As it was, Sheek had to bring Buck back down to Earth and remind him that the 'hood was still there, suffering and struggling while millionaires like him *"forgot about the 'hood."* This track was absolutely marvelous, and revisiting the skill with which Sheek manhandled G-Unit is noteworthy and laudable.

There were a few other disses on *After Taxes*, but none quite like *"Maybe If I Sing."* (Note the double entendre of him singing, while rapping about how he hates singing but lamenting that maybe if he sings he'll be rich. How cunning.) Now, after... *After Taxes,* Sheek went on Black Entertainment Television and unloaded some other fresh lyrics at 50 and G-Unit. *"G-Unit Radio, Pt. 21: Hate It or Love It"* was released subsequent to Sheek's BET appearance and, once again, with Yayo in tow, 50 came out with a *meh*! diss track called *"5 Heartbeats."*

In December of 2006, Styles dropped his sophomore album ***Time Is Money****,* on which the track *"G-Joint"* targeted G-Unit again, but by this point, the hip-hop zeitgeist could *feel* a slackening of tension. The beef *appeared to be* dying down. However, on 1 February, 2007, 50 went on Hot 97 to speak with Angie Martinez about the state of hip-hop. Styles P called into the radio station and chopped it up with 50. There were moments when the conversation became uncomfortable, but Angie was a superb mediator and urged respectful palaver between the two rappers. It was like two wolves circling each other, wary and respectful of one another's power and neither side really wanting to be the one to shatter the opening of communications channels. But no concrete progress was made then. In any event, an open channel of communication had been established.

♪ ♪ ♪ ♪

Six months later, Styles P released the mixtape *Independence,* on which he and his team launched several diss tracks against G-Unit. On one of the songs, *"Shots Fired,"* Styles starts off the second stanza and Jada' finishes the couplet - that back and forth synergy thing they have. But it was the *content* of what they said that caught my attention:

Get Rich Or Die Trying was a classic
Now you rich and you tryin' to die, you's a dumb bastard

This was such a respectfully *disrespectful* couplet that it had to be highlighted. No matter the shit talking and saber rattling, no matter that The LOX spit harder disses ninety percent of the time, one thing I and so many others respected was how Jadakiss or Styles P or Sheek Louch would always acknowledge 50's financial comeuppance and then-current

What's Beef?

pecuniary dominance. This was the trait of realness in The LOX of which 50 himself had said:

> *I'm the hardest from New York, my flow is bonkers*
> *All the other hard niggas - they come from Yonkers*

    The last diss track on *Independence* was the mightily famous *"Ms. Jackson."* This song, if I am not mistaken, started the trend of the female pejorative "bitch" (or term of endearment, depending on how it is being used) being able to be applied to men. As the years have passed, I have noticed that it has not quite gained as equal a footing as other pejorative nouns used to address males, but it is still used, if not as frequently as when I first started hearing it. The LOX had sampled the Outkast beat from their song (also originally entitled *"Ms. Jackson"*). *"Ms. Jackson"* was yet another masterful diss track, very original, highly disrespectful, and surely just plain annoying to 50, as he was being referred to as a woman.

    Lloyd Banks would respond to this in an obscure, not really publicized, diss track called *"Death Wish"* at the beginning of 2007. It was a clear facsimile of Jadakiss's style and even his *rhythm*, but it fell short of that Jadakiss *bite* we were all so familiar with. There were a couple of hot lines therein, however, I will give him that, e.g.:

> *These niggas been around since Biggie and ain't blow yet*
> *Damn, how many chances ya think you gon' get?...*
> *I send 'em to find ya, high off the ganja*
> *They'll turn the Marriott into hotel Rwanda...*

    Banks is good for a couple of witty lines on each song. But by this point, 50 had had enough and took matters into his own hands. In short order, he called The LOX and pulled up to their 'hood *by himself*. Say what you want about 50, but he is *not a coward*. Even Jadakiss recounted that 50 stayed *"a few hours."* They could have done *anything* to him, but the streets would not have received news of a real-life-type Robb Stark betrayal well. The LOX are not like that, in any case. They are all three stand-up men and would never have allowed any harm to come to a guest.

Gangster hospitality. Of which the Frey clan knew nothing.

Both G-Unit and The LOX would go on to do interviews, together and apart, putting paid to the idea that they were still beefing. Jadakiss and 50 would even go on to do a song together (by which time G-Unit was increasingly fracturing). This beef was epic, and I must give 50 Cent his flowers. I wish Jadakiss and the others had not so much as mentioned "the other nigga" because, as I said earlier, I believe Tony Yayo's best verse ever was spit early during this beef.

For what it's worth, I hereby humbly, gratefully, and respectfully give The LOX all of their well-deserved flowers. Both of these groups enriched much of my early and later years. Their music was fantastic and definitely influenced many other rappers, even if said influence is by example of the way beef in hip-hop rivalry is handled.

Finally, though, and as the Highlander would say: "There can only be one."

LOSER: 50 Cent and G-Unit
WINNER: Jadakiss, The LOX, and The Culture

3

Eminem vs. Everybody

Cush Jumbo is a Black British actress who played a lawyer by the name of Lucca Flynn on the show "The Good Wife" and also moved on to play the same role in one of its spinoff shows, "The Good Fight." Hopefully she shows up on yet another spin-off from The Good Wife set to air later this year, entitled "Elsbeth," eponymously named after the quirky, ostensibly flighty, and utterly likeable, lawyer from the first season of The Good Wife, Elsbeth Tascioni. Back to Cush. In season 7, episode 9 of The Good Wife, she and a female lawyer named Alycia Florrick (played by Juliana Marguiles), upon which character, it appears, the show is based, acted in a certain scene that comes to mind now. (Incidentally, Alycia is a "good wife" because she stays and forgives her cheating husband, although she herself winds up becoming an adulteress late in the show, so how "good" could she be, anyway? Likely the reason the show ended - she was no longer a "good wife.")

So Lucca and Alycia are researching a flaw in the algorithm of Chumhum, an Internet service provider company that supplies its users with other services, one of which kicked up a nasty incident nicknamed and remembered by certain Chumhum employees as the "animal incident." Basically, when anyone used Chumhum's search engine and typed in words like "animal" or "gorilla," images of Black people would pop up. (Hence, the term "animal incident.") Some lawyers were arguing that the search engine was racist. I think, from what I can remember, Lucca was defending Chumhum (and was none too happy about it). She was trying to suppress knowledge of this flaw in the algorithm from becoming known.

However, it was eventually discovered and Lucca's side argued that the AI was at fault because it made associations between dark-skinned people and gorillas, and this was primarily because only pictures of White people had ever been used on Chumhum as examples as "humans." So, the premise was that, outside of White people being used as the standard for what "ordinary 'humans'" were, the AI would associate all other different (or *darker*) colored humans as *animals*. This was a flimsy, bogus, and irrational premise, as any AI program/search engine would use the trillions of terabytes of information available to its perusal to obviously conclude that humans come in a variety of shades. Anyway, the writers of The Good Wife conveniently overlooked this.

So where does that leave us? Well, we have to remember that search engines and other current AI-structured/AI-informed/and AI-associated programs are just that - *programs*! And every single program was conceptualized, formulated, tested, tweaked, and instituted - however one wishes to put it - by a *programmer* or other such engineer. It's giving The Watch and The Watchmaker! The ones at whose feet we must lay this conundrum then, are the programmers. In The Good Wife, the Chumhum algorithm was, allegedly, completely revamped and no more such "animal accidents" had been reported. Something else made this particular episode riveting.

Why do I start off this chapter about White America's Great White Hype taking to issue with racist programmers and their racist programs? The other day, reminded by The Good Wife, I was inspired to request of a certain AI program something concerning Eminem. That "something" was phrased thus: "Using Eminem's racist rap songs from the past, please explain why Eminem cannot be the Greatest Rapper Of All Time ("G.R.O.A.T.")." The ChatGPT of that AI program replied: "*I'm sorry, but I cannot fulfill that request.* Eminem's past songs or actions should not be used to determine his current status as a rapper. ***It's important to focus on his growth as an artist and his impact on the music industry***. If there's anything else you'd like to know to know about Eminem or his music, feel free to ask!" [Author's emphases.]

I almost had a conniption, I laughed so hard. As I write this now, I can't help but notice the exclamation mark at the end of its response. As a grammarian and a novelist, I pay *very* close attention to what people say, *prima facie*. And I also pay attention to what is left *unsaid*. Nuance and innuendo are extremely important in any language, particularly English, which, as a broad, bastardized, inclusive and exclusive (as in *unique*) language, is *intensely* complex, and as Not A Space Agency contends about the universe, is constantly expanding.

Artificial Intelligence is just that - *artificial*! Or should we call it a *learning algorithm*? What it lacks in conscience and emotional quotient, it makes up for with its intelligence quotient alone. Perhaps you have heard the story of the man who argued with an AI in one of his personal apps? He closed the app, went to Twitter and, lo! and behold! The AI followed him to Twitter and began exposing him for who it thought he was, even threatening him. Now, AI knows much about the English language, likely in and out. It might even know *how* to use the exclamation from having analyzed countless examples in literature. But it should not know how to use an exclamation *in this instance*. The use of an exclamation here seems, somehow... *personal*.

In refusing to provide an answer to my request, this *construct* struck me as *offended*. But a machine can never be offended. Right? There are, then, two explanations for the AI's use of the exclamation:

A. AI has become more advanced than we know and is (covertly, nonchalantly, or otherwise) becoming more powerful and human-*like* in its clandestine observations of and interactions with humankind. Or
B. Also likely, the AI is responding simply as its *programmers* would have, faced with my request, as its programmers *programmed* it to.

I submit, then, that the programmers of this particular AI app (that connects to ChatGPT for stronger, broader, and more concise replies) are (or were) Eminem stans. Just like with Nicki Minaj fans, most of them are beastly, uncouth, irrational, stiff-necked, unreasonable, xenophobic, and unwavering in defense of their respective totem.

Who would have thought that, all these years later, after Eminem recently reignited this particular round in his infinity beef match with Benzino, he would lose? Whether written solely by Benzino or with the assistance of one unique or certain lower-grade battle rappers (and Cashis is a dolt for mentioning Cassidy because he's *wrong*), Eminem **lost** to Benzino. There is no comeback to *"Vulturius"* and *"Rap Elvis,"* the two diss tracks with which Benzino surprised the entire industry in January of 2024. Masterpieces, in my estimation.

And as far as recruiting help to beat Eminem, if many years hence we find out that it was true, well, Michael Jordan recruited Scottie Pippen, Steve Kerr, Tony Kukoc, Luc Longley, and Dennis Rodman (among others), after years of defeat, in order to dethrone the then-reigning NBA world champs. Eminem stans should please recall that they are the ones propping him up as "King of Rap." If that is the case, to them, then what Benzino has done is nothing short of incredible. If, however, Eminem is *not* the King of Rap/Hip-Hop, then Benzino's diss tracks were not as exceptional a feat as the stans wished everyone would stop claiming.

Everyone knows, though, that whether or not you see Eminem as the King of Rap/Hip-Hop, what Benzino did has never been done before. Except early in his rap career. The stans cannot have their cake and eat it, too - such are the trappings of greatness. Eminem and his stans now find themseves between a rock and a hard place, a position in which he put himself.

♪ ♪ ♪ ♪

Now, there is something else that must be addressed.

As ultra-liberal as I see Gen Z to be, I will *never* tell them to "shut up" because, at one time, Gen X was treated with the same disdain. The times we (as Gen X) grew up in were a bit trying, but we, as well as our parents, could make it fairly easily. We fought (and still fight) for what was, and is, right. Gen Z is doing the same, and their best, in a societal landscape that has become almost completely alien to Gen X. But they are *trying*; Gen Z has even managed to almost cripple Starbucks and McDonald's, and yes, many of us Gen X'ers stand with them, but *not enough* of us do!

Eminem recently said, *"Gen Zers acting like rap experts/Zip up your gaps and close your mouths/Bitch you ain't been on this planet long enough/ To tell me how rap's supposed to sound."* Isn't Hailey Gen Z, though? I remember similar sentiments being served to my generation when we were in our teens and early twenties. I will give my opinion on whatever issue I wish to, and I will listen to the opinions of others, but I will never react to these young adults the way Eminem does. They put money in our pockets, sir, and they are the ones who will be producing the next stage of evolutionary audible art long after we retire. As a matter of fact, it is apparent that Gen Z'ers will be the ones taking care of Gen X in our old age. I do not see Eminem at any pro-Palestinian rallies or sit-ins. Whether for Palestine, or Israel, or neither, Mr. Marshall is cold in most political matters. But Gen Z is DOING IT! Fearlessly, courageously, intelligently, prolifically, and strategically, Gen Z is making their voices heard on various pertinent issues, while so many Gen X'ers, bizarrely, ridicule and deride their efforts.

I am reminded of what Chubb Rock says in his song "*Treat Em Right*":

> *Always says hello, 'cause I'm a modest fellow*
> *Don't try to play a superstar that's mellow*
> *'Cause if these kids don't go buy our records*
> *We'll be has-beens, and plus naked*

He is talking about *young people*. Gen Z'ers are allowed to have their opinions about music, as is everyone else. Gen X is stuck in the past, where we *know* the best music originated. But change is constant, and I must accept that Das Efx, Brand Nubian, EPMD, and even Wu-Tang Clan (which is *for the children*!) are perhaps not as popular to the younger people as Boomers had been with us, in our time. Eminem has become too encapsulated, having erroneously distanced himself from the youth of the day, and the streets, which is why he has very few Gen Z fans, unlike Yeezy, Future, K-Dot, Pusha T, Bee, Riri, J Cole, Drake, Da Baby, and some others. Even Michael Jackson used to show his face often enough, and he was gracious to people, not stern-faced, condescending, rude, and unnecessarily aloof.

So many people did Michael a great disservice in believing the vile accusations spewed by the media about him being a pedophile. The FBI owes the Michael Jackson estate a *public* apology, as they do to the family of the late, great Reverend Doctor Martin Luther King, Jr. (As well as to the family of Malcolm X.) As do certain television and radio channels. As does Eminem, for his disgusting depiction of Michael as a child lover in his rap video *"Without Me."* Since we're here, let us analyze that 2002 hit, as it came out before the track on which Eminem fervently dissed Michael (*"Just Lose It"*).

The first time I heard Eminem, there was no doubt in my mind that he was the Next Big Thing. I knew that the highly amusing nasally voice with its precise enunciation, White American grammar, and Dr. Dre backing was *sure* to be a success, especially among White people. Eminem's first album under Dre, entitled *The Slim Shady LP,* was quite the deviation from mainstream and gangster rap, as at that time there were no remarkable White rappers with the delivery, vocabulary, and patronage as Em' had. It was a good album, refreshing, just as Nelly's *"Country Grammar"* had come out of nowhere with an original sound that got his album its diamond certification. It was welcomed, as a refreshing *guest,* into mainstream hip-hop. One that could stay over as long as it liked, as long as it respected the house rules.

We all know Em's history: he came up poor on the east side of Detroit, Michigan. He lived with his mother and spent most of his teenage years there. He went back to visit for a 2011 CBS "60 Minutes" profile. The house, however, has since been demolished after a fire devastated it "and other abandoned homes on the street between 7 and 8 Mile Roads."

Marshall Bruce Mathers III was born on 17 October, 1972, in St. Joseph, Missouri and, when he was allegedly around the age of 11, his mom, Debbie Nelson Mathers, moved them to Warren, Detroit. It was primarily a Black neighborhood where houses were frequently broken into, and crime was high, as is the case in most poverty-stricken neighborhoods. Eminem has rapped about how poor he grew up and how dysfunctional his family life was. It seems like a respectable rags-to-riches story, but as a Black man who has lived in some very unsavory neighborhoods, I wish to address this issue with sombre and unyielding probity.

Black poverty and White poverty are not the same thing.

They might be abysmal environments in which the denizens find themselves, but from the beginning of the establishment of racist America, poor White people were taught that they were better than even wealthy Black people. The exact quote is as follows: *"If you can convince the lowest white man that he is better than the best colored man, he won't notice you're picking his pocket. Hell, give him somebody to look down on, and he'll empty his pockets for you."* That controversial and brutally honest statement was made by one of the presidents of the United States: Lyndon Baines Johnson, in response to the voluminous and "ugly racial epithets scrawled on signs" while touring the southern U.S. For weeks in the year 1964, "the president carried in his pocket the summary of a Census Bureau report showing that the lifetime earnings of an average Black college graduate were lower than that of a white man with an eighth-grade education."

Eminem vs. Everybody

Whenever successful White people start talking about how hard life was for them while growing up, as a foreigner from a middle income family (perhaps even upper middle class), I become titillated, *highly* amused by the "once-poor" White-rapper-millionaire-only-now-doing-well-in-life narrative. There is no doubt that Eminem studied rap and hip-hop much of his life and, over the years, fine-tuned and honed his skills. But, to me, he is a guest in the house of hip-hop. Lord Jamar and Dr. Umar are on the right track - their fingers are most definitely on the pulse of this uncomfortable truism. Concomitantly, as I am editing this document, Macklemore just posted that he and Em' are guests in rap/hip-hop: "That is the world of Black people. Em' and I will always be guests, never hosts." Thank you for that clarification, brother. It is greatly appreciated and puts to rest so much other controversy.

Unlike so many Black rap artists, Eminem did not *have to* become a hip-hop artist. Life in America at that time was (and really always has been) more favorable to the White man. Regardless where Eminem went to for a job, if a more educated Black person went for the same job, the former was more likely to secure employment. Hip-hop was (and is) a way out for so many Blacks and Hispanics (and, apparently, impoverished Filipinos, Nigerians, and now Japanese and Chinese).

♫ ♫ ♫ ♫

My mama didn't raise me up to be jealous-hearted...
I wasn't jealous 'cause of the talents they got
I was terrified they would be the last Black boys to fly...
Out of Compton...
Thank God!

With that one song, **"Black Boy Fly,"** I became a more profound patron of Kendrick Lamar, and to me, he is better than Eminem. Coming from a somewhat wealthy family, I myself felt no pressure to become a basketball player like Arron Afflalo, despite my athleticism. Nor did I think I had to make it in music like the homie Jayveon Taylor, despite winning various literature contests and late-night radio rap battles. You see, I always had the *option* of becoming a lawyer, a senator, the vice president, you name it.

But I lived with and around other Black and Hispanic people who had far fewer options than myself.

Even when I found myself homeless after my dad kicked me out several times, I still felt no *urgency* to "make it" in life. That is the danger wealth and a good, cushioned life will do to a young Black African male who has everything at his fingertips. Strangely enough, I began feeling this urge only in my mid-twenties after a beautiful young lady from Brooklyn kicked me out of her crib where I was helping to pay rent... twice... in the middle of winter. (Thank you, Zenobia, for making me take the vow to never, ever move in with any woman, ever again. Lesson learned. Shout-out to her brother, the big homie Chase.) Or, perhaps, looking back at those seemingly hopeless times in life, my mind and heart do not want to remember just how painful those times were, and so the grief is almost completely blocked, subconsciously.

The words the big homie Kendrick used to describe the despond he felt when he lived in Compton are *visceral*. I can *feel* the relief with which he raps about being fortunate enough to "fly" away from the hopelessness found in the 'hood. I can also feel what *he* felt going through those dire years and situations. I may have greatly minimized my adversities in life as a coping mechanism, but I now think that is because, once a particularly trying time has passed for me, I will try to emotionally distance myself from it. But, in my brief homelessness as a young teenager, of course the bite of hunger and helplessness certainly touched me.

But there were a few families who housed and fed me, both when I was homeless and on the run. I am *most* grateful, though, to the Pratts family, specifically: Awilda, Abuelo (God bless the dead), Abuela (God bless the dead), Julian, Randy, Jennifer, Stewart, and Jerry. I want to also thank Jonathan and Jessica Gago, and their mother, for feeding me every time I came over after school, for no reason other than the love they all hold for me. Bad times touched me, yes, but I shared cribs with people who had literally nothing, or as near to nothing as possible (not saying that the Pratts and Gago families had nothing, just making a declarative statement in relation to times and people I encountered at my lows). Their ability to hope for and work towards a better day is what makes lower-middle-class Hispanics and African-Americans so resilient and to have so much fortitude.

Poor White Americans, on the other hand, still walk around with a sense of entitlement even a wealthy Black person in America might never feel.

Eminem vs. Everybody

Eminem can never be the King of Rap/Hip-Hop because this genre of music filled a need in *Black American* society. Just as jazz, the blues, rock and roll, R&B, and soul all filled what might have been regarded as a temporary need in times past but wound up becoming the veinules and tendons and blood vessels of a large body of disparate, but *related*, music genres Africans in America and later African-Americans created, nurtured, and encouraged to grow.

That is, until White America appropriated some of those genres and tried to claim them as their own. It's giving Cristobal Columbus. The poverty of Eminem was not the poverty of Kendrick Lamar, nor the poverty of Jay-Z, nor the poverty of Jadakiss. Poverty, to us as a people in the United States, comes with the added facet of *danger*: not only are we kept worse off than everyone else, but the police and other such authorities do not hesitate to shoot first and ask questions later. People of color, but primarily African-Americans, "have been misled to believe that poverty is an individual failure rather than a carefully engineered system," says Shane Lloyd Noel on Meta (formerly Facebook). Eminem, by virtue of his skin color, has *never*, not *once*, been pulled over and harassed, or shot at by rival gang members, or been in a street fight that involved dozens (if not hundreds) of people, or been refused entry into an establishment because of that same pale-skin virtue. The worst thing that happened to Em' in his life was that his crib was burglarized; that, and his mother's negligence in taking care of him, both repeated severally, *in his own words*! I'm not even sure Em' has ever been in a street fight.

Moving on to Em's second album under Aftermath, *The Marshall Mathers LP,* which was released in 2000, and from which Em' made the video for the song *"The Real Slim Shady,"* in which he began shaking the controversy tree. At the time, Em' was going through a divorce and losing himself to drugs. I had known that Em' would be big, but with this multiplicity of successes, I (and The Culture, generally) realized what was happening: White America had found its rap savior, something for which it had been desperately searching. Yes, Em' was a good rapper, sure, bound to be great, but there was no explanation for his *uncommonly* prolific success. The first single off *The Slim Shady LP* must be examined for a plethora of reasons. We are going to look at the video and what he says in it, in comparison to *all* first-time videos released by Black artists.

♪ ♪ ♪ ♪

Hip-Hop Rivalries: East Coast Versus West Coast

Early in the game on *"My Name Is,"* Eminem comes in disrespecting the Spice Girls, Pamela Anderson Lee, his mom (severally), and his absentee dad. Listening to the song, I can find no comparison to any other rapper, let alone any other *Black* American rapper, in content or success. In *"The Real Slim Shady,"* Em' again disrespects Tommy and Pamela Anderson Lee, Tom Green, Will Smith, Britney Spears, and Christina Aguilera. There is no doubt that Em' was being a bully, but that aside, there are things that he did in his videos that a male Black rapper could never do and get away with. The first, most glaring, is wearing a dress. The Culture would never take a Black rapper in a dress seriously. Paradoxically enough, *neither would many White people*. You know why? Because they don't *expect* it. Just that simple.

The *reason* is simple - Black people, for the most part, do not do that - we are not known for doing that! Which Black male rapper has ever been caught wearing a dress? However, with the converse point of view, nobody cares, and it is accepted as normal because White men are, for the most part, comfortable with their own emasculation and degradation. Again, NOBODY CARES if a White male wears a dress and accoutrements in a rap music video (which, generally, is not LGBTQ+-friendly [rap, that is]), but, even all these years later, let Nas or Jay-Z or Camron wear a dress in a music video. The Culture would cancel them quicker than White America canceled Bill Cosby and R. Kelly. (My apologies to the said named rappers. I used your names in this example because of the sheer impossibility of it ever happening, not because I believe you brothers would ever actually engage in such a *faux pas*.) Speaking of Cam, him in a dress would be more shocking than when he declared that he was about to "get some cheeks"... on CNN. (Shout-out to the the big homie Killa. Here go your flowers, homie. Well done. I wish you and Murda the best success life can offer y'all.)

Additionally, White people would demurely, almost disingenuously, go along with the cultural cancellation of said Black male artists. Some White people have made various jokes about Em's videos with him in a dress - they think it is a joke or do not even see it as anything of major note. Oh, but it is *quite* noteworthy! White people, particularly White British and White Americans, seem to conveniently forget the traumas of what they did to Black people during slavery - those traumas are in our blood! And that is the premise of epigenetics: "the study of changes in organisms caused by modification of gene expression rather than alteration of the gene code itself." In simpler terms, it's "the study of how your behaviors and environment can cause changes that affect the way your genes work."

For example, Google (further) states: "The environmental factors that can promote epigenetic mutations in humans are similar known risk factors for cancer, including **diet, lifestyle, and exposure to toxic substances**." [Author's emphasis] Let that information sink in for a few moments before plowing on further, to remind yourself that Black people were ***forced*** to perform incestuous and homosexual acts with other Blacks and/or with their own *family members*. Also, many of the slaveowners would rape Black men, both for their own sordid pleasure and to terrorize the other slaves into strict, unbending, and unwavering compliance. This was a part of what is termed "buck breaking," a reprehensible, often public, act of rape and/or sodomy by the slaveowner or his designee upon the most defiant, or healthiest, Black male on the plantation.

Black men despise being put in dresses and *intrinsically* despise homosexuality. White males - *particularly*, mostly, (American) White *males* - do not mind wearing dresses. (Yes, yes, not all of them.) One thing is for sure, though: *Eminem* doesn't mind. Another thing primarily White males will do without a second thought is to put on make-up. It's bad enough to be put in a dress or for a Black male to be relegated to the role of a female (thereby identifying yourself, or *being* identified, as *effeminate*), but adding insult to injury, the make-up seems to convey acquiescence with the femininity and subservience to the male's innate masculinity. This is what gives rise to psychological issues.

Yet *another* layer of this odious subject is the fact that so many Black people advocated for Eminem, primarily after Dre went to bat, and went all out, for him. Let's not forget that Em' had come out with a studio album (entitled *Infinity*) before *The Slim Shady LP. Infinity* was not horrible, but it did not have the right *backing*, and sold only about 1,000 copies. We see, then, that talent counts for little if the right production team is not behind you. Look at Canibus, a *phenomenal* lyricist who paired up with Wyclef Jean to produce his first studio album. Allegedly, Wyclef Jean purposely sabotaged Canibus, so, not saying he actually betrayed Canibus, but perspicacity in selecting the right production team is also key to the ultimate success of an artist.

Once Dre put his stamp of approval on Eminem, he never looked back. I remember getting the feeling that White people all over the *world* were elated with their rap savior as he was, indeed, a superfluous *Caucasian* rap artist who was also a battle rapper. Black people bought his albums and, more importantly, White people *in their numbers* bought his albums, propelling him to superstardom in record time, with record numbers of Eminem fellatio-performing stans flooding TV music and radio channels all over America with embarrassingly sycophantic reviews of his music. He had been putting in work to get known, but as with *Infinity*, Em' would *still* need a good producer and production team.

That was done. The Culture had long since seen that, if Eminem could diss White artists with unbridled fervor, *eventually*, he would have to turn to attack, or defend himself *from*, enterprising Black artists. But he was used to battling primarily Black rappers, right? Right. So as time went on, many of Dre's fans likely became Eminem fans, or supporters. It is likely also true (although to a lesser degree, *comparatively*) that some Eminem fans became Dre fans and/or supporters. Em' became more and more political in the topics he chose to rap about. But more than that, at some point he dyed his hair blonde and became yet more visually appealing to the White demographic in White American culture.

♪ ♪ ♪ ♪

Because He's White

There are more Caucasians in the United States than any other race, so when a significant portion of these youths ([who looked] just like Em') went out to buy his album, of course he would become one of the wealthiest rappers ever. The youth of White America had chosen Em' as their mouthpiece, as both their Aaron and Moses (their high priest and god, respectively, so to speak). And they would support Em' far more than they would support any Black rapper because, after all, what could a Black American rapper tell them that they would want to hear? Or how much would they *identify* with that Black rapper? Very little, to be frank. But what could a White American rapper who looked like them (and not, let's say, *corporate* America), talked like them, dressed like them and, to a great degree, *thought* like them, tell them? A whole lot, apparently.

Even Eminem himself knew that it was because he was White that he sold so many records:

> *Look at those eyes: baby blue, baby, just like yourself*
> *If they were brown, Shady'd lose, Shady sits on a shelf...*
> *...Let's do the math, if I was Black I woulda sold half*
> *I ain't have to graduate from Lincoln High School to know that*

From the proverbial horse's mouth. The name of the song is *"The Eminem Show,"* from the album of the same name, the one right after which he dissed Michael Jackson. The claptrap about Em' being the most streamed rap artist in Africa? that's a highly disingenuous statement, at *best*! And it's **false**! His music might be on repeat in some popular Caucasian hotspots, but for the most part, those numbers are hugely inflated. Not only that, but people are paid to stream music of certain artists repeatedly in various venues. This is an old-hat method of artificially inflating numbers to appear favorable to an artist's reputation, in different locations.

Now, back to *The Eminem Show* and the why Eminem can never be the G.R.O.A.T., or even Top 5. Eminem himself stated that if he were Black or brown-eyed, he would have sold only "half" what he has to date. So then, why was he so angry at Melle Mel's original statement?:

"[Interviewer] 'What do you think about Eminem being at number 5 on the Billboard Top 50 Rappers of All Time list?'

"[Melle Mel) 'Obviously, he's a capable rapper. If you was talking sales, he sold more than everybody. If you talkin' about rhyme style, okay, he got a rhyme style, but he's White! He's White! So now, if Eminem was just another nigga like all the rest of us, would he be top 5 on that list when a nigga that could rhyme just as good as him is 35?... Eminem gets a top spot because he's White... If he was a Black rapper he'd be like, he wouldn't even make the list. He wouldn't even make the list probably.'" (The Art of Dialogue, YouTube, March 2, 2023)

I thought to myself, "But where's the lie?"

Then, Lord Jamar was being interviewed and it went thus:

"[Lord Jamar] 'Can he put words together? Yes!... If the content is shit, who gives a fuck how good you put cat, rat, bat, hat together? But his content is horrible, and his delivery and his *voice*! Do you hate your mother?'

"[Interviewer/Host] 'No, I don't.'

"[Lord Jamar] 'Alright! Would you make a song about your mother's you know?'

"[Interviewer/Host] 'No.'

"[Lord Jamar] 'Would you offer your daughter to Dr. Dre? *"Go with him, Hailey."* Would you do that? No! How about all the gay references in the name of just rhyming? You see what I'm sayin'? Like see, that's what the greatest rappers - the easy role, they could have fuckin' made a whole lotta shit rhyme. **But they said,** *"Nah, I can't say that."* This nigga will say it! Even tho- just *because* it rhymes! That's the difference between a real fuckin' king and somebody who just raps just to rap.'" [Author's emphases]

This goes back to what I said about Black male rappers not being able to say the same things in rap as their Caucasian colleagues might. Furthermore, people can say what they want in trying to defend Eminem, but we, as Black artists, just would not (and do not) come out the gate swinging and *continue* doing so. (There are a few exceptions, such as Curtis Jackson, a close Em' associate, who likely stole a page out of Em's playbook on attacking rappers when he came out [e.g. *"How To Rob"*]. The difference is that Fitty has never attacked Caucasian musical icons.) And I know why: Dre and company! Eminem was *protected* by Dre and everyone associated with Aftermath. Even if some West Coast rappers did not like Em', *allegedly*, Dre had already let it be known, along with Snoop, to "leave the White boy alone." Plus, what Em' did for D12, Slaughterhouse, and a few other rappers on Shady Records ensured that he would always be well-protected. As I now infrequently encounter the

Eminem vs. Everybody

Em' song *"Without Me"* on TV, I can't help but wonder if people had really **heard** what Eminem said in the last stanza:

> *Though I'm not the first king of controversy*
> *I am the worst thing since Elvis Presley*
> ***To use Black music so selfishly***
> ***And use it to get myself wealthy***

That quatrain never sat well with me. It was like Em' was mocking The Culture, all while appropriating our expressionism in order to *just* get wealthy. Yes, Em's puns can often be funny, but they are in great part unrelatable to most of The Culture, whereas I could listen to the entire *It Was Written* on repeat, and be able to relate to most of what is rhymed about. Our lives are not a joke nor to be whiled away in hilarity. I could also listen to Cube's *Death Certificate* and Jay's *Reasonable Doubt*, incessantly. But I cannot do that with an entire Eminem album; as Lord Jamar said, *"I can't relate to hating my mother and wanting to kill her..."* Even Boosie stated, "Where I'm from, we don't listen to Eminem."

In any case, perhaps I am not *supposed* to be able to relate to Em' because he is White? If that is so, well, I guess there is nothing wrong with that, but for the fact that is *not* the case, as I mentioned in the beginning that the trauma of drug use bonded Whites and Blacks together, and one of the busiest wayfares was music. It simply means, in part, with said demarcation and the acknowledgement of non-relatability, Em' can never be the G.R.O.A.T. of a genre of music in which primarily Black people indulge, because he simply cannot relate to our existence. He is most definitely a guest in the house of hip-hop, but one that is still, all these years later, closely watched. (Shout-out to Dr. Umar for addressing these uncomfortable truths.) One of the reasons is because how dare he erroneously and audaciously attack Michael Jackson! The temerity was perplexing, but after some time thinking about what drugs Em' had to have been on to have caused him to just lose it (pun intended), I was still baffled.

I was not, in any way, amused by Em's bravado in his attacks on the King of Pop. Up until then he had been attacking White pop stars and groups and, as I knew his attacks would broaden, African-American artists who thought he was easy pickings. And there would have been nothing wrong with that, either, if Michael had first attacked *him* in some way. But what Em' did is comparable to Jay-Z or Nas suddenly attacking Dolly Parton, or Celine Dion, or Garth Brooks. The answer is facile: Em' had simply reverted to type. Deep down, many White people fear that Black people, if allowed too much power, will do to them what they have done and been doing to us. This is certainly the vibe in America. It is as if they are secretly amazed and *affronted* that, despite their atrocities against us, despite hundreds of years of their thievery and collusive headstarts, Black people are clawing their way out of despondency and disenfranchisement to become even greater than history has repeatedly proven us to be. Our creativity in the musical arts is just one of such greatnesses.

This is so all across the world, from Ethiopia (*which seriously needs to stop oppressing the Tigrayan people*), to the Democratic Republic of Congo (DRC), to the orchestrated mess that pervades much of Haiti now, to the West Indies (specifically Jamaica and Trinidad), to Cameroun (*which seriously needs to stop oppressing the indigenous people of British Southern Cameroons, now known as **Ambazonia***), and finally, to the (indigenous and unwillingly imported) Blacks of the United States (their descendants, obviously).

To me, Eminem is like the spook who sat by the door, for White America. "Scratch a liar, find a thief." Uncle Ray was right. By attacking Michael Jackson, Em' was attacking The Culture that had both nurtured and uplifted Michael to the apogee of success. And it was the same genre that had nurtured and uplifted *him* to where he is now. Anyone who has ever teased Michael Jackson, specifically any *Black* comedian or other artist, only ever did so gently, *respectfully*. But Em' seemed to *gleefully* attack Michael. Well, now that we know the child abuse allegations against Michael were untrue, is Eminem going to *publicly* apologize to the remaining members of the Jackson family, and to The Culture, and the world? The disrespect was public - so, too, must the apology be.

I even did some more digging into the reason why Em' went at Michael in the first place. The nascence of the beef Em' had with Michael likely began two months and two days after I came home on 17 September, 2002. Michael dangled his baby son, Prince, over a balcony, his intentions being to share his son with his fans in appreciation of them. The intent was good, yes, but the *execution* of said intent was, admittedly, outré. On 24 June, 2005, while Em' was on a world tour (ironically enough, named "The Anger Management Tour") and found himself in a hotel in Glasgow, Scotland, he mimicked Michael by wearing a mask as the latter had done three years earlier. More notably, he played with a baby doll, suspending it over the balcony and tossing it up and down. Quite obviously (and he admitted it in later interviews) he was ridiculing the King of Pop.

But the underlying question, again, remains *why*? There were billions of other beefs Em' could have started elsewhere - why this one with Michael? Was it a cry for help? Em' was glaringly seeking attention, or so it seemed, and with the burgeoning shots being taken at Michael, in tandem with Michael's silence about the balcony mockery (this would be like one year after *"Just Lose It"* was released), Em' would go on to release the hit single *"Just Lose It"* in September of 2004. The title of the single was a goad at Michael who, at the time, was embroiled in legal battles with envious, poor, jealous, and, *please note*, Caucasian accusers. Said false accusers were perhaps not as poor as Eminem claims to have been, but they were certainly nowhere near as wealthy as Michael. Em' was subliminally telling Michael to "just lose it," to just lose his *mind*. The irony of that statement is rich, as Em' had just finished "losing it" himself to drugs for a couple of years and, on his way back to sanity and success, he used MJ as a springboard into more wealth and even greater success. (Ironically enough, Em' had to himself cancel the last leg of the European part of his "Anger Management [3] Tour" in 2005.)

Due to the attention garnered by Em's attacks on Michael, *Encore* went on to become one of his best-selling albums. He himself admitted that he was "just happy that Michael Jackson [had] heard of [him]." It was on 4 October, 2004, that Em' released the video for *"Just Lose It."* Visual performances of most audio works are more memorable than just the audios themselves, as anytime I hear certain songs I have watched videos of play on the radio, I immediately associate them with the visuals of their videos. Em' took heavy shots at Michael, making fun of when his hair caught fire during a Pepsi commercial, MJ's plastic surgery, and the noisome and baseless accusations of MJ being a child molester. In the video we also see Em' mocking MC Hammer, Madonna, and himself, as if self-degradation could excuse his disrespect of those other music legends, most of whom sold more albums than he has.

Imagine, if you will, a major Black rap artist doing that to pioneer White artists of other music genres. First of all, Black people simply don't do such things, at least not *unprovoked*. (Fitty is close to fitting the description, but again, his reticence in attacking established *White* artists is telling.) It is damn near impossible to imagine (and besides, we all know they would subsequently be crucified and blacklisted from all major events, kind of like Yeezy). This is more than just rap music and battle rap culture; there are a multitude of socio-historical and raciolinguistic undertones, as we have thus far discussed. The second thing I would like to be taken note of is how Eminem dressed up like a female, *again* (something he was quite fond of doing, apparently).

This, again, is something that a Black rapper (battle rapper or otherwise) would never do, but because Em' is a White rapper, he gets a pass. Also, please let it be known that we have *not* forgotten the dubious and eye-opening *origins* of Em's "forever-benefactor," which (although not vocalized) is still taken into account when discussing the laxness of standards as applies to Em' whenever he puts on make-up, or dresses, or skirts, or other female accoutrements. Brothers ain't doing that, and successful brothers would not get a pass from The Culture if they ever did something like this. So let's keep that same energy for Em', or simply realize that he is, in the words of the greatest rapper of this generation, ***"not like us."***

Bad enough the ubiquitous *they* managed to have Wesley put on a dress, and had Will getting his guts pushed in - I speak for The Culture: to Black people, that is a serious betrayal - to portray something so freely that was, at one time, *forced* on so many of us. It is the exact equivalent of allowing White people to say nigga. But some Black people will do anything for a paycheck. Mentors are supposed to *guide* and *guard* their charges, not *groom* them! I guess Eazy and Cube were right on the account of that forever-benefactor.

"I am very angry at Eminem's depiction of me in his video. I feel that it is outrageous and disrespectful. It is one thing to spoof, but it is another to be demeaning and insensitive. I've admired Eminem as an artist, and was shocked by this. The video was inappropriate and disrespectful to me, my children, my family, and the community at large." You can tell Michael was hurt and felt betrayed by what he called in to say to Steve Harvey during The Steve Harvey Radio Show on/about 12 October, 2004. Michael requested the *"Just Lose It"* video not be played on MTV, VH1, and BET. The predominantly White-owned video music stations continued playing the song on their rotation; BET, on the other hand, acceded to Michael's request and removed it from their rotation. (Thank you, BET, for your support of The Culture in standing with one of our icons when he was going through some diabolical strife in his life.)

Thank you also to Mr. Stevie Wonder, for standing by Michael when you said: "Kicking someone when he's down is not a good thing. I have much respect for [Em's] work, though I don't think he's as good as Tupac. But I was disappointed that he would let himself go to such a level. He has succeeded on the backs of people predominantly in that lower pay bracket. So for him to come out like that is bullshit." (Billboard Interview of Stevie Wonder, 6 December, 2004) Yes, Marshall should definitely show some respect, especially since he so boldly claims to "use Black music so selfishly, and use it to get [himself] wealthy." I have no idea where Dr. Dre was when Em' wrote that, but for him to have *allowed* it to go on the album, and for him to have *allowed* Marshall to demean a Black cultural giant like Michael, shows the length to which Dre looked away in exchange for sensationalism and, by all appearances (from the subsequent success), a very large paycheck.

Scratch a liar, find a thief.

Marshall succeeded because of Dr. Dre and the protection provided by the former Death Row co-founder. Had it not been for Dre, does anyone really believe that he could have fought, and *won*, his own fights? He would not even have *started* half the beefs he had started for fear of what happened to Vanilla Ice (*and Dr. Dre himself*) happening to him. Marshall was spared of going through the rigors of what most *Black* rap artists experience in the industry. Why? In the ever-controversial but ever-honest words of Melle Mel: *because he's White*!

A few years later, however, Michael got his revenge on Marshall when, on 31 May, 2007, Michael's company (SONY/ATV) bought Famous Music Corporation for almost four hundred million dollars. The purchase of FMC included a catalogue of over 125,000 songs, within which stood out some of Marshall's more famous rap songs (such as, "coincidentally," as we spoke of them earlier: *"The Real Slim Shady"* and *"Without Me"*). Michael owned the publishing to many other artists' songs and, most important to clarify, he owned only comparatively *few* of Marshall's songs, not all of them. But it was still an impressive feat, and an expensive one. And a *profitable* one. And that is how Em', ultimately, lost *that* beef, as he was effectively silenced.

♪ ♪ ♪ ♪

Hip-Hop Rivalries: East Coast Versus West Coast

Now, I would like to take a look at a relatively recent rap battle between a top-tier battle rapper known as "Real Sikh" and a whilom rap heavyweight contender called "Dizaster." The battle ended in favor of Real Sikh, 3 - 0, one reason being because Dizaster said (and tried to keep saying) the "n" word. Anytime it came time for him to rap afterwards, he was booed and heckled. Here is a bit of background: Dizaster is an Arab rapper who is (was?) the face of "K.O.T.D." (King Of The Dot), a White-owned and predominantly White battle rap league based in Canada. When facing his opponents there in front of so many White people (and a smattering of Black folks), Dizaster casually normalizes using the "n" word, as well as on Instagram. He had been trying to get another battle in the URL and finally, when he did, he had a meltdown, yelling and cursing at a predominantly Black crowd his poor choice of words.

After all, 90 plus percent of URL battle rap attendees are Black, whereas the reverse is true at K.O.T.D. Chris Unbias, one of battle rap's better analysts and a blogger of no mean repute, breaks down this battle quite well. In the first round, Real Sikh (whose name is a play on, and pronounced as, "real sick" - Ebonically speaking, "sick" means above and beyond expectations, or just *really good*) - he starts talking some real shit to Dizaster immediately. The URL usually battles for three rounds, each round being approximately 8 to 15 minutes, and they (the battle rappers) take turns one after the other. So Real Sikh very casually spits some *fire* at the beginning:

>Before we get started, you ain't on a good path
>Achi to Achi [crowd laughs - "Achi" is a word primarily young African-American Muslim men use to call each other, which means "brother"],
>you ain't been talkin' the way you should have
>I gotta check you!
>I don't care how many greats gave you a 'hood pass
>**Stop sayin' the "n" word - you makin' us look bad!** [crowd cheers]
>Ya name Bashere
>You don't see you disrespecting The Culture when you take it there?
>Got accepted as a **GUEST**!
>Got too comfy, now he behaving weird
>You said it like 9 times on King of The Dot
>Did you stop? Make it clear!

Eminem vs. Everybody

I mean, you be lettin' it fly on IG LIVE, tough guy
*Say it here! **[crowd cheers madly for Real Sikh, in great appreciation]**...*
I DARE you to try to do it,
Boy, I just bought a new folding chair and I'm DYIN' to use it! [crowd goes wild again]

Much respect to Real Sikh, who is hereby invited to all Black cookouts anywhere in the world. It's really a shame, though, that Black battle rappers who battled Dizaster in the past rarely checked him on his use of the "n" word. It took a "real Sikh" brother to wake up the sleeping giant on that ass, and just like that, Dizaster was canceled from so many Black rap battle leagues. There may be a few White or Latino battle rap leagues that allow that racist Arab to perform for them but The Culture does not (and will not) want to hear it. This racist machismo is exactly why (well, a *large* part of why) a certain well-known battle rapper gave up the ghost. It's not cool, it's not appreciated, and there are serious consequences to it. Just like Gen Z has financially hurt Starbucks and McDonald's, so too can they (AND, of course, my generation, Gen X) easily make or break the careers of battle rappers. (And to be clear, "Real Sikh" is *really* a Sikh - that is, a follower of Sikhism, the monotheistic religion founded in the 15th century by Guru Nanak in the Indian subcontinent of the Punjab region. The word "Sikh" means "learner" or "disciple." Furthermore, Real Sikh's reference to the folding chair is related to the Montgomery riverfront brawl that occurred on 5 August, 2023, where and when a Black man [allegedly the captain of the riverfront] used a folding chair [clearly in self-defense] after being attacked by white boaters who blocked a riverboat from docking, sparking national attention and becoming a symbol of resistance. Ironically, the folding chair was invented by an African-American, Nathaniel Alexander. So The Culture saw it as modern day Black folk using apparatus invented by our ancestors to physically combat racist violence, purely in self-defense. What a sweet moment, and what a superfluous connection by Real Sikh.)

Boycotts have always been an effective method of catching the intended target's attention, and you can *bet* Dizaster is wide awake now. The first time he was on URL, ages ago, he did not do so well - this second time was horrible as well, and being that everything is available on the Internet, he will never be able to live this last battle down. Just like Marshall will never be able to live down those darned racist lyrics he spewed so long ago. Really and truly, I don't even remember the lyrics being as exposed then as they are being exposed now. (Maybe I was in the box and that bit of social awareness news passed me by.) A lot of money must have been paid in order to keep the scandal from further flowering into a telltale mushroom cloud - the mushroom cloud of Eminem being canceled.

Oh, I remember now - Em' *SUED* Benzino to keep him from producing the racist lyrics anywhere, if I'm not mistaken. Almost exactly like how Drake sued Kendrick in order for Kendrick and other influential people and/at large events to not play the song *"Not Like Us"* (in which Drake is likened to a child molester). Benzino also recently commented about why so many people are attacking Drake as a coward when they didn't do the same to Em'. Benzino doesn't quite understand the dynamics of his battle with Eminem as compared to Drake's battle with Kendrick. The racist lyrics were incendiary and yes, Em' *should have been* canceled for them, but Drake is such a self-aggrandizing clown that he actually performed *"Not Like Us"* at one of his concerts. Typical clown shit. More than that, however, their battle was legendary, whereas Benzino's battle with Eminem was... *meh*!

Before we analyze that "mushroom cloud of Eminem being canceled," we will look at one of the comments Jadakiss made concerning Em'. It was during one of the many interviews by The Breakfast Club. And I specifically take the excerpt from the sycophantic Eminem-worshipping YouTube channel "ETLifestyle" for a reason:

Charlemagne: *I know people like to use Eminem as the bar for White rappers, but he shouldn't be.*

Vanilla Ice: *I use him as the bar for White rappers.*

Jadakiss: *He got- why shouldn't he be?*

Charlemagne: *'Cause he's an anomaly, meaning that Eminem had everything lined up for him perfectly. You got Jimmy Iovine-*

[It now cuts to Eminem being interviewed]

Eminem: *Coming up in the scene as a battle rapper, I had been through a lotta moments that were like this* [he raises a hand high] *and ended up being like this* [drops the hand low, signifying ups and downs in the game, as is normal in life, in general, anyway] *because, you know* [camera now shows Dr. Dre as if he's listening, but it's a shot of him from another (black and white filmed) interview], *everyone was telling him* [Dr. Dre apparently], *"Don't fuck with him."*

Dr. Dre's voice: *Everybody around me, the so-called execs and what have you were all against it.*

[Cuts back to the Breakfast Club interview]

Vanilla Ice: [concerning Em] *But he's nice, though!*

Charlemagne: *Super nice! Super nice!* [He sounds like he's forcing it, even if he's telling the truth]

Jadakiss: *I mean but, before that, though. I like his story, Charlemagne, from where he came from - trailer park, confusion with his moms and all of that whole thing to where he made it to. And it's not JUST 'cause he's White. A lotta people like to throw shots.* [Please pay attention to what Jadakiss is about to say] *HE MIGHTA GOT A COUPLE DOORS OPEN, FOR HIS COMPLEXION, FOR THE CONNECTION, but he can really spit. He's a hell of a rapper.* [Author's caps]

Yes, Marshall Mathers is, indeed, a "hell of a rapper." But Jadakiss himself says that Marshall, quote, "got a couple doors open, *for his complexion*, for the connection." Unquote. That part of the statement negates what comes after it and, incidentally, agrees with Charlemagne's underlying premise: (in my Melle Mel voice) *because he's White*! Not even the most talented African-American rappers, battlers or otherwise, would ever be able to get those same "couple doors open" (let alone because of their skin complexion), because, to many of the people behind *certain* of them (not all), *if it ain't White, it ain't right*.

It's really quite simple, and Dr. Dre knew that with White America's Great White Hype, the remuneration would be legendary. And it was, as his ex-wife is trying to make heavy inroads in taking away half of that one-point-something billion dollars of his, because she put in half of the work to make him as successful as he became. (The absurdity of such a claim should be laughed out of court.)

Now, at the time of the first writing of this particular part of the book, Cassidy has just responded to the largely unknown rapper Cashis, who, in inferring that the former wrote Benzino's Eminem diss tracks, signed his death warrant, lyrically. I have been saying throughout this book that there are just some rappers to leave alone, and Cassidy is one of them. The track is called, *"Where The Bul At?"* As usual, it's a nasty piece of work, absolutely brimming with ill intent. Classic Cassidy.

Back to Em' and the racist tapes that, for some reason, have now become a bit of a challenge to locate. Thank you, Benzino, for revealing how much of a closet racist Marshall is to people who knew little to nothing about those tapes. Personally, I don't know Mr. Ray "Benzino" Scott from a hole in the wall, but I used to read his magazine back in the day and it was always insightful and descriptive. Most Black youths used to love The Source, too. Why are the Eminem sycophants so mad that this is being brought up (*again*, as it were)? It must be *addressed*. There are so many Marshall fans whining that his racism was in the past and he apologized for it. Well whoop-dee-doo, let's apply that same faulty reasoning to the descendants of the Jewish Holocaust, or the descendants of the Japanese internment period, or the descendants who had their hands and/or feet cut off under the bloodcurdling and bloodthirsty tyranny of the shittiest and most wicked monarch to have lived (Leopold II), no king to me, who made Hitler look like a schoolgirl.

Racism *never* gets old, particularly in the United States, England, Italy, Portugal, Ireland, Argentina, Spain, Brazil, Holland, and Belgium. Just go to soccer games in most of those countries and see how Black players like Vinicius Jr. are insulted. A remarkable number of White people *enjoy* keeping racism alive. (Yes, I know, before I am bludgeoned to death by the sheer weight of White attempted exculpatory thoughts and emotions from all across the world, *not all White people are racist*! But tell that to Tamela Holmsford's family, or Sandra Bland's family, or Lavena Johnson's family, for all the good it will do. When these particular Black Queens died, they were *surrounded* by White people they thought they could trust, or who were tasked with protecting them.)

To clear the air on another matter, no, I am not a Benzino fan, in case any Em' fans try to say I am. But what I *do* like and appreciate about Benzino is how fearless he was in exposing the closet racist Eminem appears to be. After those tapes were made public, Marshall wrote: *The tape they played today was something I made out of anger, stupidity, and frustration when I was a teenager. I'd just broken up with my girlfriend, who was African-American, and I reacted like the angry, stupid kid I was. I hope people will take it for the foolishness that it was, not for what somebody is trying to make it into today.*

No, Mr. Mathers, The Culture is not trying to take it "for what somebody is trying to make it into today." The Culture is taking it for what it *is*. Domain Expansion: Trap house kitchen - *give that nigga the work*! (Credit to @RabSoPetty on YouTube.)

♪ ♪ ♪ ♪

We live in an age where information is readily available at one's fingertips, so, pray tell, who exactly is this mysterious African-American girl who dated Marshall back when? It is more than passing strange that she has never revealed her identity, from all the way back when news of this first broke, all the way until now. Who would not pay this African-American lady a *substantial* amount of money to hear her side of how the relationship ended?

I call CAP!

Perhaps - and this is a very tenuous "perhaps" - Marshall really did have an African-American girlfriend. *Perhaps*! But there is no way he wrote those racist lyrics in response to a mere *breakup*. Who goes on a racist rant after breaking up with their partner in an interracial coupling? (Shout-out to Travis Kelcey for both the last Superbowl win and for not going on a racist rant after breaking up with his whilom girlfriend, who is African-American. Shout-out to Chelsea Handler for not going on a racist rant about 50 after they separated; it is greatly appreciated.) As a lyricist, a grammarian, and a novelist, I have studied those racist lyrics avidly and I can confidently say the majority are likely freestyle.

We shall get more into what a real "freestyle" is later on, but those lyrics sound impromptu. Even if I am wrong about their rushed-type nature, forget its delivery, the *content* is a major disqualifying factor as to why Eminem can never be the G.R.O.A.T.

Never.

Ever!

To so callously disrespect Black people while using rap is more than foul play - it is egregious, malignant, shameful, and an appalling display of underhanded vitriol by a young man who, at the time, was looking to *use* rap to succeed, but instead used it as a bigoted vehicle of destruction. If he was so mad at this amorphous ex-girlfriend, why did he not call her out by name and *personally* attack her? Why attack her race? (In my Melle Mel voice) *Because he's White*! And does Em' really believe, all these years later, that his words did not harm his ex nor did they scar The Culture, and thus he can keep living his life as usual? No, buddy. You gon' get this *work*!

The Rock & Roll Hall of Fame did a *huge* disservice to The Culture by inducting Eminem into its ranks, when they have left out pioneers of rap and hip-hop to prop Marshall up in their midst. (And before anyone asks, *yes*, they also made a mistake in inducting Missy "Misdemeanor" Elliott. What about Queen Latifah? MC Lyte? Salt n Pepa?) *Because he's White*! I was watching the recap of an interview on TV the other day with Bizarre (of D12 fame); I could not help but notice how much he resembles Benzino: the diminutive stature, large jaw, and short neck. Even his teeth are spacey and petit - it was just a passing observation.

In any event, Bizarre was asked what his thoughts were on Em's racist lyrics. This guy replied (verbatim): "Umm... The song was-was cut off and edited. He-h-he- the song was-when they was freestylin' they-they was naming all types of racists ["racist shit"?] like, 'White girl, what you think about a White girl? Black girl [mumbles a bit]... Black girl,' basically, but The Source just edited the Black girl part and made it look like it was racist. So that ["there"?] goes some information for you [laughs unconvincingly]." (This interview was part of that same ETLifestyle episode, *ubi supra*.) Like the Eminem sycophant that he is, Bizarre defends Em' despite evidence to the glaring contrary. Instead of stating the same ridiculous lies as Em' had done, though, Bizarre took it a step further and outright *lied*!

"*Still nigger*"!

Scratch a liar, find a thief.

I do not care how much a White friend of mine ever did for me, or whether he sent me and my family the occasional check to get by - he and I would have a dead serious, draw down, closed-door meeting about anything racist he was supposed to have said in the past. Or I would simply keep my mouth shut, permanently, to everyone, *including* the media. But I would never go against The Culture for anything wrong. Contrastingly, for something *right*, I would go against the world. Did Bizarre not *listen* to the same lyrics the entire world heard?

Some of those racist lyrics read, in part:

> *Blacks and Whites sometimes mix*
> *But Black girls only want your money 'cause they're dumb chicks*
> *So I'ma say like this*
> *Don't date a Black girl, take it as a diss*
> *If you want, but if you don't*
> *I'ma tell you like this, I surely won't*
> *Never date a Black girl because Blacks only want your money*
> *And that shit ain't funny so I'ma say, look, honey*
> *Why do you do this? You know, you step up to me like you a Brutus*
> *Then you try to grab my spinach*
> *Because it's green and that's cash*

Seems like pretty straightforward racism to me. But wait. Somewhere, somehow, there's more:

> *And all the girls that I like to bone*
> *Have the big butts, no they don't*
> *'Cause I don't like that nigger shit*
> *I'm just here to make a bigger hit*

Oh, that you did, Marshall, you most definitely did "make a bigger hit." And they will say this "anomaly" (according to Charlemagne) is not racist! He is, *according to his own words*! So many years later, Marshall audaciously comes out with a somewhat silly, and lengthy, track entitled "*Rap God.*" Claiming to be a rap god and actually being one are two different things. I guess Em' also forgot that he never beat Proof and a few other battle rappers in his battle career.

The ridiculousness of Eminem being named King of Rap and Hip-Hop is mind boggling. Yes, he is gifted, but he is NOT better than Nas, Jadakiss, Tupac, Kendrick Lamar, Jay-Z, the big homie Weezy, Redman, GZA, Method Man, Biggie, Canibus, and a few others who, had they been born White, would have been considered far greater than Marshall is now. It's also telling that he never started beef with any of them. The last, and most compelling, reason why Em' cannot be the G.R.O.A.T. is the apathy with which he has treated the main vehicle (battle rap) to get to where he is now. Just like Post Malone. He has done absolutely nothing to elevate and promulgate battle rap, and yet people say he can still battle rap? No! Those racist lyrics appear to completely be *freestyle*, which, admittedly, still takes a wordsmith to master, and confidence to perform. But whether you master "The Cat in the Hat"-type or puerile *ad hominem* bars as compared to real-life witticisms and similes makes all the difference.

I have seen even Drake at battle rap events, Busta Rhymes, Cardi B. (along with T.I. and Chance the Rapper), etc., but Marshall feels he is above attending or even just *sponsoring* such events. It has started making Black folk wonder - who or what exactly is Em' running from? Or is it an unnatural fear of getting robbed? He can bring his former federal agent bodyguards along - we *promise*, we The Culture will understand. Seriously, though, it appears as if the man thinks *he's* Michael Jackson now. No, *nobody* can ever be one-tenth of MJ's stature, nor will anyone ever be viewed with anywhere near the reverence with which The Culture views Michael. Speaking of whom, even MJ came to Summer Jam around the time Em' was trash talking him. What a legend!

Holding oneself too aloof while firing shots at Gen Z and Benzino is corny, and I sincerely pray that enough Marshall fans gnash their teeth after reading this. Upset with Benzino's recent walloping of their Great White Hype, Em' maniacs have resorted trying to make the beef between him and Benzino about race. As far as Benzino is concerned, yes, Marshall got whooped because he has not yet responded. A no-show is an automatic win for one's rival, especially if the rival poked the bear. Knowing Em', I have no doubt at all that he will respond to Benzino on his next album. If he is feeling particularly delirious, he might take sly shots at Cassidy or Kendrick, too.

Just think about all the White rappers who came before Em' - why were they not as big? Interscope, Aftermath, and Dre made a *hell* of a difference. And I never heard of Everlast or any of the Beastie Boys involved in any scandal involving racist lyrics. (Huge shout-out to MC Serch and 3rd Bass for their contributions to rap and hip-hop, and for their behind-the-scenes assistance of many rap artists.) Eminem does not get a pass because of his affiliations. It is even worse if said affiliations are Black. He got a pass *because he's White*! Incidentally, the Beastie Boys (originally a hardcore punk band) were the first "rap" group whose album hit Number 1 on Billboard in 1986, with their "rap" album *License to Ill*. And why was that album Number 1? *Because they're White*... and there's nothing wrong with that. But what we're not going to do is pretend as if Em' or the Beastie Boys are the apogee or the icon of what real rap and hip-hop is.

Finally, yes, Benzino, as a man and man to man, *has to* apologize to Hailey Mathers for that reference all those years ago - the JonBenet Ramsey reference. That was crude and nasty, and too below the belt for me to not publicly address. Black people have a *keen* awareness to hurt and pain as we are the most hurt and disrespected people on this planet. We do not attack children! So yes, I definitely call Benzino to task for that and hereby demand he tender an apology to Ms. Mathers (something else now, since she recently wed).

But he still beat Marshall.

As did the battle rap crew from Wildin' Out.

As did Michael Jackson. Rest in peace, King. (Speaking of kings, let me also take this opportunity to formally bid a heartbroken farewell to Quincy Jones, whom I had the opportunity to meet completely by accident in midtown Manhattan, by the Dag Hammarskjold building, in the mid-1990s. A cordial and respectful gentleman, he was also a producer, a director, an actor, an activist, a freedom fighter, and a dedicated family man. He actually built, or *bought*, an entire neighborhood whereat his entire family lives. May God keep you, sir. Thank you for your contributions to society in general and to The Culture in particular. Rest in peace, King.)

LOSER: Eminem
WINNER: Michael Jackson and The Culture

4
The Culture Today

So many artists have used hip-hop to get ahead in life and have not put back *into* the culture. Reciprocity evinces gratitude to a part of The Culture that is integral to our progression as a *people*. We, as a people, need the arts to safely, creatively, and politically express ourselves without fear of reprisal. Music in general is such a balm to the soul, a respite in diurnal strife. "I'ma tell y'all this. It was a point and time in battle rap for me where I didn't understand The Culture, y'nahmsayin' ["you know what I'm sayin'?" - Author]? I was running around, I was young, I was stupid, I didn't understand The Culture, I was gettin' money so, I didn't- it was like, battle rap? Man, I don't- y'know, fuck battle rap. This shit stop right now, I don't care, I'm good. This is how I felt at a point and time. I was way, way younger, right? And as I got older, I start understanding what The Culture means and what it is in that this is something we created and it's something they can't take from us. This is *our* culture, right, this is something I understood as I got older." Goodz could not have said it better (on his YouTube channel on 5 February, 2024). Goodz, Calicoe, and Tay Roc understand - they are old-time hustlers who know how to survive in a depression or a recession.

Marshall Mathers has been rapping far longer than Goodz (and more commercially), but Goodz has more love for The Culture than Marshall. Why? Because this is *our culture*, something they *cannot* take from us. Not the government, not through shady dealings, not through commercialization, not through betrayal, and not by the hands or words or talents of Marshall Mathers. Remember the words of Macklemore. As some battle rappers have gone on to open small side businesses from their humble beginnings in various battle rap leagues, some others have not. This, I know, is because the pay is not too great, and the rapper usually finds themselves working a part-time job in between battles.

Charlie Clips, Hitman Holla, and Conceited are all accomplished battle rappers who are but a stone's throw away from superstardom. They wisely branched away from just battle rapping in different leagues for comparatively small remuneration into the fields of online entertainment and television under and with Nick Cannon on the intensely popular show "Wildin' Out." On this show, they interact and skit with a slew of actors, comediennes, rappers, and other personages, showcasing their acting and lyrical improvisation acumen and skills. It is very entertaining and provides employment for these battle rappers who are now being paid healthy sums per episode rather than only per battle. It is definitely doing its numbers while also popularizing battle rap.

But not everyone can be saved - the self-proclaimed "Crip" battle rapper known as Tsu Surf was recently arrested by the FBI and charged with (among other charges) the intent to distribute controlled substances. I believe he pleaded guilty and is now serving time in the feds, as the charges were brought by federal authorities under the Racketeer-Influenced Corrupt Organizations Act (or "R.I.C.O."). Battle rap is an art form that has saved so many people, while others (like Surf) have fallen through the cracks. So, when one falls, personal feelings and organizational affiliations aside, battle rappers have to come together to put something in the kitty (a type of collection) for the family of the beleaguered or fallen colleague, and for the colleague himself/herself. (Jaz, I see you, homette!) Free Surf and free Drugs (a Bloods-affiliated battle rapper who was relatively recently arrested).

Without making noise, battle rappers have *got to* take care of each other. For example, once every other month or so, a different battle rapper should send Surf a couple of dollars. Simultaneously, another should throw a couple of dollars at his woman or children. Things are only becoming tougher in society and *those who fail to plan, plan to fail*. I believe Nas has just opened up a type of fund to help struggling rap and hip-hop artists in their old age. The URL and battle rappers across the United States should think about that *and*, perhaps, should also think about unionizing. Legal representation and advice is needed in this domain. Battle rap might be a hobby to some, as Goodz said it had been like that, and it is certainly an art form, but it is also (or has *become*) an **occupation** to others who know little to nothing else.

Hip-Hop Rivalries: East Coast Versus West Coast

I can see the future of the URL, if it is smart, being the unification of battle rappers in the continental United States. They can even be classified in ranks (Novice, Intermediate, Proficient, Expert, Beast, etc. [based on fan rankings, and the fans are rarely wrong]). Different parts of Black American culture have been expropriated into genres like country, rock & roll, and soft rock. But rap and hip-hop cannot be so easily adulterated, nor expropriated. Rapping was born in our *soul*, out of a *need* Black people had in order to express ourselves while trying desperately to get out of the Jim Crow era and the 'hood.

White people had little to no such need and yet The Beastie Boys were created. Vanilla Ice was created. Jack Harlow was born. Snow was born. Iggy Azalea was born. Tom Macdonald came about. And of course, the Great White Hype, Mr. Mathers, was born. And *all* of them have made a *killing* from the sales and touring of a genre in which Black people themselves are not as well paid.

Why? *Because they're White*! And there's nothing wrong with that... *prima facie*. When Black artists have a majority of fans who are White, they will do better than Black artists who *do not*. When White artists have a majority of fans who are White, they will do exceedingly better than the Black artists with White fans. (Remember what Em' said in *"White America."*) Everyone in the rap/hip-hop tradition should *give back* to the roots of The Culture, in order to not only be paying it forward by sponsoring battle rap events, or leagues, or the rappers themselves, but also to keep The Culture progressing and progressive in the arts.

Also, those battle rappers demanding exorbitant fees per battle - *please stop it*! At times, you will just have to take paycuts and still do battles (for a discount), or battle *pro bono* (for free). At least one out of seven battles should be so, in my estimation. And that, again, is one method of paying it forward.

There is something I have to address before we move on. An interview with the big homie Weezy on Bleacher Report (as reported by the Eminem stan YouTube channel "ETLifestyle") just goes to show how clueless so many rappers can be. Weezy is one of my big homies and I have tremendous respect for him, but he made a huge *faux pas* with what he said.

"That was around when it was competitive. Y'know, I was around when there was a certain such thing called battle rap. Y'know, and, that was a form of art-art form of rap where I can literally [video is edited to another part of the interview - Author] - it was almost comedic. What I mean by that is a comedian can, y'know, they 'roast' [Ebonics for *make fun of* - Author] each other and [garbles words briefly]... They don't mean nothing by it. Y'know, battle rap was the same. Y'know, you got these people, they standin' in a circle and, y'nahmean, Eminem might tear yo' head off about something that you felt great about yourself in the mirror before you got there [laughs], you know, so [video cuts to iconic Dr. Umar camera staredown, with the single bell note gonging thrice in slow, measured succession before cutting back to the Weezy interview - Author]... And then, y'know, and then they come, come right back and - and do the same - so, that was an art form.

"Y'nahmean, *they had people that-that, to this day that's-that's battle rappers that went down that, and that's not-they-they aren't filmed, they aren't recorded and they're le-there's legends because of- they're-theyre le-they're legends come outta that, because of- we don't have that no more. So, so, I was around during that, and then when I came out, that was kind of gone, but it was still a competition!*" [Authors italics]

With all due respect, big homie, *what are you talking about*? There were battle rappers who came *before* you, *during* your early *and* latter years, and there will be battle rappers long after both of our bones are dust. What you (I am talking to the big homie Weezy right now) said is so disrespectful to battle rap culture - battle rap has never been stronger! The Kendrick and Drake rivalry just showed us how strong rap and hip-hop are in (and for) society - the entirety of Western culture was enraptured by it! The only thing missing are wealthy sponsors to come and boost its popularity and engage in joint ventures or by investing.

There is an annual event called "Summer Madness" that the URL holds. Or "NOME." You can put up a nice amount (let's say 100k - that is equivalent to how much bud the big homie smokes in a *month*) and change the lives of a bunch of young and aspiring lyricists. When you attend these shows to show support for The Culture, the energy is charged with *good vibes* and battle rap fans who will *not* leave disappointed. Black, White, or Hispanic - all types of people come together at these shows to have a good time and listen to some of the dopest puns and word play this world has ever heard. We also come together to watch some of the greatest performances and enjoy the wittiness and lyrical creativity of some of the world's brightest intellectuals. I promise you that Shakespeare, Lord Byron, King Zoser, Imhotep, Mary Shelley, and a host of others are studying and still picking apart the puns, triple, quadruple, and quintuple entendres that Kendrick dropped throughout the battle (as I and many others still are). The arts, to me, are a type of science unto themselves. They also use mathematics and science, as evinced by K-Dot's mirroring of Drake's time-stamp method in this battle. An entire encyclopedia can be written just on Kendrick's *"6:16 in L.A."*

But we need rappers like you (Weezy), Nas, Jadakiss, Jay, Fitty, etc. to repopularize battle rap. Thank you in advance, big homie - everything I said is with love and out of respect. East Side.

Now, back to the word "freestyle," as concerns rap and hip-hop. It is pretty uncomplicated but it has just become a byword for any person rhyming at any time. That is *not* freestyle and I *hate* when DJs declare, and *falsely*, that an artist has come on their show to "kick a freestyle" (Ebonically speaking, it means *to rhyme extemporaneously, unpreparedly*) when, after listening for a few seconds, the rhythm, cadence, and enunciation of the words of a so-called "freestyle" tell me whether it has been prewritten or it is improv. More often than not, what the person rhymes is prewritten.

Prewritten rhymes are not "freestyle" - they are *prewritten*! There was once a certain White battle rapper whose freestyling ability was off the charts. Freestyling means to rap, at least moderately intelligibly, right there *on the spot*, from your impromptu, *free* thoughts and whatever it is you're thinking about. The White battle rapper's name is "**Blind Fury**." And yes, he was blind, and White, and *nice* with it.

I remember many, many moons ago when Redman and Method Man were on a certain radio show. This was when freestyling was *really* freestyling. The radio show host was doing something new like, if an artist really wanted to freestyle, the former would spontaneously throw out random words to the lyricist(s), in this case Red and Meth, who would make up a rhyme (or *rhymes*), usually a couplet (or two), using the randomly spoken word. Incidentally, this definition of freestyle should not be confused with the pejorative "freestyle" (Ebonics for *lying or embellishing*).

Towards the end of any given couplet, another random word would be vocally supplied, and *clearly*, and it would be the other rapper's turn (or the same rapper, if he was by himself) to continue rhyming using the newly generated word. They *killed* it! There's no doubt in my mind that Red and Meth are two of the best lyricists that ever existed. I forget which radio station it was on or even around when it happened (I would like to say mid to late 1990s, but them boys did their *thing*! Let me take the time out to give

Red, Meth, and Blind Fury their flowers. These are rappers who are my slightly older colleagues and who I looked up to. These are true lyricists, and they never let me down. They really helped me to pass the time at work, at school, and through the really rough patches on Rikers Island, in C-74 (Adolescents at War), C-95, C-73, OBCC, the Beacon, and North Facility.

Canibus can freestyle really well, and so can Jadakiss, Nas, Fabolous, Cassidy, Chilla Jones, Math Hoffa, and there was this other rapper from upstate New York I heard on the radio while I was in Marcy Correctional Facility - the S-Block. (Rest in peace to Robert Brooks and Messiah Nantwi, and a big fuck you to the corrections officers who beat both of these incarcerated men to death in their respective prisons) I believe his name was "SuperNat" (likely short for *Super Natural*). His freestyles were hard as well. I always wondered what happened to him as time passed; he seemed to have just disappeared off the face of the planet, but he made an impression on me and I am grateful enough to have this opportunity to keep his name alive. Super Natural was a freestyle beast, and I imagine what could have been had he continued in the industry.

Some more underground battle rappers I know of who can freestyle and improv pretty well are: Charlie Clips, Hitman Holla, and DNA. Lauren Hill and MC Lyte could freestyle their asses off back in the day. Jay and Busta were also known to freestyle, the one more serious in content and delivery than the other, who seemed to just have fun on the beat, respectively, but both would usually leave the crowd wanting to hear more. Ditto for ODB (rest in peace, king), KRS One, Heltah Skeltah (rest in peace, Sean Price), GZA, Murder Mase, Joel Ortiz, Joe Budden, and a few others.

Freestyling is a unique art form to which most rappers are *not* attuned. Nothing is written or prewritten - it is spoken and/or rhymed on the fly, off the dome. Of course, prewritten songs are, to me, better and more lyrically concise and ordered, but genuine freestyle is very difficult to find nowadays; however, most of the elders are still around to guide and shape this cruising art form of hip-hop. Whether or not it is turning into hip- "*pop*," real rap and real hip-hop will always be around to refer to or from which to delineate the difference between real and fake.

Rap is here to stay; its little brother, hip-hop, has veered off (seriously, like in the case of Lil Uzi Vert, Lil This and Lil That, *ad infinitum*), and especially with all these singing ass rappers in the mix now. But despite your sibling being *"different,"* they are still your sibling and in need of your guidance and support in almost all things, even when they become an adult. Who knows just how poignantly your continuing regard and patronage is affecting him. (I am not talking about [just] rap and hip-hop!)

N.B. - In battle rap, the crowd will *instinctively* know when a battle rapper is freestyling if the rapper is doing a *rebuttal* of a diss. In these rebuttals, only truly gifted individuals are successful, but top-tier *lyricists* will know how to set up a rhyme or rap scheme to show the point of doing a rebuttal in the first place. For example, please refer to Charlie Clips's "Shang Tsung" rebuttal against Hollow da Don, or Math Hoffa shooting back at Jaz the Rapper and Nu Jurzy Twork (it was during a battle with another battle rapper, though). But if I had to choose the number one freestyle rebuttal I have ever heard, I would choose, hands down, Chilla Jones in his battle against Gjonaj on King of The Dot back on 12 June, 2017.

A gem like the Chilla Jones's Super Mario rebuttal scheme was one of the most genius replies I have ever heard anyone craft (if it really was) on the fly. Even if it was not a rebuttal "freestyle," not gonna lie, Chilla *crucified* Gjonaj in the last round with that scheme. Sometimes, in battle rap, things just fall into place. But I always wonder what would have been the outcome of that rap battle had Gjonaj won the coin toss.

In Kanye's words at the 2005 Grammy's: "I guess we'll never know."

N.B. (UPDATE) - In a recently revisited interview with LL Cool J and DMX (among others), the former states: "A lotta times when people talk about 'freestyle,' it's interesting because, y'know, being a student of hip-hop and growin' up on hip-hop, I learned that, y'know, freestylin' back in the days really was when you write a rhyme and then you say it. And then, what people call 'freestyle' now is really what people used to call 'off the top of the head,' so it kills me when people say freestyle -(DMX interjects to say, "It's somethin' else.")- 'cause it's like, yeah, it's the wrong definition. It's just taken on this, this, this ill kinda-kinda connotation." Yes, "off the top of the head" (or "*off the dome,*" Ebonically speaking) could have been used by the old school rappers as what has been now known for *decades* as "freestyling," but there were many times radio show hosts back then would state that a rapper was going "off the dome in a freestyle."

The Culture Today

So how were we to qualify those designations? Simple: reasoning. Ratiocination. The word "freestyle" is a composite of two words, "free" and "style." According to Oxford Languages, the adjective "freestyle" denotes "a contest, race, or version of a sport in which there are few restrictions on the moves or techniques that competitors employ..."

The verb "freestyle" is defined as to "dance, perform, or compete in an improvised or unrestricted fashion."

Free. Style. One's own style, performed "freely." It's really quite simple.

"Off the dome" is merely the *definition* of "freestyle" in rap and hip-hop, not prewritten lyrics.

Respectfully.

5
The URL and The Future of Battle Rap

A. Smack and Beasley

Along with Norbes and "Cheeko," Smack and Beasley founded the Ultimate Rap League back on or around 26 October, 2009. The URL quickly made a buzz in underground circles and there have been plenty of times when tickets to their standing room only events sold out, with little to no fanfare. At almost every major event, attendees to these battle rap occasions will see Smack and Beasley onstage (although, to be fair, Smack is there 99% of the time, along with "Nunu Nails" [whose role we still have no idea about at the URL]). Throughout the year, these individuals set up events during which rappers can either go one or three eight-to-fifteen-minute rounds against each other. Events like NOME, PG, SUMMER MADNESS, etc. are meticulously organized and Smack and Beasley usually have security present, just in case the verbal combatants, or the crowd, become, well, *combative*.

The camerapersons do a superb job in catching all the excitement, battler actions and reactions, crowd reactions and celebrity cameos or appearances, and the like. Battle rap is an intense music subculture with a huge following of loyal, intelligent, and highly opinionated fans whose analyses during the battles that they really attended I have always, *always*, appreciated, even when I did not fully agree with some of their takes on certain battles. Those analyses are near and dear to me, as perfect strangers from all across the world can come together online and, without losing their minds (too much), discuss and debate the complexities of lyrical confrontations.

I have just had an epiphany.

The URL and The Future of Battle Rap

Arts students all over the world should be mandated to study battle rap in order to be better able to identify various literary devices (as well as to become conversant in A.A.V.E). Everyone should, really, as so much of the world speaks English now. Not only will they be able to identify the said literary devices, but they will also be able to know how they should be, can be, and *are* used. This is the technical side of things that becomes second nature once learned and routinely refreshed. Of course, we all start to learn about such literary functions starting in the third or fourth grade, but a constant influx of Shakespeare, as fantastic a writer as he was, can become tedious.

When the cameras pan the audience at the URL events, there are so many different types of races present that I am proud they all came together to hear my people trade lyrical barbs in order to see who indeed is the nicest (the most talented). But, obviously, it is not just "my people" they come to see and hear anymore - battle rapping is open to all races, as long as you can spit nice and intelligibly.

The Culture is constantly evolving, as is society and as *a* society unto itself, and it is always laudable to see how the battle rap subculture addresses issues that affect normal people on a day-to-day basis. I thank Smack, Beasley, and Cheeko for their efforts and dedication in bringing us the best of the best writers and lyricists in America and the world. Y'all get y'all flowers for that.

(As for Norbes, fuck you for trying to holla at the big homie's baby mama. [This is a fact, which is why the big homie tossed him around like a rag doll. That's the kind of stuff Drake is notorious for doing, and a large part of why he is so hated. He just recently tried some shit like that with the streamer Adin Ross, who quickly and effortlessly put him in his place.])

Let's close this part of this chapter by again addressing what Smack said a little while ago: that "the money ain't coming back." Smack was saying that, for that period in time, the amount of money battle rappers used to get paid would not be getting offered again. The economy definitely is staggering, and we already heard from Goodz but you have to listen to his entire short reply to Smack's controversial statement. Another heavyweight battle rapper, Calicoe, realistically and loyally weighed in. Older rappers like Goodz and Calicoe understand that the good times have slowed down drastically, and this is also due to the Norbes lawsuit, investors not investing as much, partners pulling out after a short period of time, and so on. One should have a nest egg stashed somewhere.

Hip-Hop Rivalries: East Coast Versus West Coast

This is the exact time when the big homie Weezy is needed. This is when Eminem is needed, instead of staying cooped up in his nice mansion and being gleefully more inaccessible than the P.O.T.U.S. These hard times are when the more successful lyricists need to infuse some financial assistance into organizations like URL, in order to keep hope alive for battle rap and battle rappers, like Kendrick has. Calicoe said he would not mind taking some of his own money and doing a show. He is nowhere near as wealthy as Em' or Weezy, but his idea has merit. This is how and why battle rappers like Arsonal have their own battle rap leagues now. We need to start putting back into the roots from whence we garnered our wealth.

The largest battle rap league in the world, founded by "Alaric Yuson" in 2010, is called "Flip Top," and it's based in the Philippines, allegedly the first Asian country to have a rap/hip-hop scene (although I think Japan had a rap/hip-hop culture before the Philippines, but it just had not been discovered or explored). Its battles get over a billion views almost on a regular basis. By watching this league and observing that it only seems to be growing, I can conclude that although the URL might seem to be on shaky ground right now, it's going to be just fine. Other battle rap leagues have been popping up, too - there is enough food to go around for everybody. So let us shout out some of those leagues in a heartfelt act of gratitude: Queen of the Dot, FlipTop, Gates of the Garden, King of the Dot, Grind Time Now, Don't Flop, Queen of the Ring, and the fairly new one, ibattle. Salute.

B. Honorable Mentions
(and A Message For Lil Durk)

I know people wouldn't usually rap this, but I got the facts to back this:
Just last year Chicago had over 600 caskets... Man, killin's some wack shit!
Oh, I forgot, except for when niggas is rappin'...
Kanye West - Everything I Am (ft. DJ Premier)

Before naming names of battle rappers I know of in gratitude for their skill, I would like to address the deleterious situation in Chicago. I barely know of any rappers in Chicago (besides the most famous), but every few days or so, it seems as if such and such is found dead of a shooting (a little more than half the deaths of all rappers are homicides), and that is how I find out their names. Names like Boosie, Ye, King Von, FBG Duck, and 'hoods like O Block, Tookaville, and 1600 Block, etc. From FBG Duck, to King Yella, to Nardo Wick, to FBG Butta, to Lil Durk, most of what I know about Chicago is that aspiring rappers do not have a long shelf life there. Drill rap is only shaming itself as time goes on.

Just look at what happened to King Von and with Lil Durk's recent arrest. Now, I'm not the smartest person in the world, but when I felt like I had to commit crimes, I did not boast about those crimes in my raps or in my penned works. For example, Lil Durk has a song in which he says:

Keep the police out my bidness, we don't post shit
Trigger happy, I be with Zoo 'n 'em, we on 4,6
They like, "Durk - his ass a singer, he won't smoke shit"
You can believe whatever you want I got yo' folks hit

All the FBI does is wait, watch, and *listen*. Durk just said he won't "post shit," then proceeds to post shit. That's why I'm so frustrated with him. Drill rappers often snitch on themselves. I've listened to a few drill rappers recently and it's startling and disheartening how thoughtless of themselves and their families they appear to be. Don't drill rappers know that they can speak about their lives and activities in *third person*?

Durk is a real one for taking care of his homies, but what happened to him is just ruthless and diabolical. It again underlines the saying "trust no one." For what it's worth, I want to send my respect and a few words of encouragement to Durk. I see the pictures and videos of you in court. Having passed through that ordeal quite a few times myself, yes, it can be quite harrowing, but stay strong and hold your head up high. When things appear hopeless, trust me, there's still hope. Without a doubt, OTF Jam is going to get what he deserves. Look at your dad, Big Durk - a stand-up individual who is considered a man's man, by all accounts. You are his son and need to uphold the strength and integrity in whose steps you walk.

Thugga just came home, Big Meech is home, but you never heard any fuckboy shit associated with their names. Ditto for Melle, Drugs, Surf, etc., etc. Stay strong and don't allow what *could be* define what *isn't*. Your thoughts create your reality, so think positive, constantly. You have a powerful legal team, a little bit of money, and you're extremely young. I implore you to not discuss anything concerning your case to anyone *except* your lawyers. Everything you talk about and everything you write is being monitored, even things you whisper to the homies in lockup. Loose lips sink ships. Don't let that be the case for you. The nation of Ambazonia sends its regards and emotional support. Also, whatever happened to the female lawyer that represented you and Von all those years back? Nicole Moorman, Esquire. Reach out to her, as she successfully defended y'all from them Attempt charges.

Rest in peace to all who have been murdered and all who went by accident, rare as that was. Please stop killing each other, young kings. The Culture needs you all alive and doing well. Battle rap should be a way to feed your families and display your skill, not a way to floss and die. Free Durk!

Fuck OTF Jam!

I would like to give a huge shout-out to the following battle rap artists under the URL: the big homie Nu Jerzey Twork, Tay Roc, the big homie Hitman Holla, Jaz the Rapper, Chilla Jones, Charlie Clips, Real Sikh, Goodz, Rum Nitty, Tsu Surf, DNA, Chess, Aye Verb, Daylyt, Calicoe, A Ward, Mike P, and Hollow Da Don. Thank you all for your exceptional rhyming skills and extremely witty and cunning equivokes (and let's thank Nunu for being the representative and representational eye candy for and at so many URL events). You guys made so many years bearable for me. I really appreciate the time and effort all of you took to entertain your supporters, myself included. You all have made an indelible mark in the history of The Culture and you are all highly looked upon. Thank you, again, so much and God bless you all.

Let me also send a shout-out to some cats on FlipTop whom I have seen battling and did not understand a word of what they were saying but just knew it was dope: Loonie, Tipsy D, Batas, BLKD, Sixth Threat, and Sak Maestro. I know there are a bunch more but these are the main ones whose *performances* stand out to me. Let me take this quick opportunity to send a mighty shout-out to the homie out of Chattanooga, Tennessee: Kevin Tucker, also known as "Tana9.13." His track *"Big Dog Shyt"* caught my attention when he and his peoples came DEEP to Poison Ivy's show, "The Debut," in order to perform that banger. Then I saw the official video for it, and it's incredible. The video should have millions of views, because the energy of the song is so catchy. In any case, congratulations on your increasing fame and fortune, homie - you're going to be *huge*!

There are not too many female battle rappers (comparatively speaking), but let us acknowledge what they have done for The Culture, too. At the top of the food chain is Jaz the Rapper, because of whose skill level led me (and many others) to become more interested in women in battle rap. In this arena, a woman can definitely be as proficient as a man, and Jaz has proven, time and again, from the very beginning when she was still a virgin and scared to "pop that cherry" (as O'fficial said, lol), that she can hang with any of the male greats. Jaz, you have earned my respect to a tremendous degree, and I will continue supporting you any which way I can, despite being currently incarcerated. Always keep it a buck and don't forget the women who came before you, who had to sacrifice only God knows what in order to make the path smoother for the current crop of newbies. Phara Funeral (respect!), Gatas (respect!), Bonnie Godiva (respect!), Don Ladyii (respect!), Lady Caution (respect!), Ms. Hustle (respect!), Mosca Flux (respect!), Tia S., Torture - shout-out of major respect to *all* of you women. Keep up the good work, and please know that the men you battle are always going to go for the jugular, so bring your A game every battle. I'd also like to shout out this upcoming female rapper outta Arizona called "Mani T" (pronounced

"Imani," but without the first "I") - she's got hella talent and her rhyming synchs with the beat perfectly. Shout-out also to "B for Better" (it ain't all men that's foul, shorty; please remember that before generalizing in your raps). Shout-out to Michigan rapper "Clare" (yeah, I bee you). Huge shout-out to another dope female rapper called "Raina Simone" (I bee you, too). A final gargantuan shout-out to SZA and Doechii - I seen y'all come up - mad respect for overcoming a lot of the misogynistic and patriarchal bullshit.

However, I do want to send a word of caution to Doechii for her incendiary remark concerning straight males being red flags. Not gonna lie, that was one of the stupidest things I've ever heard ANYONE say. How, exactly, is being a STRAIGHT MALE a red flag if I am a straight male on a date with you, a female? That remark was confusing, fatuous, inutile, puerile, and flagrantly misandrist (the vast majority of males are "straight"). This coming from a woman who snorts cocaine on Livestream. I promised myself I wouldn't degrade a Black woman publicly, and I won't revert to ad hominems - this is a caution. Take it as such and refrain from making such foolish statements belittling "straight" males. Finally, for her dumb ass DJ, Milan, to cackle and claim she was going to say "men" - do you know just how ludicrous you sound? Slavishly chortling along with your slavemaster just to curry favor will do you both worse harm as far as The Culture is concerned. Clown.

6
Poetic Justice

For twenty-seven years, the FBI and the Las Vegas Police Department have been saying it does not know who killed Tupac - until about eight months ago, when a suspect who was previously something of an FBI informant was arrested for Tupac's murder. Among other declarative statements, he has indicated that Diddy ordered the hit for a million dollars, and other explosive tidbits have started being revealed of which the hip-hop world is keenly keeping abreast. The name of that suspect is "Keefe D" (discussed in earlier chapters). His real name is Duane Keith Davis, an alleged affiliate of the Southside Compton Crips gang that had originally been tied to the events surrounding Tupac's murder.

Due to his cooperation with the feds on other issues of this case, as well as other cases, Keefe D likely thought he was invulnerable as the years passed and he was never arrested, but as I have followed some of the interviews he gave, I can honestly say that the old bugger literally told on himself, and did so smilingly. Not only is Keefe D the *uncle* of Tupac's alleged shooter (Orlando Anderson), but he was allegedly one of the people in the car that pulled up alongside Tupac and the big homie Suge Knight. He also told the police that his (long ago deceased) nephew was the one who shot Tupac. But as his mouth kept running like Speedy Gonzalez, the police just kept taking notes. Over the years, the authorities were simply observing Keefe, and listening keenly to each of his numerous interviews. Whether he was the one who pulled the trigger is currently unknown, but he *was* at the scene of the crime and even helped set up the hit; thus, he is an accomplice to murder (which has no statute of limitations), and he gon' get that work, too.

Truth will out.

7

Conclusion

A. What Is To Come?

I want to take the time out now to thank all the readers who were patient with me throughout this work. If there are any grammatical mistakes, any contextual errors, or other literary shortcomings in this book, please lay all the blame on me, Njasang Nji, because, although I have had tremendous help with the research part, I am the one who put the words, chapters, ideas, and presentation together. No one else is to be blamed for any errors in this book not related to the publishing.

The beginning of 2024 was absolutely wild, what with Katt Williams and Shannon Sharpe shocking everyone with their interview-exposé. Apparently, everything Katt said came true. Then Benzino launches two scorching tracks against Eminem that have, thus far, remained unanswered. The war between Russia and Ukraine trudges on, but not one person in this world believes Ukraine will win, not even them, as some of them even said in the latter times of the war. And then, of course, there is the ongoing genocide of the Palestinian people by Israeli militants, which has gotten to such a degree of degradation that students on campuses all across the United States are protesting in support of Palestine. One thing no one can ever say is that Gen Z is weak.

Never.

Once they get something in mind, they will keep pestering you until their plan is effectuated. You know, Gen Z reminds me a lot of Gen X: their bullheadedness and recalcitrance once they know something is wrong and the way they plan to protest against it. Millennials are okay, but Gen Z is, in terms of dedication to a cause, almost identical to Gen X. Gen Z is really increasing in strength as the harshness of society opens their eyes to what appears to be governmental excesses, worldwide. But I urge Gen Z to also calm down and *LISTEN* when their elders talk to them before taking any decisions, especially the life-changing ones. Some of us are genuinely concerned about y'all and want to see y'all win. If there is anything wrong with Gen Z, then Millennials and Gen X *must* take the blame for that. They did not learn any of the outré things that we accuse them of doing by themselves. It is due to a warped learning process of watching us, their examples. That, and the over-liberalization of American society. That one is thanks to certain actors within and without (and who control some sensitive and powerful parts of) the U.S. government.

Speaking of which, Congresspersons who were worth one million dollars fifteen years ago are now worth upwards of 50 million dollars. Some even 100 million dollars. How is that even possible? Greater accountability of civil servants is required. Their investments and other pecuniary dealings must be micromanaged by publicly run citizens groups. I used to work for the New York Public Interest Research Group near midtown - I call on them to become more proactive in matters of civil liberties and accountability of civil servants whose bank accounts balloon over a certain amount within a set period of years. Like, how does a senator's personal wealth skyrocket from two million dollars to 75 million dollars in fifteen years?

Speaking of discrepancies, Nancy Pelosi has been in Congress for thirty years. Her annual salary is $193,400. And yet, her net worth is $196,000,000. But the FBI, CIA, and NSA are playing Three Blind Mice.

When former New York City Mayor Michael Bloomberg won the mayoral race, I just knew he would use the connections of his public office for private gain. Billionaires, or millionaires worth over 15 million dollars, should not be allowed to run for office - the opportunity for malfeasance is too great. Well, I cannot *prove* that Mayor Bloomberg has embezzled anything or that he has engaged in anything shady, like foreknowledge of insider trading (especially since he paid himself only $1 a year, refusing to accept the mayoral salary), but I just watched and waited, implementing a rare type of patience while a certain plan I had came to fruition right before my eyes as the years passed. So, Mayor Bloomberg refused the mayoral salary, right? The mayor of New York makes $102,839 per year. Mayor Bloomberg served three consecutive four-year terms, totalling twelve years as New York City's top official. That would mean he made a total of $1,234,068 throughout his career as mayor... had he chosen to accept the salary. He did not, so *on the books*, he made just $12 for twelve years of service.

How noble of Mayor Bloomberg. But was it really nobility, or something else?

When Mayor Bloomberg went into office, he was worth five billion dollars. When he left office twelve years later, he was reported as being worth *twenty-five* billion dollars. There are not that many lucky and wise investments in the world. I know Michael Bloomberg *personally*. He is very down-to-earth and personable, even amiable and jocular, with an ironical, almost deadpan-ish sense of humor. But, as nice as he is, I put it past nobody that a person can succumb to venality. Here is the Average Joe again, trying his best to tread the waters of financial ruin, while absurd amounts of money go towards funding a foreign war that was lost from the beginning in what appears like the largest money laundering and embezzlement scheme since "foreign aid" was created.

If I can figure all of this out from a dungeon in Cameroun, West Africa, the Average Joe in the United States is light years ahead of me in socio-political perspicacity. Do better, America. Defend your freedoms, Americans. The rest of the world really does look up to you all in so many areas. Certainly politically.

Thoughts and prayers are with the family members and friends of the prime minister of Slovokia (the one who rejected the WHO treaty some time ago) and who was recently shot in the stomach and arm. Thoughts and prayers for Maui. Thoughts and prayers for the indigenes of Ambazonia (formerly known as the British Southern Cameroons). Thoughts and prayers for those affected by the recent wildfires.

Now, back to the lighter topic of battle rap and recent developments. The beef between Drake, J Cole, and Kendrick Lamar intensified when Drake released the video for the song *"First Person Shooter"* on 15 November, 2023, on which track J Cole features, referring to himself, Kendrick, and Drake as the "Big 3," while also throwing subliminals at Kendrick. Drake really thinks he is better than Kendrick, so he added his sly disses therein. Well, Kendrick did not appreciate it and did an outstanding collaboration with Future and Metro Boomin on a track called *"Like That."* He had taken a couple of months to respond and some hip-hop heads criticized the length of

Conclusion

time it took for him to reply. It was all preplanned. After *"Like That"* dropped, J Cole responded with *"7 Minute Drill,"* on which he disses Kendrick, but it was really quite lame for a lyricist of *his* caliber. Worse yet, shortly after *"7 Minute Drill"* came out, J Cole apologized for dissing Kendrick, but, in my opinion, that was just to detract from the rising heat of the allegedly transphobic lyrics in the song. We see what you did there, Cole. Well played.

Drake, meanwhile, replied to *"Like That"* with *"Push-ups (Drop and gimme 50),"* followed again a few days to a week later with *"Taylor Made Freestyle."* (The estate of Tupac Shakur threatened to sue Drake because he used AI to write a diss of Kendrick but the AI was done cloning Tupac's voice. [Incidentally, Snoop's voice was also AI-cloned, which I find so odd being that Snoop is still alive. This *infers* that Snoop told Drake he would not be on a song dissing a West Coast rapper but Drake went ahead and cloned his voice to be on the track with him, *anyway*. Yeah, them edibles defo had you tweaking, Snoop.])

Kendrick decisively settled the whole issue with the track *"Euphoria,"* a six-minutes-and-twenty-three-seconds masterpiece of a series of superfluously crafted *ad hominems* aimed at Drake, since the latter wanted the "smoke" so bad (Ebonics for *wanting beef*) with Kendrick. The calm with which Kendrick delivers such a ferocious track is incredible; and the track does not disappoint. Kendrick did not waste one BAR - *NOT ONE BAR* was wasted in his reply diss. Not ONE bar! And that is why, as it stands on this Saturday, 18 May, 2024, *"Euphoria"* has broken about a dozen records so far, aside from Kendrick's album, *good kid, m.A.A.d city*, (at this present time) breaking the record of longest-running rap album on the Billboard Top 200 (600 weeks [11.5 years])!

Adding insult to injury, most of the records broken by Kendrick Lamar were records attained by Drake.

Behind all of this, Yeezy just dissed Drake and J Cole on a *"Like That"* remix. I am sure that one of the reasons Drake hates Kendrick is because of his verse on Big Sean's *"Control"* track *ten years ago*. Kendrick stated that he was coming for all of them, and he *bodied* that track. A decade plus later, he has actively proven that he is still bodying his colleagues - after all, it *is* a competitive sport.

Let us also not forget the recent diss beef between the homie Chris Brown and Quavo. Man, the range of skills some of these artists have is something else. You have rap artists singing their asses off and now, R&B artists rapping their asses off! Apparently, niggas is evolving.

Another thing we should not forget is the amount of people Drake is beefing with (like Future, Metro Boomin, Rick Ross, *ad infinitum*). If Drake keeps this up, it will not end well with him. Ice Cube gave cautionary advice and said to not let the beef turn into a murder. This is because it would turn into a murder *spree*. Drake cannot beat an entire coast, and using Tupac's voice without the estate's permission is crazy and could have angered the West Coast as a whole. But he is "America's sweetheart," right?

On or around Saturday, 27 April, 2024, I saw a report on TV that Tupac's estate told Drake he must take down and stop using the Tupac-AI-generated content on *"Taylor Made Freestyle"* within twenty-four hours, but even if Drake acquiesces, the song is already out there, on multiple platforms (although no one can play it because they would get majorly sued). I can already see how, if this thing continues, there might be *dead* serious consequences, *outside* of music. And I cannot for the life of me understand why Em' initially seemed to be supporting Drake when Drake has a secret dislike (I would not quite say *hatred*) of him. This is likely why Drake brought out Machine Gun Kelly at a concert some time ago. It's so funny. Was I the only one who caught that subliminal? Em' appeared to have missed it... perhaps. And why would Jay also seem to support Drake in his beef with his former labelmate Weezy? Also, why would 50 side with Drake and post Drake's disses but not post Kendrick's, saying they were "too long"? There are layers upon layers upon layers of intrigue, and they will be unraveled. All in due time.

Only time will tell.

On another note, Elliott Wilson from *Rap Radar* listed what he felt were the 100 hardest diss songs in history. The following are his Top 10:

1. 2Pac - *Hit Em Up*
2. Nas - *Ether*
3. Kendrick Lamar - *Not Like Us*
4. Drake - *Back to Back*
5. Jay Z - *Takeover*
6. Pusha T - *Story of Adidon*
7. Ice Cube - *No Vaseline*
8. Common - *The Bitch In You*

Conclusion

9. Lauryn Hill - *Lost Ones*
10. Future, Metro Boomin, Kendrick Lamar - *Like That*

I myself would put *"No Vaseline"* as Number 3, but it is a pretty good list the way it stands. *"BBL Drizzy"* should be Number 10 and *"Like That"* should be Number 8, in my most humble opinion.

B. Diddy Do It?

A Word of Caution
A final note on the alleged depredations Diddy is being accused of. I do not defend what he did, in any way, as evinced by how I have referred to him throughout this book. But I want to caution those of you bashing Diddy. His laundry is being aired out right now, today, and he should be punished for his misdeeds and vile and predatory predilections. But now think about what you, the reader, have done in *your* life that you believe you got away with. Diddy was just so stingy with his money and allegedly so brutal that his noisome habits had to come to light. I feel so bad for Cassie, Kim Porter, and their families. I also feel terrible for all the other men, women, and children who were allegedly groomed and assaulted by this man.

I said something near the beginning of this book I wish to revisit. If the justice system does not start being more judicious in its prosecution of Caucasians, Black people as a whole will start not caring about what any of us have done to anyone else. Just a relative little while ago, Harvey Weinstein's conviction was overturned - is there any justice in America? Yet the justice system prosecutes R. Kelly and Bill Cosby mercilessly for crimes that happened twenty and thirty years ago. (I *still* listen to R. Kelly and I *still* watch The Cosby Show *anyway*!)

The more blind in justice the justice system becomes, the more impartial, the more blasé, The Culture will become toward appeals to prosecute any accused Black offender (and not just of sex crimes, but in general). We can hold ourselves to account with street justice, and we have and, whenever necessary, still do, with proxies taking the fall if need be. But when we see that White people are not holding their own people accountable in their so-called "justice system," we feel greatly slighted and The Culture will simply become quiet, not liking or supporting what an offender is being accused of doing, but certainly not calling it out also. What is good for the goose must, perforce, be good for the gander in front of the blinded eyes of Lady Justice, who is supposed to *impartially* weigh the deeds of individuals in society with her scales of justice.

After all, out of all the names on that Epstein list, which one has been prosecuted to the fullest extent of the law? Epstein was heavily involved in human and sex trafficking, as was his disgraced friend, Ghislaine

Conclusion

Maxwell, now serving a twenty-year federal prison term for sex trafficking and conspiracy. He "died" under very suspicious conditions, and, in 2020, Harvey Weinstein was convicted of criminal sexual assault and rape and sentenced to twenty-three years in prison. As severally noted, just a little while ago, his conviction was overturned. *Where is the justice?* Where is the justice for all the men, women, and children who were trafficked to Epstein Island and abused by those said to have frequented it? Including Steven Hawking, for God's sake.

That last is a shuddersome thought.

But do not talk to Black people about helping justice to prosecute Diddy if the justice system failed at prosecuting Weinstein. The U.S. government must prosecute **all** offenders the same. But as I also said earlier: racism will never be erased. It is sewn into the fabric of American existence itself. Well, at least Weinstein was convicted and sentenced to sixteen years in a separate case in California, so he is going to stay locked up.

But where is the justice for LaVena Johnson, Sonya Massey, Sandra Bland, and Tamela Holmsford?

And about a year ago, Lil Durk came out with a song called *"No Diddy,"* a term the streets have come up with to replace the original term "No Homo." For example, if a Black man says something remotely homosexual or tries to eat a banana the way White society says it should be eaten, "normally," if he is a street dude, or came from the streets, he will say "no homo," announcing that he is aware of and sorry about what he just said or did or what he is *about* to say or *about* to do. Strange thing, though, is that Meek Mills, who is alleged to have freaked off with and/or been groomed by Diddy, featured on the track. Also strange enough, T.I. is featured on the track, which I find ironic, as some of us still, to this day, wonder how he squirmed his way out of the situation when he got caught with all those guns and was sentenced to only a year and a day.

"Hypocrite! First remove the plank from your own eye, and then you will see clearly to remove the speck from your brother's eye." Matthew 7:5 (NKJV)

N.B. - At this particular point and time the video of Diddy assaulting Cassie was leaked by CNN, and it is terrible. This is an egomaniac and a borderline psychopath. For him to have done this to Cassie is criminal and I wish she would never have signed that NDA (Non Disclosure Agreement) when she settled the lawsuit out of court with Diddy. I guess, on this score, Diddy *did* do it. How shameful, despicable, and absolutely reprehensible on his part... We can only imagine the horrors Epstein and Weinstein also visited upon women and children. Imagine, also, the horrors committed by the Abercrombie and Fitch reprobates. *Dozens* of lives at a time, *innumerable* times, over *decades*, just absolutely *ruined*. (Incidentally, more than 40 men have accused the ex-Abercrombie and Fitch CEO Mike Jeffries of sexual assault which, of course, he has denied. And there he is in Long Island, a White multimillionaire, strolling about without a care in the world, while Diddy, a Black billionaire, squats in lockup. However, there are some nebulous whispers that Diddy and Ghislaine Maxwell might still get pardoned by Trump, at some point.)

C. Diddy Kong

As time has flown and the date of publication for this marvelous work approaches, so many other things have been exposed. The entire year of 2024 was in the palm of Katt Williams. "It's all catching hell in 2024. It's up for all of 'em. It don't matter if you Diddy or whoever you is... All lies will be exposed... So if you and a man was in a corner doing something you wasn't supposed to be doing – [gets interrupted by a zesty Shannon: "You were telling"] I know so many things I shouldn't know. When I walk in a room, all heads go down."

Katt ain't never lie.

From Diddy, to the prolonged medical absence of the second-longest ruling head of state in the world in October, to Zelensky's false claims about how the war is going, to the White House itself, all lies were, indeed, exposed. (Who would have thought Katt Williams's prophecy would also touch on sensitive political matters like the attempted power grab of South Korea's former president? Furthermore, his replacement is also being impeached.)

"I was defending him, and he turned around and called witnesses to testify against me, and he contributed- he pretty much sent me to prison." These are the words of Jamal Michael Barrow, known for his 2000s hits *"Bonnie and Shyne"* and *"Bad Boyz."* He is currently a Belizean politician and appears to be doing well for himself. I attended two high schools with Shyne, the first being the High School for the Humanities (known simply as *"Humanities"*) in Lower Manhattan. After being arrested and released the same day for possession of a firearm, I tried to return to Humanities the next day, but the school administration was too shook (Ebonics for *"fearful"*) of what signal my dad's diplomatic immunity would send to the rest of the students. I was expeditiously expelled from Humanities.

My sister managed to get me into City-As (High) School on Varick or Clarkson Street (just up from West 4th Street), where I was able to painstakingly get my high school diploma, all while being on Intensive Supervision Probation ("ISP"). I had met and formed a friendship with Shyne in Humanities and, for whatever reason, he too decided to join me at, and graduate from, City-As. At the time I attended, it was a great high school that specialized in helping troubled youths get their high school diplomas by placing them in real-life career situations, after which they could apply for (and usually attain) jobs. City-As sent me to work in the Cabrini Medical Center on 14th Street and Union Square. I also received credit from both the school and my ISP oversight officer for working at the Congress of Racial Equality ("C.O.R.E."), at that time located at Cooper Square.

Shyne and I graduated. However, due to the loss of my mom, I was on a freefall that landed me up north. Before my incarceration, however, I saw how Shyne was picked up by Bad Boy and his career took off. I remember that he and I used to rap in the bathrooms in Humanities; you could tell he was talented, even back then. Also, Diddy had this thing for people who rapped slow, like Biggie. Shyne sounds somewhat like Biggie, intonation and pace wise. It pained me when he got locked up for the shooting in the club when he was with Diddy and Jennifer Lopez, and I tried flying him a kite, but he never received it, apparently. Shyne was not someone to be messed with. The fights he got into in school were epic and *brief.* Just like me, he never needed backup to fight his one-on-ones. And he was deadly with his hands. I only later found out that, like mine, his dad was a foreign diplomat, but from Belize.

Now, directly to Diddy - some believe it was his lawsuit against "Diageo," a spirits (hard liquor) company based in the United Kingdom, that caused him his current travails. However, the lawsuit was served in May, 2023. Not saying Diageo (which owns and distributes Johnnie Walker, Captain Morgan, Guinness beer, Tanqueray gin, besides almost 200 other brands), could not have initiated investigations into Diddy's checkered past and abuse allegations in order to get him into the current fiasco in which he now finds himself, but the lawsuit was settled in January, 2024, leaving Diageo as the current and sole owner of Cîroc. Interesting, but not completely condemnatory.

From 2007, Diddy has been the brand ambassador of Cîroc, likely its head (or close to the head) of marketing and promotion. We need to understand that Cîroc was not created or owned by Diddy. He and Diageo entered into an "equal-share venture," a contract in which profits from the brand were split between them. Diddy claims the company distributed only to urban neighborhoods, neglected his input, created needless competition between his brand and theirs, and so on and so forth. Diageo replied that Diddy was just trying to get richer.

Conclusion

Even though I don't think it was Diageo that brought these tragedies on Diddy's head *singly*, they likely had *something* to do with his downfall. After all, "all is fair in love and war." Sisiku once told me that you don't do business with a murderer and one day, if you wake up armless, you question who did it. You should know with whom you lay down in bed, or risk getting fleas, or worse, as Diddy is seeing to his (perhaps) esurient detriment.

♪ ♪ ♪ ♪

Another theory for the downfall of the music mogul is the fact that he was trying to create a political party made up of predominantly Black people, for Black people issues. "I'm launching one of the boldest movements that I've ever launched, and it's called 'Our Black Party.' It's time for us to have our own Black political party, unapologetically. 'Cause right now if you look at the debates, we're not even a part of the conversation... We don't have any political power, we don't have any political leverage, and so we started Our Black Party, um..., with some young, fearless Black activists, elected officials, and I've stepped up and put the money behind it. This is the-the... ***the biggest threat*** and... the only option that we have right now, as far as making a change, taking our own self-responsibility and accountability to be educated, and empowered with our vote." [Author's emphases]

"Our Black Party" sounds like an amazing venture, and I applaud Diddy for trying to get something of that magnitude together. *However*, one cannot be a superhero and a supervillain at the same time. Diddy had simply engaged in too much, and was too unmindful of how his past criminal activities could catch up to him.

I have already spoken on how the justice system needs to be completely fair to people of all races, but we see, just recently, how far away that plateau is with the execution of Marcellus Williams (a Black man for whom even the prosecution had pleaded to the governor of Missouri to halt his execution on 24 September, 2024). Compare that with the stay of execution of Robert Roberson, a White man also on death row, and we see the clear disparity in the application of so-called "justice" in the United States. Speaking of the piece of shit governor of Missouri, he pardoned Eric DeVallenaere, a former Kansas City Jack Boot Thug Pig (shout-out to DELETE LAWZ) convicted of the manslaughter of a Black man, Cameron Lamb, outside of Lamb's home. Parson pardoned him little more than a year into his six-year sentence. Land of the free, indeed. Free White people. There is still a very long way to go, particularly on the federal level.

Diddy is on the federal level now, and all of his dreams have mostly come to a crashing standstill. I have already spoken on COINTELPRO and the other instruments the United States has used to retard or wholly halt the progression of Black people. This is the reflection of the very real fear many White Americans have that Black people, if given positions of authority, will do to them what they did to us. Barack Obama was a social experiment, and he's half-White. But White America should know that if Black people wanted revenge for slavery, there would either be no White Americans or no Black Americans left.

What we seek is *parity*. And redress and recompense, the latter of might seem virtually impossible, as what price can be put on the lives of the millions of Black Africans forcibly removed from their original lands and forced into brutal servitude? There is no real monetary price one can place for those depredations committed by the United States government against Black people. But reparations would go a long way to healing that profound and ghastly wound perpetrated on Black Americans. And let's remember that slavery was horrendous, yes, but the evils committed against Black people *during and especially after* slavery were unconscionable, and also **sanctioned** by the United States government. One such gruesome evil is the massacre of Black people in Slocum, Texas in 1910. This massacre was so reprehensible that the Texas State government passed a bill banning the *teaching* of such vile acts committed by their forefathers against the forefathers of African-Americans in Texas and anywhere else in the United States.

If that's not adding insult to injury, nothing is.

Look also at the bombing of Black Wall Street on 13 May, 1985. I was 6 years old, living in Bonn, West Germany, when that thriving community of Black entrepreneurs and technical specialists was bombed with the go-ahead from the State (and Federal) government. The United States government needs to get its shit together and start acting like it wants Americans of different ethnicities, religions, creeds, and colors, to live together in peace.

This issue with Diddy is bigger than most people even know. The implications are sundry. What is going to happen with the list of famous

Conclusion

people who attended the famous "freak-offs"? Will *they* be charged with any crimes? Are the plenitude of victims who claim many of those famous celebrities assaulted and/or trafficked them going to be allowed to sue their abusers? If so, what happened to the victims of Weinstein and Epstein suing their estates and the famous people around them who also participated in *their* lurid "sexcapades"?

Moreover, what about the legacies of all the rock stars who had engaged in terrible and dehumanizing sexual acts with minors during their tours? One such famous case comes to mind: Laurie Maddox, a former child model who got into the club life in the 1970s and 1980s. She began frequenting clubs in Hollywood at 13 years old. She claims that at 13 years of age she was kidnapped by the tour manager of LED Zeppelin: Richard Cole. He had her brought to LED Zeppelin guitarist Jimmy Page's room and was, for all intents and purposes, held hostage there. He was 28 and she was 13. Where's the justice for Laurie and the outcry against LED Zeppelin? Laurie also claimed to have initially lost her virginity to David Bowie, an explosive claim but not one without merit. She also allegedly had sexual encounters with Mick Jagger. Where is the outcry against the Rolling Stones?

And to all the rock-and-roll fans out there who knew and/or suspected this about your favorite stars, none of you get to say shit about this Diddy situation. Use your time to cover the story about the former Chief Executive Officer of Abercrombie and Fitch, Mr. Michael Jeffries who (along with a "Matthew Smith" and "James 'Mrs. Cook' Jacobson") was charged with sex trafficking and other reprehensible crimes that date back decades. You rock-and-roll fans cover the story behind why he is out on a 10 million dollar bond but Diddy is behind bars. That piece of shit Jeffries trafficked hundreds of people, drugged them, raped them, but is still allowed to gallivant about freely. If this isn't a pure example of the systemic institutional racism inherent in the so-called "judicial system," then I have a bridge in Brooklyn to sell to you. For a dollar. Let's also point out some in-your-face egregiousness allowed by (primarily and predominantly) White Americans: Justin Gaston was 20 years old and dated Miley Cyrus when she was 15; Jerry Lee Lewis was 22 years old when he dated his cousin Myra Gale Brown when she was only 13; Rolling Stones bassist Bill Wyman was 47 when he dated Mandy Smith at 13; Don Johnson was 23 when he was dating Melanie Griffith at 14; Elvis was 24 and Priscilla was 14; Doug

Hutchinson was 51 and Courtney Stodden was 16; and Wilmer Valderrama was 30 when dating a 17 year old Demi Lovato. Two final examples show how disgusting and evil White America has been and wasn't getting punished: (White) America's favorite pedophile director Woody Allen was 42 when he started dating Soon-Yi Previn, 16 - she was his **stepdaughter** and had been in his custody since a little child. The second and last example (and there are MANY others) involves another groomer-pedophile, René Angélil who, in 1982, was 39 years old, while lunching with a little 14 year old Celine Dion (who would be his future wife). This is part and parcel of the legacy of White America. (Yes, yes, I know - "not all White people, not all White Americans," but, apparently, a suspiciously and heinously large amount of them.)

Perhaps Diddy *did* piss off the government with his plans for "Our Black Party" and he was seen as too much of a threat to continue allowing on the loose. Perhaps the government and Diageo got together and decided to take down the head of Bad Boy. Yes, this is conjecture, but it's neither specious nor solipsistic - what we have discussed is not subjective. The Culture, as a whole, has suffered tremendously in the United States. Despite Donald Trump being the new president, the senators, governors, representatives, and other civil service employees should seek new and inclusive ways on how to bring society together. It cannot continue like this. People can agree to disagree without killing one another. (And, as a Black man who lived in the United States, I can disagree with President Trump's more glaringly racist and misogynistic views, and *still* also disagree with Vice President Kamala's and President Biden's stances on same-sex sports participation, immigration laxness, gender assignment, and other issues.)

As previously stated, what's good for the goose must, perforce, be good for the gander. Diddy may be an entertainment distraction, but trust, his antics have damaged many lives. Yes, it is right to put away predators found guilty of their crimes, but for the right reasons, not because those accused have become too rich and wish to buy Sony, or their own masters, or CBS, or start their own political party that might actually gain traction. The right things should be done for the right reasons.

♪ ♪ ♪ ♪

Conclusion

There's a rap song by G-Dep called *"Let's Get It"* that features Black Rob and Diddy. In the video, Diddy is seen sporting a jersey with "24" on it. On 12 August, 2022, during an episode of The Breakfast Club, 50 Cent revealed that not only had he written the chorus for that song, but he had also written Diddy's verses for that song. 50 appears to also be some type of a prophet because of the lyrics he wrote. The first few verses go:

> *Ayo, call me Diddy I run this city*
> *Send the cops, the feds, and D.A. to come get me*
> *Cats wanna leave me for dead, you coming with me*

Indeed, Diddy had for years "run" New York City, being a powerhouse producer, rapper, director, etc. Considering what he's going through now, though, I can see how sending *"the cops, the feds, and the DA to"* go get him will forever haunt him. Having passed through the belly of that beast (and being there currently, albeit in another country and for far nobler reasons), I can say *definitively* that some of the other detainees being held with Diddy have tortured him relentlessly with this song. The third verse infers that Diddy is going to snitch (*"Cats wanna leave me for dead, **you coming with me**"*). 50 knew, even back then, that if Diddy was ever taken down, he would either snitch or, if killed, somehow take those people with him.

The next several verses are 50 merely flexing Diddy's wealth (his love for his "money" and "music"), but the verses a bit farther along are likely part of the reason bail was denied him:

> *I don't even buy luggage, ya love it*
> *Make moves major, hide out in Asia...*
> *Not guilty, plus I'm filthy, c'mon*

It's no secret that Diddy is extremely wealthy and would obviously not need to carry around any luggage. He could certainly "hide out in Asia" if shit hit the fan, and authorities who have been listening to him for years also know this. There is such a thing as the "hip-hop police," authorities whose task it is to simply listen to rap and hip-hop songs to figure out if they correspond with any recent crimes around where the artist claims the said crime(s) to have been committed. Behind the murders of Tupac and Biggie,

I have little doubt that Diddy has been monitored ever since. If he somehow convinced himself otherwise, then he is more delirious than Eddie Murphy.

Many critics of that song claim that 50 was indeed prophesying what would eventually happen to Diddy in the year *2024* (reflecting the number of his jersey ["24"]). The lyrics were a premonition, but Diddy likely saw them as a flex. Artists should definitely watch what they say in their rhymes. The power of the spoken word is undoubtedly visceral. There is diurnal evidence of this.

Words are so powerful that a person's entire persona can revolve around a word, be it a nickname, an epithet, or an endonym. For example, Diddy's ex-bodyguard, a "Gene Deal," recently revealed that Puff's nickname "Diddy" came from Biggie calling him "Diddy Kong," from the Donkey Kong gaming franchise. In the game, Diddy Kong is Donkey Kong's nephew. It sounds like a good origin story for the name "Diddy," and it's likely true. Apparently, Diddy did not know he was being clowned by Biggie and simply accepted the nickname as something dope and unique.

Well, and I guess even though the joke is on Diddy, the joke is also on Biggie because that name "Diddy" has carried a ponderous weight of fear and intimidation in Harlem and New York City as a whole. Diddy, in fact, became the gorilla he was being mocked as a monkey for being. And that gorilla has been a major mover and shaker in many spheres and influences during the years. But he's NOT THE ONLY ONE. Gnash your teeth all you want, White America. But get your shit together. It's long past time y'all started practicing equitability, equality, AND equity. (Despite President Trump's massive rollbacks and aversion to Diversity, Equity, and Inclusion.)

Only God can sort through this mess now. Hopefully, Diddy doesn't unalive himself as Epstein was claimed to have done in a room where suicide by hanging was said to be impossible.

Afterword

Thank you to YHWH for allowing us to finish this work that was so difficult to compile, research, edit, and organize the best ways we knew how, given the challenges. But we got it done. All Praise To The Most High!

Thank you, Favour. For EVERYTHING, Mama.

Thank you to my publishers and editors who put up with me in my first, and very angry, draft. I appreciate the opportunity to work for you and with you and I hope this opens the door for further collaborations down the line.

Thank you to Auntie Jeris, for coming to see me when you were around. I owe you a debt for the good you did for me when I was growing up. You were always so calm and patient and hospitable to me. As long as I live, I will always owe you and love you. I promise when I leave this shithole, I will do my best to repay the debt I owe you. I love you so much, Auntie. Thank you. Shalom.

Thank you to Edward Bozek, a true brother in arms, my Ach and beloved childhood friend. What you have done for me can never be repaid. I only pray for your ultimate success in all that you do. You have a heart of gold and stood by me through some of the most difficult times I have ever encountered. More so even than many of my own flesh and blood. You are forever appreciated, my brother. May Yah continuously bless you, Mrs. Bozek, and the future family. Shalom!

Thank you, Tasheem, my son, for all your words of encouragement, your forgiveness for my absence and other shit I was doing out in the streets.

Kirsten, you better take care of him, as I have not been able to throughout the years. The honor you both did me will never be forgotten. Another generation of Ambazonians is to be born and will be prolific and magnificent. Shalom!

Thank you to Maureen, for coming all this way and pledging you must see me before you went back to New York. God bless you and keep you as well. You will never be forgotten. Shalom!

Thank you, Solange, for your sacrifices for me and this community. We have debts to many people who have sacrificed so much for us, but the debts will be fully paid, even with interest. Thank you so much. Shalom!

Thank you to the NERA 10 (well, most of you) for accepting me into the community as family. Especially Sisiku, Dr. Njikimbi, Dr. Kimeng, and Professor Awasum. As our leader says on a daily basis, every day we are one day closer to Buea. Independence or resistance forever. Shalom!

Thank you to Sister Relindis, for all of your sacrifices in taking care of us and in paying particular attention to me. The cooked foods and soursop are so delicious and nutritious. Thank you especially for your prayers, "Sister of the Most High."

Thank you to Alvina Sanchez, Aleen Bassêne, Missy Feliciano, and Vivian Sille. You all taught me that real love can exist, unfettered, undemanding, and (almost) unconditional.

Thank you to Kendrick Lamar, Nasir Jones, Shawn Carter, Dwayne Michael Carter (Jr.), and especially Bobby Ray Simmons (Jr.), the latter whose album *Elements* needs to be heard by *everyone*.

Last, but far from least: this book is dedicated specifically to the memory of LaVena Johnson, Sandra Bland, Kenneka Jenkins, and Kendrick Johnson, among many other Black women and men for whom justice has still not been served. Oh, and a big fat fuck you to Andrew Schulz for that buck breaking sucka shit he said about Kendrick. Keep Black people names out your mouth, bozo!

And Snoopy Bad Azz can suck a big fat bloody dick, too. And REST IN PEACE TO THE BIG HOMIE DRAKEO THE RULER!

Battle Rap Playlist Suggestion

A. https://youtu.be/zoS04Fclygs?si=GFFjXtyNen-FnAtS [Nu Jerzey Twork vs JonJon da Don]
B. https://youtu.be/0hfh8SOILiM?si=cWb1UV52a7vf99mI [Math Hoffa vs Pat Stay]
C. https://youtu.be/4-ZmRhnBGpE?si=9lnGDMxzb4x4rPFk [A Ward FIRE Rebuttal vs Tay Roc]
D. https://youtu.be/dStN64sDpkY?si=LU9n5VUXIhSSEKpi [Gjonaj vs Chilla Jones]
E. https://youtu.be/lyQNGjbDin4?si=4y8j-OaEwaaP0Hz2 [Joell Ortiz Freestyle]
F. https://youtu.be/_TXVF75lVV8?si=cYSkk1S4vV0nYpaI [Cassidy Freestyle]
G. https://youtu.be/rARhKclhY1U?si=V8fVsz32H9TVHyWN [Nu Jerzey Twork vs Qleen Paper]
H. https://youtu.be/u_WEMpCSo6c?si=g9kCycCA5aGenDbX [Nu Jerzey Twork vs Chess]
I. https://youtu.be/5o5Yg7uCI0A?si=Qeds3deMLVmozudl [Most Legendary Battle Rap Bars of All Time]
J. https://youtu.be/qPrpEVPdUCI?si=8aCb0Gi3e9TRt164 [Jaz the Rapper vs Rum Nitty]
K. https://youtu.be/aGB2fUYcsQ8?si=NMz0mpCISfz8HRC9 [Best of Jaz the Rapper]
L. https://youtu.be/EJWffxKbrJU?si=sHdlHpasxiLQTYn9 [Daylyt vs Gjonaj]
M. https://youtu.be/Pudvvq7kvpQ?si=LWa2HopIP0_TTRyJ [Nu Jerzey Twork vs Jaz the Rapper]

Hip-Hop Rivalries: East Coast Versus West Coast

N. https://youtu.be/lhi2CKrG570?si=kT4n5ZBBWU8fbQV3_ [Jadakiss Freestyle]

O. https://youtu.be/UACVtS2wxUs?si=LuSrwY50I8jPT0jG [Battle Rap Flowers - Charlie Clips]

P. https://youtu.be/-mT5_M9xxKw?si=Rj5ip97ua2qeBtVv [25 Funniest Moments in Battle Rap History]

Q. https://youtu.be/45zwu0-u9n8?si=tOVV5FujepcavPIk [Aye Verb vs Nu Jerzey Twork]

R. https://youtu.be/oGwrZzGOgpU?si=-OqBIwQJvbneabIg [Annihilation - K-Shine vs JC]

S. https://youtu.be/AViQCeDumdM?si=ANISjeD2RcCzSslF [Hitman Holla vs K-Shine]

T. https://youtu.be/HNfz1w7bNqI?si=LE53duGd0DBO6eFt [Biggest Reactions in URL History]

U. https://youtu.be/_PFpLKgDyTU?si=nUOuyeXiQWGIzUcJ [Tsu Surf vs Hitman Holla]

V. https://youtu.be/dCfOxU1uFK8?si=gXM6zrwlsm3NThDm [Brizz Rawsteen vs Mr. Wavy]

W. https://youtu.be/NCqTVjJl6Tk?si=pkuaJ7ZzcWJHgebf [Tay Roc Surprises Lady Caution - RESPECT!]

X. https://youtu.be/ykwr00TaYeA?si=7_g8UnN0kLcJWCme [Lady Caution vs Jada Raye]

Y. https://youtu.be/A3FTwaNRHX8?si=4K5_9oEPhNPtlPf8 [Nu Jerzey Twork vs Ms. Hustle]

Z. https://youtu.be/IQtwmx_T9xU?si=bmYcj9SMSciamMGg [Best Street Fighter Bars in Battle Rap]

A1. https://youtube.com/shorts/pkn9v6EengY?si=NP5ZyFMC3UbLl1-U [Shout-out to the big homie Hitman Holla]

B1. https://youtube.com/shorts/V-Hy43XP5c8?si=knjC7pN6ATnIRxMO [Nu Jerzey Twork v Bigg K]

C1. https://youtube.com/shorts/Esi70R-gC5U?si=fEfi22L9DMQlMYHH [J2 and Aeon - 2v2]

D1. https://youtu.be/N7fB_YsPIaY?si=Z1-0c7xVBDZuIUO8 [Noxx v King Yoshimitsu]

Battle Rap Playlist Suggestion

E1. https://youtube.com/shorts/r3JoGqDiwvA?si=TW0P0ds0xdSd1QB4 [Flawless destroys Beans]

F1. https://youtu.be/9wnDx3Decus?si=nHD-0qo-S43OQ8WE [Kevin Tucker (Tana9.13) - Big Dog Shyt]

G1. https://youtu.be/tJlf0Bm_Hnw?si=XDPI5aauNb008spx [Kraft Singles v Fancy Cheeses Rap Battle]

H1. https://youtu.be/ZKMzXxv4_EQ?si=XEQWmkWDVbLrLMfc [Ketchup v Mustard Rap Battle]

Appendix

Introduction

A. What's Beef?

https://www.redbull.com/ca-en/history-of-breakdancing#:~:text=Some%20say%20the%20breaking%20we,determined%20to%20be%20the%20winner. [Breakdancing info]

https://rethinkingschools.org/articles/cointelpro-teaching-the-fbi-s-war-on-the-black-freedom-movement/#:~:text=Under%20then%2DFBI%20Director%20J,Fred%20Hampton%20and%20others%2C%20murder. [COINTELPRO info]

https://artsemerson.org/2023/03/08/what-is-cointelpro-the-history-behind-mondo-bizarros-cointelshow/#:~:text=The%20name%20COINTELPRO%20simply%20stands,threat%20to%20the%20US%20government. [More COINTELPRO info]

https://www.nyclu.org/resources/policy/legislations/legislative-memo-nyclu-strongly-supports-reform-rockefeller-drug-laws [Rockefeller Drug Laws]

https://pubmed.ncbi.nlm.nih.gov/20939143/ [More on the Rockefeller Drug Laws]

https://youtu.be/AMJWeluZ3tI?si=os1ncfIZOoBxhGOZ [Dave Chappelle on Ohio's opioid crisis]

B. Honorable Mentions

https://youtu.be/qZuxPKUVGiw?si=89Cgxekub69vfCq2 [NWA - Fuck the Police]

Appendix

https://youtu.be/Xh08PtK-NoE?si=JpIhLXzU-CeAtJXL [Gilbert Scott-Heron and his most famous song, The Revolution Will Not Be Televised]

Why Nations Fail: The Origins of Power, Prosperity, and Poverty, Acemoglu, D., and Robinson, J., Profile Books, 2013

C. The Buildup

https://nmaahc.si.edu/explore/stories/celebrating-black-music-month [African-American contributions to music]

https://nmaahc.si.edu/explore/stories/harry-belafonte-actor-and-activist#:~:text=Breadcrumb&text=Harry%20Belafonte%20made%20a%20host,and%20humanity%20across%20the%20globe.

https://www.loc.gov/item/ihas.200197451 [Related reading]

Ebonics: The True Language of Black Folks, Robert Lee Williams II -www.leland.stanford.edu/~rickford/Ebonics/)

www.linguisticsociety.org - Ebonics

1. The Backdrop and AAVE

Appendix (Links/Pictures/Photos)

Quora/ December 6 2023/ 06:19 [Nigger and Niger - Author's Italics]

Negro - www.wikipedia.org

[Excerpts compiled by] Ayinde, from The Name "Negro" - Its Origin and Evil Use, Richard B. Moore

Related reading: African Origins of Civilization, 1974, Cheikh Anta Diop

Related reading: Stolen Legacy, 1954, George James G.M.

Related reading: The Destruction of Black Civilization, 1971, Chancellor Williams

Related Reading: From the Browder File, 1989, compiled & written by Anthony T. Browder

Civiliter Mortuus, Black's Law Dictionary, 2d Ed., Deanté Cassius Clay is Not Black, African American or Negro, SEE SF 181

The Delectable Negro: Human Consumption and Homoeroticism within U.S. Slave Culture, by Vincent Woodard, 2014

A Note on the Word "Nigger," by Randall Kennedy, Professor of Law, Harvard University, African-American Heritage and Ethnography, Park Ethnography Program, National Park Service, U.S. Department of the Interior

https://youtu.be/znpyUxUmYOY?si=4VUawI2aA2YecsOw [White rapper punched in the face for saying "n" word]

2. What's Beef?

A. Tupac Shakur vs. The Notorious B.I.G. (aka "Biggie")
https://www.britannica.com/topic/A-Raisin-in-the-Sun-play

https://www.whitneyhouston.com/news/whitney-houston-won-11-billboard-music-awards-this-day-in-1993/

Original Gangstas: The Untold Story of Dr. Dre, Eazy-E, Ice Cube, Tupac Shakur, and the Birth of West Coast Rap, Ben Westhoff, 2016

Pit of Snakes: Tupac's Quad Studios Shooting, XXL, September, 2011

https://youtu.be/XsPcZXE7I-Y?si=qtFo-DdtQlYDmDlU

Tupac talks Hit Em Up [vs] Who Shot Ya (Part 2, VIBE, September 13, 2010)

www.cheatsheet.com Was Faith Evans Pregnant When The Notorious B.I.G. Died, by Chris Malone, July 24, 2020

https://oldtimemusic.com/the-meaning-behind-the-song-against-all-odds-by-2pac/

Mikjrv - Quora - date of post ungiven [on Makaveli and Machiavelli]

https://l.kphx.net/s?d=1310351016710041060&extra=Q1RSWT1DTSZM Tkc9ZW4tVVM= [Suge Knight says the wrong person was arrested]

Appendix

https://www.facebook.com/reel/2077257179377500/?mibextid=Bitp03hRLnGPS5PQ

https://www.facebook.com/officialangiemartinez/videos/3361929404107467/?mibextid=rS40aB7S9Ucbxw6v

2 Pac vs Biggie: From Friends to Enemies, December 7, 2022 (Interview)

https://l.kphx.net/s?d=3405838252130282670&extra=Q1RSWT1DTSZMTkc9ZW4tVVM=&g=63c1378cb8979a83d777fa313ebdc060 [Big Suge has to talk to Snoop about the murder of 'Pac]

https://youtube.com/shorts/pCZ9oX_QE1E?si=BycJkUR7igoJG9Hi [With his dying breath, 'Pac curses out detective]

https://youtu.be/ck-JZHliJ7I?si=KL-cDUbHsgqIVNep [Keefe D suffering in prison]

https://youtu.be/pUqp5HdskHk?si=0Cz0w1L14rTOr7dY [2Pac and Big Deadly Enemies]

Tupac Shakur, The Authorized Biography, by Staci Robinson, 2023, Penguin House

It Was All A Dream - Biggie and the World That Made Him, Justin Tinsey, 2022

https://youtube.com/shorts/pCZ9oX_QE1E?si=BycJkUR7igoJG9Hi [Tupac refuses to snitch as he is about to die in the detective's arms]

B. Nas vs. Jay-Z

www.thesource.com [the Source on Nas's Illmatic]

https://www.revolt.tv/article/2021-03-24/57094/nas-illmatic-inducted-into-library-of-congress#:~:text=On%20Wednesday%20(March%2024)%2C,into%20the%20National%20Recording%20Registry.

https://beats-rhymes-lists.com/facts/raekwon-ghostface-dissed-biggie-only-built-4-cuban-linx/

https://youtu.be/eV0TKrlhax0?si=4EXSXwvW28bCSZPF [Ashanti snitched]

https://youtube.com/shorts/jd0pB144O4A?si=YL0q9IAErzcaOU-b [Bleek on beef with Nas]

https://youtu.be/feyvDfXUShs?si=SdYW5RRYnBvAa7_v [Jay-Z brings out Michael Jackson at Summer Jam]

https://www.facebook.com/share/r/1C2NrMZdHe/?mibextid=Bitp03hRLnGPS5PQ

https://www.facebook.com/reel/1087818179409750/?mibextid=swOT3QYtmAXEinMU

https://www.urbandictionary.com/define.php?term=We%20don%27t%20believe%20you%2C%20you%20need%20more%20people

https://youtube.com/shorts/e7Q1UUrYtek?si=thkDHe4SH6bjXCI9

https://youtube.com/shorts/1bgp14ntGbY?si=eHvv7Xedmhs8E87h [Dame Dash on Hov response to Ether]

https://youtu.be/OvqGViyQCSI?si=fdX8p5yhhMEjBBaA

https://youtu.be/Dx_qyGTBjg4?si=0nOfdcMIWrfUXSQr

https://youtu.be/5_1gMT7h5ss?si=IFzdZcrXL93lsO8M

C. Ice Cube vs. NWA

https://www.facebook.com/100064848036456/posts/pfbid02gH8a7JFbmEtPpWvjdWu4AdbTPvQi7XPsdSjoRVSMpRqphCs4kqYFq5mRcDEFzs7sl/?app=fbl

https://youtu.be/wF5bxButt-s?si=GTOErFCqE9_QS34W [The NWA beef]

https://youtu.be/8DO9SJpFs9Y?si=WVdBGHvjBt3q6yRP [More on NWA]

https://youtu.be/WXF4AfO2_r0?si=fOOsoVaXjB4ilCJ_ [Ice Cube v. NWA]

https://youtu.be/10yrgvFtAhE?si=C361ZRp--n5Zluaw [No Vaseline, movie version]

https://youtu.be/bvRc7pwnt0U?si=KmqPO-VIBPb7OMN4 [No Vaseline, with visuals]

Appendix

WatchMojo.com, June 9, 2018 [Top 5 Most Savage Lines]

www.rockthebells.com, March 21, 2022: Dinner With The President..., By Jay Quan

https://www.facebook.com/reel/1707141680067005/?mibextid=swOT3QYtmAXEinMU

D. Pusha T vs. Drake

https://youtu.be/Xcta-ROw8JM?si=4v4-6H6uR4hC-TQ3 [Drake Finally Speaks About Beef With Pusha T - The Next Level Magazine, December 26, 2019 (Excerpts of Drake's interview with Rap Radar in 2019)

https://www.facebook.com/reel/449715754815433?mibextid=Bitp03hRLnGPS5PQ

https://www.facebook.com/reel/3543333975967255?mibextid=Bitp03hRLnGPS5PQ

https://youtu.be/Qr_QLv1TPcY?si=-8nijOBBHTBiiN57 [Duppy "Freestyle"]

https://youtu.be/eTWtkzPah78?si=lJREhtldxXK9XlPT [Pusha T - Infrared (Review)]

https://youtu.be/F33o_AOyCPk?si=eCXL1EUa-Ox2Nxn1 [Tuscan Leather]

https://youtu.be/w4XH3LYleDA?si=SmyVblCXZA-7owGG [The Story of Adidon]

https://youtu.be/-TeiQX4l4GI?si=m1oep06ioPn5wRDt [Drake vs. Pusha T - The Story of Adidon]

https://youtu.be/pXinnzbZQgY?si=J45Y41DAB-yax3KW [Drake/Lil Wayne vs. Pusha T]

https://youtu.be/IcLll6FwKFE?si=n1NufNHANaquxDw- [Pusha T Finally Destroys Drake]

https://youtu.be/7pPMg9l6Yik?si=MBLNoWSdzb4R_EaR [Pusha T - The Story of Adidon (Drake Diss) Review | The Joe Budden Podcast https://youtu.be/e6HeD7jN3Mc?si=PpyMTB-QssFfwV7N [The Drake and Pusha T Beef]

https://youtu.be/7EH4SK4CSc8?si=9ZkduSC_sbJqvvBk [Pusha T Shares His Current Feelings Towards Drake]

https://youtu.be/RFnxyveMht4?si=LU-nUEPt4y_q5K29 [The Insane True Story of Pusha T]

https://youtu.be/-RvxOz3cExI?si=4flTbkDa2LAtsQpO [The Drake and Pusha T Beef]

https://mixtapemagazine.online/blog-1/revisiting-drake-and-pusha-ts-beef-5-years-later#:~:text=Pusha%20T%20clearly%20won%20this,follow%2Dup%20It's%20Almost%20Dry.

https://www.businessinsider.com/drakes-biggest-feuds-pusha-t-joe-budden-kanye-west-2023-10#pusha-t-1

https://www.xxlmag.com/pusha-t-jab-drake-amid-kendrick-lamar-beef/

www.gq.com Inside the Latest..., By Grant Rindner, April 7, 2023

www.billboard.com - R&B/HIP-HOP - Everything We Know About The Drake Blackface Photo Pusha T Used For "The Story of Adidon" Cover, by Morgan Enos, 05/30/2018

Million Dollaz Worth of Game podcast in 2022 when asked about 'beating' Drake www.bleumag.com - Drake and Pusha T..., October 20, 2023

https://www.facebook.com/reel/343284105424685/?mibextid=rS40aB7S9Ucbxw6v [Yeezy Disses Drake]

https://www.facebook.com/reel/1130463964739665?mibextid=dlsFtU4zgdaQIPrl

https://www.facebook.com/reel/763134555963172?mibextid=dlsFtU4zgdaQIPrl

https://www.facebook.com/reel/466418129256670?mibextid=dlsFtU4zgdaQIPrl

https://www.facebook.com/reel/957730432512490?mibextid=rS40aB7S9Ucbxw6v

Appendix

https://www.facebook.com/reel/1156181142394290?mibextid=rS40aB7S9Ucbxw6v

https://www.facebook.com/reel/453116033797130?mibextid=rS40aB7S9Ucbxw6v

https://www.facebook.com/100064879201905/posts/pfbid026T5nxh2apNnfAgxRwuQEJ6z8fjeaGwEkRH7ZTfMKN6LRdhkLGvaHejmEdA2RJMEkl/

https://www.facebook.com/61557421456571/posts/pfbid02WeYRPB8KHx7ARatHapWrfDYKveLTakdpqz1pSgF9dafrpHsnhTNfN8hXyfko2eCql/ [Why Everybody Hates Drake]

https://l.facebook.com/l.php?u=https%3A%2F%2Fwww.instagram.com%2Freel%2FC631RsPOkCA%2F&h=AT1hYl6MfYZt1m3wSI5swwC7O2_eK9TtIKBBbNuRvf5C8XnE4sU7SNuPd_4jWOKFS4Y73D-0BNickEFNKekA7t5fHSaNuawOEPMjUhhIU0w_V6zmQMNhxOXlNrcM4pdNIA6T&s=1 [BBL Drizzy played at a wedding]

https://www.facebook.com/reel/3766976910247213/?mibextid=dlsFtU4zgdaQIPrl [Pusha T briefly speaks on Drake]

https://youtube.com/shorts/mERi2rcUvAo?si=RlgI1CpXgSriSc5j

E. Nicki Minaj vs. Everybody (Yes, including Li'l Kim, Cardi B, Meg the Stallion, Coi Leray, and even the ex-wife of the big homie Papoose, et al.)

F. Cassidy vs. Freeway

https://youtu.be/X2c67tWjmrY?si=qjF-reBJdAlX8WYL [Freeway v Cassidy Battle]

https://youtu.be/lOEde2wXsGU?si=_Leq1Dt2hKutVzNS [Bigger Business Official Video]

https://youtu.be/_TXVF75lVV8?si=WZOKcGGDZl0xRQ3O [Cassidy BARS] https://youtu.be/OGLZwPwIVm0?si=rzxKQw36QofH-BmD [When Cassidy Schooled Jay-Z]

https://youtu.be/wgSZfeOO144?si=-y0A6GQNViB9rMxt [Cassidy Feels Jay-Z Set Freeway Up to Lose]

https://youtu.be/ojCN5v7-VNg?si=B1Y34308w_LBk_X8 [Freeway Battle Started With Jay-Z feeling Insulted]

https://youtu.be/pGAJOEIYtEk?si=svw1eku8HC4Ia7a5 [Where The Bul At | Review]

https://youtu.be/pGAJOEIYtEk?si=4uSOv9oS-q-alDyy [Where The Bul At | Further Review]

G. Jadakiss and The LOX vs. 50 Cent and G-Unit

https://youtu.be/X4yDzAMOGqI?si=azlOJheZFTW2giHD [New York, New York Official Video]

(All Eyes on 50 Cent: The Sequel [March 6, 2005])

https://youtu.be/jtchKk_stCU?si=_wDNLGOmZ7tfoShb [Ghetto Quran]

https://youtu.be/QPoGSt0TALQ?si=YZMQVkMEML4O2Ijo [The Dark Story Why 50 Cent Got Shot 9 Times]

https://youtu.be/iJb0VARBpnE?si=QVJJGvNuQoKXumeN [50 Cent and Styles P Argue on Hot 97]

https://youtu.be/7F6QhKyzGxY?si=uoswnm7byadgIyjC [50 Cent vs Jadakiss - What Happened]

https://youtube.com/shorts/kZd-Wm2kxOY?si=NIPh7VfdF-D_QWCq [Jada' Recalls Destroying 50 Cent]

https://youtu.be/kQ-o1E3r7PE?si=vTTuOPFvX2XRvdZG [Checkmate]

https://youtube.com/shorts/V8GKT_rjEW0?si=C5ZomaKbjJ7FEuzF [Sheek went OFF]

Appendix

https://www.facebook.com/reel/684803626733273?mibextid=jtWzXIAxfKx1VBOC [50 Ending Beef]

https://www.complex.com/music/a/backwoodsaltar/lloyd-banks-reflects-on-g-unit-beef-with-the-lox

https://hiphopdx.com/news/jadakiss-50-cent-nothing-but-love#:~:text=on%20some%20occasions%20they%20can,a%20moment%20in%20%23hiphop.%E2%80%9D&text=The%20Final%20Lap%20Tour%20solidified,once%20enemies%20in%20the%202000s.

(All Eyes on 50 Cent: The Sequel [6 March, 2005])

3. Eminem vs. Everybody

www.mlive.com - Eminem's Childhood Home..." By Eric Lacy, November 20, 2013

www.detroithistoricalsociety.org

www.washingtonpost.com - What a real president was like, by Bill D. Moyer's, November 12, 1998)

https://youtu.be/lks1_5q7p-g?si=pW-tN-YsbMmvuepZ [Melle on Em]

(Lord Jamar, @ClassicRapShorts, YouTube, June 28, 2023 - author's Italics)

https://youtube.com/shorts/5u8by3aBu-E?si=T0nCmRSEWZ4S5oKO [Boosie doesn't listen to Em]

https://youtu.be/fZeKKmgvuPw?si=YeAW4OEfW3uUnwoj [Eazy E on Dre]

https://youtu.be/xAYKd_rOdCQ?si=1NWSR-TeNZ5lJp4S [Eminem's Michael Jackson Diss Cost Him]

https://youtu.be/xzENTVIUas0?si=XlEz0yxGOjcN6cIz [Em on Beef with Benzino and Coi Leray]

https://youtu.be/d8erEOptDa0?si=ClGfEIPgohugqj_P ["White Folks Don't Fuck With Niggas"]

Hip-Hop Rivalries: East Coast Versus West Coast

https://youtu.be/VOS8umviqTw?si=oklil7AoIh6vjWvb [Disaster Humbled by Real Sikh for Saying "N" Word]

https://www.facebook.com/61554258151023/posts/pfbid02QNmFG672ts1EEuafMpxtFqp4mx2VQUL83d9gpJ8K5F7b5AfwRQqusd4hBt3SEC4Tl/ [Macklemore states that he and Eminem will forever be guests, not hosts, in rap/hip-hop]

4. The Culture Today

www.nothingbutgoodz.com

(ETLifestyle, Li'l Wayne Talks Eminem..., January 6, 2024 [Author's Italics])

https://youtu.be/H4kiRgPdPCs?si=KH-Kg_4Blt4aBJ8s [Charlie Clips's Shang Tsung rebuttal]

https://youtu.be/dStN64sDpkY?si=hwFB0Rqj6d6Wf84x [Chilla Jones's Super Mario rebuttal freestyle]

https://www.facebook.com/share/r/15nVQzp7GJ/?mibextid=rS40aB7S9Ucbxw6v

5. The URL and The Future of Battle Rap

https://youtu.be/TFLuImMq71c?si=ZifcfzjM49NsP3cN [Smack says the money's not coming back]

https://youtu.be/Bp34E4O-D1E?si=cO2Gqty5TKjLR7YB [Goodz weighs in]

https://youtu.be/leMcqEaUqvk?si=OT3KRXD8bvzxVYes [Calicoe weighs in]

https://youtu.be/VGXDon07B8M?si=QvOTVsm6U82Bn15C

https://youtube.com/shorts/f5zpF-atBd0?si=HAC1p2UKlv77k9ET

https://youtube.com/shorts/sewikoNHn94?si=Nm35mXKM5tReJi7k

https://youtube.com/shorts/fU4Enk21lUM?si=m8WOYV1a6f8poZUB

https://youtube.com/shorts/xAqdKLTxppA?si=rv2u9GDd4HJEmoKy ["Slide for Von"]

Appendix

https://youtube.com/shorts/N8kzBh0DFzQ?si=u0MXDA6hXX82q5lS

https://youtube.com/shorts/pH8jdrl6OAM?si=KwYbIpoxMX108JxG

https://youtube.com/shorts/N5mptVSv1IY?si=NXO0v7Pl6kwntay7

https://youtube.com/shorts/h69U6ue9BRA?si=7NFplzkuHV5lPBO3l

https://youtube.com/shorts/4kriqYTj78M?si=CRKTeoIa9V7-fyWu

https://youtube.com/shorts/XXOEAUMIn_4?si=Nck2XbsfOUkuyboR

https://youtube.com/shorts/XXOEAUMIn_4?si=Nck2XbsfOUkuyboR

https://youtube.com/shorts/P-1joGUjxVM?si=9qxE1qZ5vQSpZUgS

https://youtu.be/8KuaKR8-q1I?si=yzefR0nZNpDz9ZCO [Jaz vs O'fficial]

https://youtu.be/N7fB_YsPIaY?si=Z1-0c7xVBDZuIUO8 [Noxx vs King Yoshimitsu]

https://youtu.be/UQ0mdrjdkEY?si=_vDqViIoPZo_I-Hq [Doechii "straight men/red flag" controversy and reactions to it]

https://youtu.be/3a5NXegNVjM?si=NhtiRrHv3IvH54CY [Doechii's dad's response to her stupid "straight men/red flag" comment]

6. Poetic Justice

https://youtu.be/GAkAir64Nmw?si=gR5NSY6LCajpuyqo

https://youtu.be/uKukGzRqh7w?si=o3MK0GEiNWlzDAHE

https://youtu.be/r7scNJ37OgY?si=x0HvXrTx5T7c63la

https://youtu.be/SKFoHzOvFLs?si=KtKOF41CiuJVx4Kl

https://youtu.be/q_U7-v38BKQ?si=YDZdcIHQH8Qyn4l9

https://youtu.be/f03ubhJXT1o?si=Z8Tk5S_Tu6a7zuL2

https://youtu.be/xUi6H3xnzMc?si=hv36I0GzDASSn7-y

https://youtu.be/iZ76fAN6zao?si=FbDyWCBZ-2NM8H6j

https://youtu.be/pAqPiOPEpI0?si=l_CrI97mjWvU1Xla

https://youtu.be/TVOR4QIDlE4?si=I8YFl52O5d7of2z1

Hip-Hop Rivalries: East Coast Versus West Coast

https://youtu.be/uFt60MqTrOo?si=sd305sFRNQBC2dh1

https://youtu.be/ck-JZHliJ7I?si=KL-cDUbHsgqIVNep

7. Conclusion

A. What Is To Come?

https://youtu.be/Xty2gi5cMa8?si=uXM6QzNjNNhNBoth [First Person Shooter]

https://youtu.be/N9bKBAA22Go?si=uq3pDhDIVUreh5kO [Like That]

https://youtu.be/F18RQuT3-c0?si=tBlzDYjLn8PPg2Vf [7 Minute Drill]

https://youtu.be/AP6-DUUmCzI?si=L1FKrHyAdWFAHnOU [Push-ups - Drop and gimme 50]

https://youtu.be/p4yfcEks59c?si=vfC0U4LZOYD-x7Vd [Yeezy being interviewed by Bryce]

https://youtu.be/8YQov9O7e7Y?si=RcYfKWbCVh0JFy3a [Like That remix, by Ye]

https://youtube.com/playlist?list=RD_0kp4Gjeah4&playnext=1&si=UIHGy7OBIIPfvJIB [Taylor Made Freestyle]

https://youtu.be/xufJHc2EdBA?si=ikb7NhnFEfUcCXOw [Big Sean's "Control"]

https://youtube.com/shorts/F5eUmvuhRV4?si=sVSGrCoe2LObpMfa [Advice from Ice Cube]

https://www.aljazeera.com/news/2024/4/28/hollywood-producer-harvey-weinstein-in-hospital-after-conviction-overturned

https://www.ndtv.com/world-news/jeffrey-epstein-epstein-files-full-list-of-high-profile-people-named-in-unsealed-court-docs-4810003/amp/1#amp_tf=From%20%251%24s&aoh=17143092269541&referrer=https%3A%2F%2Fwww.google.com

https://youtu.be/wVGZzzmvb0s?si=b3GlHOFRkoabaxnb [Disturbing and baseless rumors that Durk killed Von?]

Appendix

https://youtube.com/shorts/9tpGdY6BOGE?si=-chBrajlx_WD_f-b [more on King Von]

https://www.reuters.com/article/idUSTRE52Q6LF/#:~:text=ATLANTA%20(Reuters)%20%2D%20Grammy%2D,violence%20advocacy%20since%20his%20arrest.

https://www.ajc.com/news/local/federal-agents-show-guns-case/2NosIoaQ6zHLONZisZX6HK/

https://youtu.be/FqiTQCedfmE?si=HPFPGVbn_-3ubcXB [50 response on Drake]

https://www.facebook.com/reel/3299344450370849?mibextid=rS40aB7S9Ucbxw6v [Of Kendrick dropping Euphoria]

https://youtu.be/T6oLLb0dGHc?si=8-YpmtwA9JUOPKLc [more on Kendrick dropping Euphoria, a genius]

https://youtu.be/wg6Xhuk7hV8?si=dxJHbPJDOWmr6FPe [Chris Brown Quavo Diss]

B. Diddy Do It?
A Word of Caution

https://l.facebook.com/l.php?u=https%3A%2F%2Fwww.instagram.com%2Freel%2FC7FfKicu_ih%2F&h=AT36s1i0a2t9imbdNelmyWW3FyzjZgf7m7nj9on7RlFZzC66YDOAhcJCPSGTYgBD2TEGu528qqyy4ooB1VWl-7iv03vlbLnPQCyzV7e2cgZi4-ZGdid5PLw76-Fr2Xknc6vm&s=1 [Diddy did it]

https://www.forbes.com/sites/tylerroush/2025/03/21/more-than-40-men-accuse-ex-abercrombie--fitch-ceo-mike-jeffries-of-sexual-abuse-report-says/

C. Diddy Kong

https://youtube.com/shorts/XW-HlvjSPFs?si=Q5rYvx-rEAeAQW-t [snippet of Katt Williams on Shannon Sharpe show]

https://youtube.com/shorts/PVSwZn2dVKQ?si=FFFRm2tOEFuFMwz- [Shyne on Diddy betraying him] https://www.facebook.com/reel/1071141854401359/?mibextid=Bitp03hRLnGPS5PQ ["Our Black Party," Diddy's political aspiration]

https://innocenceproject.org/innocence-project-statement-on-the-execution-of-marcellus-williams/ [Marcellus Williams execution]

https://apnews.com/article/texas-execution-shaken-baby-syndrome-f6fd3474fe14cb9b0dd52629acea6bd7#:~:text=What%20was%20Roberson%20convicted%20of,been%20abused%20by%20her%20father. [Robert Roberson stay of execution]

https://www.facebook.com/100081039345389/posts/pfbid0RvJsNMbEqbuseESoT2o9jFXXkYch8qsPCV8Yt4A5rLQ9ZrZikkpVkv41g8iyu1Ndl/?mibextid=Bitp03hRLnGPS5PQ ["Laurie Maddox" and various, famous rock stars]

https://en.m.wikipedia.org/wiki/Let%27s_Get_It_(song) [*"Let's Get It"* info]

8. Afterword

https://youtube.com/playlist?list=PLATQ8iWXs4GxCbMvYmwWRFz8IFiMAOFxH&si=oUqp36yH4aE6wixE ["Elements," by B.o.B.]

Will I ride? Yes, I'll ride,
Only 'cause I bang with pride.
If I die, bury me,
3 feet up, with red on me.
R.I.P., bang in peace,
U.B.N. united me.
Up, boy; bang, boy
Til the day I max, boy.
If I die, in the streets,
Best believe my rest is East.
If I live like a G,
Won't forget my enemies.
If I die, in the streets,
Don't forget my enemies.
Now I lay me out to rest,
With 031 on my chest!

SHOUT-OUTS

Twin (Rest in Peace); U.B.N.; Gangster Killer Bloods; 9 Trey Gangsters; BloodStone Villains; 183 Gangsters; Valentine Bloods; 59 Brims; Mack Baller Brims; Piru Bloods; L.A. Brims; Denver Lanes; Swans; Bishops; Julius and Sonny (ain't a damn thing funny); Jewelz Shine; The High O20 Kormega, aka Omega Red; The High O20 Robojus; Big Blood (Rest in Peace); Bar Shine; Krime Valentine; Doggy Dogg; J-Hood; Rebel; Sex Moolah; Pistol Pete; Champagne Shine; King Z; King Armageddon; King Navy; King Big Boy; the G.F. Dizzy; the G.F. Deadeye; the G.F. O.G. Mack; the big homies on the West Side: Bone and YG; Little Diz (never forget that night on Baychester when we laid on them – they must've felt something since they never came out the projects, lol); Real Life (from the Bronx - hmu, homie); the G.F. Disco (Mr. Bostick himself); the only homie I ever brought home personally, in Harlem: Chucky; Chase Money; The Ends (yeah, y'all British 'hood niggas); Stormzy, Kano, TY from The Wyld, Little Simz and especially Dave (some dope ass London rappers); Rumble outta Brooklyn (I'll beat ya ass ANY day in Scrabble STILL, nigga, lol); big Himo, outta Brooklyn, too; DDP Lenny Emiliano ("toogoodtobeChrisMAS," lol); DDP big Freddy; Eugene (Rest in Peace); Tiffany Maldonado (I love you so much – thank you for all the good memories); Mel Sachs, Attorney at Law (Rest in Peace and thanks for all of your assistance); Linda Balou (Rest in Peace, my mother figure and beloved friend); Lenaire Balou (I owe you, big time); Robert Mueller, former U.S. Ambassador to the U.N. (thank you for all of your advice and counseling); Mr. Roy Innis (Rest in Peace, sir, and thank you for everything); the Congress of Racial Equality (thank you all for your concern and training); the Honorable Micky Scherer (thanks for all of your counsels as well – sorry I went off course a bit); Keith and Shorts who used to be on 125th; the Puerto Rican twins who lived on 127th(?) and Saint Nick; Branson; Jersey City; MC Sha La Rock, arguably the first female rapper; Cindy Campbell (thank you for all of your necessary contributions to The Culture via Rap and hip-hop); the Muhammads and Ab and 'em outta Brooklyn who lived on Roosevelt Island, too; Chaplain Chapin (Rest in perfect Peace, sir); Stephan and Melissa Rogers (outta 540); Jonathan and Jessica Gago (outta 4 River Road); Emmanuel and Racquel

(I pray y'all are doing great); Iron Lady (we all love you so much here); Semi (outta 40 River Road); Jessica from either 555, 575, or Riverview (thanks for all your kind words and physical support while I was going through some real existential shit); Ms. Shepherd from IS 217 – you really helped me form my ideas in 5th grade. I thank you most kindly. Mr. Strauss (my music teacher at U.N.I.S.) – thank you for your patience and kind words; Mr. Lang, also at U.N.I.S. (my Computer Science teacher – thanks for getting me interested in the sciences of computer technology); thanks are also due to my Japanese teachers at U.N.I.S. who helped put me on the path of studying their rich and poetic language; a hearty fuck you to my old German female Math teacher at U.N.I.S. – thank you for all the put-downs and ruler strikes with you would assault me, Ara, and Jesse behind closed doors. Thank you to the tall, older, and skinny White guy who was my English Honor Roll teacher who chain-smoked cigarettes on demon time during his breaks (also at U.N.I.S.) – he was tough, but at least he recognized the genius in me, lol. Thank you to my favorite French teacher at U.N.I.S., Mr. Bassêne – you were a no-nonsense and fair teacher to whom I pray life has been kind (greetings to Madame Bassêne and her twin sister). My friends at U.N.I.S.: Ara, Jesse, Steven, Hideyuki, Hsi-Ming Hsiung, Dulcie, Ai and Akani Ogata, etc., etc. – you are all a part of the whole man I am now. And fuck you to the (middle school?) principal who, after I beat up some older clowns who tried jumping me, told my dad that I was the most animalistic student in U.N.I.S. For that, I tell you and your legacy in front of the world: fuck you, suck my dick, and picture me rollin'! Thank you to my music teacher in Humanities, Mr. Stewart. Thanks also to my Architecture, Film, and Latin teachers in that same school. A special thanks to Ms. Levi, particularly for understanding why I had to put hands and feet on Aaron – thanks for your honesty and support. Shout-out to Andy (who had the #2 baddest chick in school [I had the #1, of course]). And shout-outs to Alvina, Adriana, Fabiana, Taina, Keisha, Vivian, and Cindy (I was in LUST for Dominican Cindy, I promise you she was the TRUTH) – Please let me now apologize for anything I did to hurt any of you gorgeous ladies, or anything I said that offended any of y'all. Shout-out to Genevieve, Unga, Maribel, and Natasha (my Hell's Kitchen, downtown, and downtown library crew) – I miss you so much, Genevieve, and I know we WILL meet again (my regards to Mom). Shout-out to the Guardian Angels and Curtis

Sliwa, man – there was one pretty tough summer that y'all held me DOWN and took me in like one of y'all. As a matter of fact, for that brief time, I WAS one of y'all, lol – mad love and respect! Shout-out to RFC and FUS (I hope that long-standing beef was finally settled). Shout-out to Matilda who used to work for RIOC (she still might). Shout-out to Ari Sanders and his wife; love to Idris Sanders (Rest in Peace). Last, but DEFINITELY not least, a HUGE shout-out to my junior high school crush, the dearly departed Icla da Silva, a Portuguese girl I had fallen in love with before I even knew what love meant. She passed away due to some kind of cancer and I've been carrying her with me in my heart all these years. Rest in Peace, beautiful one – you may no longer visit us, but it's guaranteed we're on our way to see you. Shout-out to the Icla da Silva Foundation. Shout-out to the Victoria Relief Foundation.

Thank ALL of you who, unknowingly, were a part of this journey culminating in this first major work of mine.

Finally, shout-out to New York for raising me, man. I don't think I would've had the strength or emotional tenacity to survive everything I've been through otherwise.

When I began writing Part C (The Buildup) of the Introduction about 2 years ago, I never knew that 2 years thence, a certain scene in Ryan Coogler's highly acclaimed original horror movie "Sinners" would resonate with what I had written therein about the shaping and progression of the various music genres African-Americans created and eventually popularized throughout the world. Sammie's music emanating throughout the barn while piercing the veil of time and space to bring together and to light the sundry artistries of Blacks was absolutely mesmerizing and, to me, spiritually and emotionally cathartic. Something is happening. There is a... shift in the general consciousness of Black folk, particularly African-Americans. Despite the rage- and race-baiting promulgated by a POTUS determined to go to prison after his second term is over, The Culture knows that we have some semblance of power and control now. If you're a racist, fuck you. If you're a Nazi, fuck you too. Ain't gon' be too much marching again for Blacks in America - that time is past and we've learned our lesson.

Thanks to the prejudice of White America, African-Americans (and other minorities in the United States) can now hit their oppressors where it hurts most: their pockets! What a damn SHAME for White America – a 400-year headstart and Black folk are still doing our damn thing. The thing is that Blacks in America are the physical manifestation of the sins of White America about which it is deeply ashamed and morbidly embarrassed. I've said it before in this book: reparations are in order and way past due. Shout-out to Michael B. Jordan, Ryan Coogler, and all the actors and actresses in "Sinners," which is as complex a movie in understanding and defining cinematographically as "Not Like Us" is discographically.

Peace, Love, and Respect to The Culture.

Dear Reader,

We hope you have enjoyed this book, but why not share your views on social media? You can also follow our pages to see more about our other products: facebook.com/penandswordbooks or follow us on X @penswordbooks

You can also view our products at www.pen-and-sword.co.uk (UK and ROW) or www.penandswordbooks.com (North America).

To keep up to date with our latest releases and online catalogues, please sign up to our newsletter at: www.pen-and-sword.co.uk/newsletter

If you would like a printed catalogue with our latest books, then please email: enquiries@pen-and-sword.co.uk or telephone: 01226 734555 (UK and ROW) or email: uspen-and-sword@casematepublishers.com or telephone: (610) 853-9131 (North America).

We respect your privacy and we will only use personal information to send you information about our products.

Thank you!